50 REASONS
NOT TO VOTE FOR BUSH

By Robert Sterling

Contributions from Paul Krassner
Greg Palast / Buzzflash.com
Lydia Lunch
Sam Smith
Matt Taibbi
Robbie Conal
Brian Paisley

→ TABLE OF CONTENTS

50 REASONS NOT TO VOTE FOR BUSH

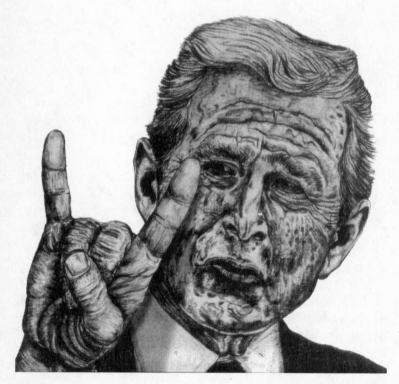

Illustration by Robbie Conal

→ PREFACE

Approaching the 2000 election, many people looked at the choice between Al Gore and George W. Bush with cynical indifference. With so little difference between the two candidates, there hardly seemed much of a choice at all. After all, both were hog-tied with corporate money and more interested in pleasing the business and political establishment than listening to the concerns of the average man. In this climate, many Americans viewed a vote for Ralph Nader of the Green Party not simply as wasted, but as an almost despairing protest against the inadequacy of the alternatives.

I was almost seduced by this line of thinking. True, I did vote for Gore, having more distrust of Bush, his family, and where his ilk were leading the GOP, but Gore and the Democrats seemed corrupt, too, and I could not really recommend any of the candidates, except as the least evil by a small margin. But those who wasted votes on Nader, and those who thought their choice did not really matter and stayed home, or perhaps chose at whim, were wrong. Far from making little difference, the 2000 election was an historical turn for the worst, steered in the end not by the American public, but by five Reagan-Bush judges on the Supreme Court.

In Bush's presidency much that is wrong with American politics comes together—a smirking contempt for people's rights, a stupidity bred in privilege, a faux-folksy condescension toward the common man while screwing him in favor of large corporations. The coming election is a chance for the beginning of reform of American politics, the first step of which is the end of Bush's reign. The alternatives to Bush are not inspiring, but despair and indifference are a trap. Lest the election be close enough to steal again, make sure that your friends go to the polls, if only out of anger. Give them this book, which, if it succeeds in conveying the essence of the Bush White House, has something to anger everyone.

I'd like to acknowledge hundreds of people, but my unlimited love for them as well as space limitations prevent it. My first and foremost thanks go to Adam Parfrey of Feral House. He has that one virtue all writers love: his checks clear.

Next, my family, starting with the Tully Clan: Nick Hamilton; Grandma Molly Tully, Aunts Martha and Shlee; Uncles Pers, Skip & Mark; John "JT" Tully, Chris, 'Dwin & CeCe Brown, and Elhi and Curtis; Ivy of T-NG2 and Honora. Then there's my Pop, Roy Peacock, my bro Greg, Denny, Uncle Billy and Tina.

Big thanks to Chris Dolan, Alex & Jackie, whose support and kindness make them virtual family. Thanks also to Scott Rose; Greg Bishop; Kenn Thomas; Jon Vankin, John Whalen; Richard Metzger, Russ Kick, Alex Burns, Gary Baddeley & Nimrod Erez; Paul & Olga Ruiz, and Stan Gates.

—Robert Sterling
February, 2004

THE 51ST REASON

→ **PAUL KRASSNER**

Robert Sterling, editor of *The Konformist* (an online publication) was sitting around and thinking one day when he remembered a *Spy* magazine cover story in 1992 titled "1001 Reasons Not to Vote for George Bush."

"Hey," he said to himself, "somebody should do that for his piece-of-shit son."

Then he realized that *he* could be that somebody.

But instead of 1001 reasons not to vote for George W., Sterling and Feral House publisher Adam Parfrey settled on 50, because: It would fit in less pages, making it more economical; it would be the best "all killer, no filler" collection; and 50 is a good number, as in the book *50 Ways to Save the Planet*.

Finding 50 reasons was the easy part. Too easy, in fact. The real problem was too much information rather than too little. Sterling's plan was to give a catchy title for each reason, then get in and get out as quickly and as painlessly as possible. He sourced over 600 books and articles, so there was a great deal of research involved.

"It turns out," he told me, "that showing what a creepy bastard Bush is takes more work than you'd think."

When I was an adolescent searching for the meaning of life—at least for my own life—I attended a meeting of the American Association for the Advancement of Atheism. There was a speaker there who looked like Tarzan at the age of 72, and he proclaimed the 11th Commandment: "Thou shalt not take thyself too goddamned seriously." So now I find myself following his numerical lead by proposing the 51st reason not to vote for George Bush.

It isn't because he has been raping the environment and is now telling us to go to Mars, attempting to divert public attention from his not having an exit strategy from Iraq by announcing that he *does* have an exit strategy from Earth. No, the 51st reason not to vote for Bush is because he's Hitler. Former President Bush may have said, "Read my lips," but George W. is saying, "Read *Mein Kampf*."

In December 2000, the newly appointed "president" declared, "If this were a dictatorship, it'd be a heck of a lot easier, just so long as *I'm* the dictator," and now it feels like his wish is coming true. But this is not about Republicans and Democrats. It's about a fascist takeover. And I don't use that term loosely. It was Hitler's ally, Benito Mussolini, who said, "Fascism should be more properly called corporatism, since it is the merger of state and corporate power."

It was Joseph Goebbels, Reichminister of Propaganda, who wrote in his diaries that it was impossible to use advertising and manipulation of the news to turn all Germans into Nazis, but that he could set the parameters of conventional wisdom and alter the language, thus altering the rationality of the population. By presenting the war as necessary to Germany's survival and prosperity, and insisting that Hitler's regime was necessary to the successful prosecution of war, he could win over the vast majority of German citizens, with few dissenters, fearful of the state's police power.

And it was Holocaust orchestrator Hermann Goering who said, "Voice or no voice, the people can always be brought to the bidding of the leaders, that is easy. All you have to do is tell them they are being attacked, and denounce the peacemakers for lack of patriotism and exposing the country to danger. It works the same in every country."

An individual whose family members were victimized by Hitler writes: "Why, now, when I hear George W. Bush's speeches, do I think of Hitler? Why have I drawn a parallel between the Nazis and the present administration? Just one small reason—the phrase 'Never forget.' Never let this happen again. It is better to question our government—because it really can happen again—than to ignore the possibility. So far, I've seen nothing to eliminate the possibility that Bush is on the same course as Hitler. And I've seen far too many analogies to dismiss the possibility:

"The propaganda. The lies. The rhetoric. The nationalism. The flag waving. The pretext of 'preventive war.' The flounting of international law and international standards of justice. The disappearances of 'undesirable' aliens. The threats against protesters. The invasion of a non-threatening sovereign nation. The occupation of a hostile country. The promises of prosperity and security. The spying on ordinary citizens. The incitement to spy on one's neighbors—and report them to the government. The arrogant triumphant pride in military conquest. The honoring of soldiers. The tributes to 'fallen warriors.' The diversion of money to the military. The demonization of government-appointed 'enemies.' The establishment of 'Homeland Security.' The dehumanization of 'foreigners.' The total lack of interest in the victims of government policy. The incarceration of the poor and mentally ill. The growing prosperity of military ventures. The illusion of 'goodness' and primacy. The new *einsatzgrupen* forces—assassination teams. Closed extralegal internment camps. The militarization of domestic police. Media blackout of non-approved issues. Blacklisting of protesters, including the no-fly lists and photographing dissenters at rallies.

"There isn't much doubt in my mind—anyone who compares the history of Hitler's rise to power and the progression of recent events in the United States cannot avoid the parallels. It's incontrovertible."

George W. Bush has served as the official cheerleader for his time-warped advisers, insane with power, reeking with arrogance, and severely in need of compassion transplants. It's acceptable, of course, for right-wing radio talk-show hosts to refer to "Hitlery" Clinton, and for Rush Limbaugh to speak of "feminazis," and for the *New York Post* to describe Howard Dean as a follower of Goebbels. However, Bush and his administration have been treated with much deserved irreverence by some of the country's top comedians.

Mort Sahl: "Bush is the first president who likes to hang around with his father's friends."

Jon Stewart: "If the events of September 11th have proven anything, it's that the terrorists can attack us, but they can't take away what makes us Americans—our freedoms, our liberty, our civil rights. No, only Attorney General John Ashcroft can do that."

Margaret Cho: "George Bush is not Hitler. He would be, if he fucking applied himself."

Bill Maher [*referring to Arnold Schwarzenegger's gubernatorial campaign*]: "Finally, a candidate who can explain the Bush administration's positions on civil liberties in the original German."

Jay Leno: "The United States is putting together a Constitution now for Iraq. Why don't we just give them ours? It's served us well for 200 years, and we don't appear to be using it any more. So what the hell?"

Harry Shearer [*referring to Bush's crusade to stamp out global terrorism*]: "It's like the war on drugs. It's a totally metaphorical war in which some people get killed. I expect the Partnership for a Terrorist Free America to start soon."

Actually, the War on Drugs—that is, the war on *some* people who use *some* drugs—has resulted in a larger number of African Americans being imprisoned than Jews incarcerated by the Nazi regime during its first several years.

According to the Drug Policy Alliance, "A little-known provision buried with the omnibus federal spending bill that the U.S. House of Representatives approved [on December 8, 2003] would take away federal grants from local and state transportation authorities that allow citizens to run advertising on buses, trains or subways in support of reforming our nation's drug laws. If enacted, the provision could effectively silence community groups around the country that are using advertising to educate Americans about medical marijuana and other drug policy reforms. Meanwhile, this same bill gives the White House $145 million in taxpayer money to run anti-marijuana ads [in 2004]."

And if you've seen that insidious propaganda in the guise of public service announcements, you've seen fascism in action. But, in the interest of presenting a fair and balanced introduction to this book, allow me to quote Dennis Miller:

"People say I've slid to the right. Well, can you blame me? One of the biggest malfeasances of the left right now is the mislabeling of Hitler. Quit saying Bush is Hitler. Hitler is Hitler. That's the quintessential evil in the history of the universe, and we're throwing it around on MoveOn.org to win a contest. That's grotesque to me."

It had only been two entries out of 1500 in the MoveOn political ad competition that made the Hitler/Bush comparison, but never mind sacrificing perspective for the sake of agenda. I mean, if Tony Blair was George Bush's lap dog, then Dennis Miller is his poodle. And yet, paradoxically enough, I am now convinced that Miller is correct. There *is* a difference between Hitler and Bush. Hitler was elected.

Paul Krassner edited *The Realist* (1958–2001) and is the author of *Murder At the Conspiracy Convention and Other American Absurdities*, with an introduction by George Carlin.

➡️ **GREG PALAST**

Interviewed by Buzzflash.com

> "Look, as a journalist, I don't like saying, *50 Reasons Not to Vote for George Bush*. In fact, I don't mind if people are Republicans in the privacy of their own bedrooms. It's just the ones that flaunt it in public, the raging, flaming ones, that give me the creeps. We shouldn't condemn Republicans; they need our understanding. At a certain income level, it is an urge that can't easily be controlled. And hell, with the new computerized voting systems, we may ALL be voting Republican no matter WHICH party you touch on the touch screen."
>
> —"Non-Partisan Waiver" asked to be included in this
>   book by Mr. Palast

Buzzflash: Is there any doubt in your mind that Gov. Jeb Bush and Katherine Harris removed 57,000 African-American voters from the registries because they knew that George W. Bush needed to carry Florida to "win" the presidency?

Greg Palast: Well, golly gee, are you telling me a politician doesn't know what happens in a state where every vote is fought over, and they were wondering what would happen when they could just erase 57,708 votes with the flick of a computer button. Did that happen by accident? My God, politicians look at every single vote. 57,000 votes is not just something that they lost track of. It's not like a laundry list that they put at the bottom of a file cabinet and forgot about it. The Republicans spent almost their entire budget in the Department of Elections on conducting this computer hunt for black voters. And that was almost the entire budget for that office. They knew what they were doing and they knew why they were doing it. We have plenty of evidence of the intent.

One of the things you'll read in the book for example, is that this law was written by Katherine Harris, and her crony Clayton Roberts, of the Florida Department of Elections. He's a kind of bullneck, red-faced, chubby character that helped her draft the law. Roberts took over the agency when Harris grabbed the Secretary of State's office and put this law that targeted African Americans into effect. And when the U.S. Department of Justice questioned whether this was gonna have a racial effect,—'cause remember this is a Jim Crow state that's under the Voting Rights Act, Roberts wrote back and said, "Aw, shucks, ain't nothin' but some administrative changes," when he knew that this was a cruise missile aimed at innocent black voters. And I want to emphasize that—innocent black voters. Just for those who don't know the story, it's 57,700 people targeted as supposed felons, purged from the voter rolls. Most of them are black. Almost all of them were Democrats. And almost all of them—about 90% plus— were innocent of any crime and have the right to vote. Their crime is being black or being Democratic.

Buzzflash: Was this Jeb's decision?

Palast: What you'll see in the book, in fact, are letters out of Jeb Bush's office in which they are directing county supervisors not to register legal voters if they had clemency from other states and were allowed to vote. Now, that's against the law; that's against the United States Constitution. Bush's operatives knew it was wrong, and it was evil and corroded, because when I asked Jeb's office for the letters, they said, "We never sent such a letter. It doesn't exist. It's not in our files. It's not in our computers." I have the letter. I quote it in the book.

Buzzflash: You actually broke the story while the recount was going on in Florida, and before the Supreme Court appointed Bush. Not one American newspaper picked up the story.

Palast: I caught them in the act, and Al Gore was still hanging in the race by his thumbs. And we figured out, working with the BBC and the *Observer* in London, exactly how the Bushes fixed the vote. We did get it in the *Washington Post* under my byline, seven months after the fact, when Bush was reading it from the

White House and grinning. And that was the big problem was that some of this information came out in the American media, but so much later and only in little teeny bits. Finally this month, I got a story in *Harper's* in which I actually show you the computer purge list.

In *Harper's*, I point out one guy, Thomas Cooper, whose conviction date was 2007. In other words, Harris had removed this guy from the voter rolls because of the crime he'll commit in seven years. And there were hundreds and thousands like that. What they were very careful about doing was making sure that they got down the race of the voters. But whether they were actually convicted or not didn't mean a hell of a lot to Harris, Jeb Bush, and the Republican Party.

Buzzflash: Greg, you state in the book that Bush spiked investigations into Bin Laden and Al Qaeda before September 11th and that Bush directed any probe to not target the Saudi government and Saudi businessmen.

Palast: That's right. With BBC television and the *Guardian* newspapers, I led an investigation which uncovered a really ill-making, sad, horrid fact that George W. Bush put an absolute block on investigations of Saudi financing of terrorism. Where do you think Al Qaeda gets their money from?

I know about meetings that were held in Paris, in which the billionaires of Saudi Arabia divided up who had to pay what to Al Qaeda and to Osama Bin Laden. The problem is that no one wanted to tell that story for fear of being unpatriotic. I'm trying to protect the flag. My God, I worked in the World Trade Center. My office was on the 52nd floor. These were my friends there. And I was trying to find out how the intelligence apparatus of the United States, on which we spent a trillion bucks in the last decade, missed any information on the biggest attack on America since Pearl Harbor? And the answer is that they were told to shut their eyes.

I don't want to get my report confused with stories alleging that Bush knew all about the September 11 attack before it happened. I've found no evidence he knew anything at all. In fact, the point is that we knew nothing because we were blindfolded by our own guys. Now, why they did it is that Bush is very close, financially, politically, socially, to the Bin Laden family. They're partners in the Carlyle Group and others. And basically you don't investigate buddies who are your friends. They invest in the same deals. It's the same social group.

I can tell you one particular investigation they killed off, which was the investigation into how Pakistan was able to build an atomic bomb, because it was done with Saudi money. The problem with killing these investigations is that we don't know who else got their hands on this atomic bomb information. So we're still trying to find that out. I'm still investigating. Let's put it this way: if I knew about the money to Al Qaeda, and I knew about the Saudi involvement in the Pakistan bomb program, you're telling me the CIA didn't know this? They were told not to know this.

Greg Palast is the author of *The Best Democracy Money Can Buy: The Truth About Corporate Cons, Globalization and High-Finance Fraudsters* (Plume).

THE WHITE HOUSE PRESS CORPS POLITELY GRABS ITS ANKLES

→ **MATT TAIBBI**

After watching a recent George W. Bush press conference, I'm more convinced than ever: The entire White House press corps should be herded into a cargo plane, flown to an altitude of 30,000 feet, and pushed out, kicking and screaming, over the North Atlantic.

Any remaining staff at the Washington bureaus should be rounded up for summary justice. The Russians used to use bakery trucks, big gray panel trucks marked "Bread" on the sides; victims would be rounded up in the middle of the night and taken for one last ride through the darkened streets.

The war would almost be worth it just to see Wolf Blitzer pounding away at the inside of a Pepperidge Farm truck, tearfully confessing and vowing to "take it all back."

This Bush press conference to me was like a mini-Alamo for American journalism, a final announcement that the press no longer performs anything akin to a real function. Particularly revolting was the spectacle of the cream of the national press corps submitting politely to the indignity of obviously pre-approved questions, with Bush not even bothering to conceal that the affair was scripted.

Abandoning the time-honored pretense of spontaneity, Bush chose the order of questioners not by scanning the room and picking out raised hands, but by looking down and reading from a predetermined list. Reporters, nonetheless, raised their hands in between questions—as though hoping to suddenly catch the president's attention.

In other words, not only were reporters going out of their way to make sure their softballs were pre-approved, but they even went so far as to act on Bush's behalf, raising their hands and jockeying in their seats in order to better give the appearance of a spontaneous news conference.

Even Bush couldn't ignore the absurdity of it all. In a remark-able exchange that somehow managed to avoid being commented upon in news accounts the next day, Bush chided CNN political correspondent John King when the latter overacted his part, too enthusiastically waving his hand when it apparently was, according to the script, his turn anyway.

KING: "Mr. President."

BUSH: "We'll be there in a minute. King, John King. This is a scripted. . ."

A ripple of nervous laughter shot through the East Room. Moments later, the camera angle of the conference shifted to a side shot, revealing a ring of potted plants around the presidential podium. It would be hard to imagine an image that more perfectly describes American political journalism today: George Bush, surrounded by a row of potted plants, in turn surrounded by the White House press corps.

Newspapers the next day ignored the scripted-question issue completely. (King himself, incidentally, left it out of his CNN.com report.) Of the major news services and dailies, only one—the *Washington Post*—even parenthetically addressed the issue. Far down in Dana Millbank and Mike Allen's conference summary, the paper euphemistically commented:

"The president followed a script of names in choosing which reporters could ask him a question, and he received *generally friendly questioning*." [Emphasis mine.] "Generally friendly questioning" is an understatement if there ever was one. Take this offering by April Ryan of the American Urban Radio Networks:

"Mr. President, as the nation is at odds over war, with many organizations like the Congressional Black Caucus pushing for continued diplomacy through the UN, how is your faith guiding you?"

Great. In Bush's first press conference since his decision to support a rollback of affirmative action, the first black reporter to get a crack at him—and this is what she comes up with? The journalistic equivalent of "Mr. President, you look great today. What's your secret?"

Newspapers across North America scrambled to roll the high-light tape of Bush knocking Ryan's question out of the park. *The Boston Globe*: "As Bush stood calmly at the presidential lectern, tears welled in his eyes when he was asked how his faith was guiding him. . ." *The Globe and Mail*: "With tears welling in his eyes, Mr. Bush said he prayed daily that war can be averted. . ."

Even worse were the qualitative assessments in the major dailies of Bush's performance. As I watched the conference, I was sure I was witnessing, live, an historic political catastrophe. In his best moments Bush was deranged and uncommunicative, and in his worst moments, which were most of the press conference, he was swaying side to side like a punch-drunk fighter, at times slurring his words and seemingly clinging for dear life to the verbal oases of phrases like "total disarmament," "regime change," and "mass destruction."

The closest thing to a negative characterization of Bush's performance in the major outlets was in David Sanger and Felicity Barringer's *New York Times* report, which called Bush "sedate": "Mr. Bush, sounding sedate at a rare prime-time news conference, portrayed himself as the protector of the country. . ."

Apparently even this absurdly oblique description, which ran on the *Times* website hours after the press conference, was too much for the paper's editors. Here is how that passage read by the time the papers hit the streets the next morning:

"Mr. Bush, at a rare prime-time press conference, portrayed himself as the protector of the country. . ."

Meanwhile, those aspects of Bush's performance that the White House was clearly anxious to call attention to were reported enthusiastically. It was obvious that Bush had been coached to dispense with two of his favorite public speaking tricks—his perma-smirk and his finger-waving cowboy one-liners. Bush's somber new "war is hell" act was much commented upon, without irony, in the post-mortems.

Appearing on *Hardball* after the press conference, *Newsweek*'s Howard Fineman (one of the worst monsters of the business) gushed when asked if the Bush we'd just seen was really a "cowboy":

"If he's a cowboy he's the reluctant warrior, he's Shane. . . because he has to, to protect his family."

Newsweek thinks Bush is Shane?

This was just Bush's eighth press conference since taking office, and each one of them has been a travesty. In his first presser, on Feb. 22, 2001, a month after his controversial inauguration, he was not asked a single question about the election, Al Gore or the Supreme Court. On the other hand, he was asked five questions about Bill Clinton's pardons.

Reporters argue that they have no choice. They'll say they can't protest or boycott the staged format, because they risk being stripped of their seat in the press pool. For the same reason, they say they can't write anything too negative. They can't write, for instance, "President Bush, looking like a demented retard on the eve of war. . ." That leaves them with the sole option of "working within the system" and, as they like to say, "trying to take our shots when we can."

But the White House press corps' idea of "taking a shot" is David Sanger asking Bush what he thinks of British foreign minister Jack Straw saying that regime change was not necessarily a war goal. And then meekly sitting his ass back down when Bush ignores the question.

They can't write what they think, and can't ask real questions. What the hell are they doing there? If the answer is "their jobs," it's about time we started wondering what that means.

Matt Taibbi was co-editor (with Mark Ames) of the notorious Russian expat mag, *The Exile*, whose best issues became the Grove Press published book, *The Exile: Sex, Drugs and Libel in the New Russia*. Taibbi now writes for the *New York Press*, where the column above first appeared.

QUESTIONS THE MEDIA WON'T ASK GEORGE W. BUSH

➤ SAM SMITH

In 1984, after your firm, Arbusto Energy, had fallen on hard times, you managed to get a job as the 30-something president of Spectrum 7 Energy Corporation, the firm that purchased Arbusto. You also got 14% of the Spectrum's stock. Meanwhile, your 50 investors in Arbusto got paid off at about 20 cents on the dollar. Is this the sort of thing your economic advisor, Lawrence Lindsey, was thinking of when he said Americans had become too greedy?

Or might he have been thinking of the deal in 1986 when, after Spectrum 7 had lost $400,000 in six months, you sold it to Harken Energy, becoming a major Harken stockholder and receiving a good salary as a director and consultant?

Or was it that time when you sold two-thirds of your Harken stock for a 200% profit on June 22, 1990, just 40 days before the start of the Gulf War and one week before the company announced a $23 million quarterly loss, setting off a 60% drop in share price over the next six months?

Why were you so valuable to these companies given your less than impressive business acumen?

When you and your Harken partners ran short of cash and hooked up with investment banker Jackson Stephens of Little Rock, Arkansas, he got you a $25 million stock purchase by Union Bank of Switzerland. Did you know that Sheik Abdullah Bakhsh, who joined your board as a part of the deal, was connected to BCCI? Did you know that the United Bank was connected to BCCI (including its operations in Panama), the Nugan Hand Bank (a notorious CIA-front in Australia), and Ferdinand Marcos?

Did you know that it was Jackson Stephens who introduced the players in what would turn out to be the infamous First American-BCCI deal?

Why do your think the government of Bahrain chose Harken to drill its offshore wells even though it had never dug overseas or in water before? Why do you think it chose Harken, with no relevant experience, over Amoco, with plenty of it? Did you ever discuss with your dad the Harken-Bahrain deal? Did any sheiks or other officials ever express any concern over the failure of Harken to find any oil? Do you think they really cared?

Tell us again why you waited almost a year past the legal deadline to file the necessary SEC report on your Harken stock deal.

You borrowed $180,000 from Harken at a low rate. Did you ever pay it back or was it included among that $341,000 Harken listed in SEC documents as loaned to executives and later forgiven?

You have worked closely with a number of persons with CIA ties. Do you think it is healthy for the country to have three presidents in a row so closely connected with this intelligence agency?

Do you think it is healthy for the country to have three presidents in a row who are Yale men?

Your grandfather Prescott was on the board of Brown Harriman which helped provide some of the financing for the Soviet and Nazi regimes. Do you think this was a wise idea?

As president would you continue this tradition in our policy toward China?

During World War II your grandfather had property seized under the Trading with the Enemy Act. Was he pro-Nazi or just a proto-neo-capitalist ahead of his time?

What is the American voter to make of the fact that two of your brothers, one father, one grandfather, and one uncle have been involved in unseemly scandals of one sort or another? How do you distinguish your ethical code from theirs?

One of your Uncle Prescott's hot deals resulted in an early but major transfer of sensitive technology to the Chinese government. Your father in 1989 lifted sanctions that blocked such ventures. Do you approve of Uncle Prescott and your father's behavior in these matters? As president would you allow such deals to continue?

Do you approve of your uncle's and father's role in what has become to be known as the "October Surprise?"

You invested $600,000 in the Texas Rangers and later sold out for $15 million. What did you do for the Rangers in between? How much of this profit reflected your ability to get the city of Arlington to condemn land for a ball park at 1/6 its true worth and then impose a 1/2-cent sales tax to subsidize your business? Is this an example of what you meant in 1993 when you said, "The best way to allocate resources in our society is through the marketplace. Not through a governing elite?"

Can you name a business deal you have been in that hasn't raised ethical questions? That has made a profit without some form of government subsidy?

Why did you have to hire private investigators to find out what dirt private investigators might be able to dig up on you?

Do you think that you have used more or less cocaine than, say, Marion Barry or Bill Clinton?

Discuss this remark by Michael King in the *Texas Observer*: "Although by his own admission George W. was an indifferent student, he was nevertheless the deserving-by-both beneficiary of the oldest most illegitimate, and most sacrosanct form of affirmative action. . . It's business as usual."

Since you want to help "instill individual responsibility" and give people a "future of opportunity, instead of dependence on government," why did you and your neighbors at the exclusive Rainbo Club development get a tax break from your government?

In what ways do such tax breaks differ from welfare benefits other than that welfare recipients are more needy?

Do you believe that being a member of a secret society dedicated to promoting fraternal nepotism in public office is consistent with being president of a democracy?

If the words "skull and bones" are mentioned at a White House news conference, will you—as the tradition of the society demands—feel compelled to leave the room?

Sam Smith runs the *Progressive Review* website [http://prorev.com/] and is the author of *Why Bother? Getting a Life in a Locked-Down Land* (Feral House) and *Sam Smith's Great American Political Repair Manual: How to Rebuild Our Country So the Politics Aren't Broken and Politicians Aren't Fixed* (Norton).

50 REASONS
NOT TO VOTE FOR BUSH

11

→ HE STOLE THE 2000 ELECTION

With a villain like Bush, it's difficult to focus all the spite he has earned on one single reason why he does not deserve your vote. Nearly everything he has done, both before and during his White House squatting manifests a uniquely repulsive character. Yet one reason screams out to be recognized as the best one for rejecting him in the voting booth: his claim to the White House is fraudulent.

Let's start with one undisputed fact: nationally, Shrub lost the year 2000 popular vote to Al Gore by over 500,000 Americans. In other words, if the office of the President were decided in a directly democratic manner, Dubya would still be stuck in Texas snuffing death row inmates. Granted, this is legally irrelevant. Like it or not, the U.S. Constitution established an Electoral College system to select the President, not a system of popular vote. While the system may seem archaic, it is nonetheless the rule of law, and nobody would argue for trumping it without a Constitutional Amendment. Right?

Actually, one group did argue this: the George W. Bush 2000 campaign. The polls leading up to the November election made it seem likely that while Georgie Boy would win the popular vote by a razor-thin margin, he would lose the Electoral College. The Bush team's strategy for this contingency was to manufacture a massive "popular" campaign of outrage to overturn the results of the election. As reported November 1, 2000 by Michael Kramer of the *New York Daily News*, the mass rebellion would be stoked by paid advertisements and a right-wing talk radio onslaught. The broadcast blowhards would inveigh against the "unfairness" of the Electoral College, which was described in another pre-election *Boston Herald* article as "an antiquated relic" by Republican sources.

The Republic anti–Electoral College campaign would go further. "Local business leaders will be urged to lobby their customers, the clergy will be asked to speak up for the popular will and Team

Bush will enlist as many Democrats as possible to scream as loud as they can." For the last part, the Bushistas even came up with a catchy slogan: "Democrats for Democracy." A Bush aide added, "And I think you can count on the media to fuel the thing big-time. Even papers that supported Gore might turn against him because the will of the people will have been thwarted." Most important, members of the Electoral College would be pressured to do the right thing and switch their vote for Dubya. In summing up the entire proposed operation, a Bush aide succinctly stated: "The one thing we don't do is roll over—we fight."

(Lest you believe the *Boston Herald* article was part of some liberal media plot to smear the Shrub campaign, the plan was never denied by any member of the campaign, and was cited with gleeful approval before the election by the right-wing GOP-linked website Newsmax, which labeled as "obvious" the unfairness of the Electoral College system.)

Oddly, when Gore defeated Dubya in the popular vote, the massive talk-radio campaign against the trumping of the people's will never happened. Instead, a campaign rallied against Gore and his VP pick Joseph Lieberman (who were quickly referred to as "Sore-Loserman") for daring to challenge the results of the Shrub "victory" as granted by an infallible Electoral College.

Gore (to his credit) never risked provoking a Constitutional crisis by challenging the legitimacy of the Electoral College. Instead, the Gore campaign focused its challenges on the official voting results in Florida, where a supposed win by Dubya granted 25 electoral votes toward his Electoral College majority. (270 votes were needed, and Bush finished with 271 to Gore's 266.)

At face value, the 2000 Florida election stinks. The Governor of the state then was Jeb Bush, Shrub's brother, who is still in office. The Secretary of State, whose job was to certify the results and ensure the election's integrity, was Katherine Harris, a right-wing hack with ties to both Bush brothers. (She was co-chair of the Bush 2000 campaign in Florida.) The official margin of victory in Florida: 537 votes out of nearly six million. Even without any further evidence, such results would have deservedly met with snickers and skepticism had they been announced in some backwards banana republic.

Further worries were soon noted. The most infamous example was the "butterfly ballot" in Palm Beach County. Presidential candidates were listed on two pages in the county, with Pat Buchanan's name listed in between Bush's and Gore's in a manner that confused many voters, who weren't sure which hole was for Buchanan and which for Gore. The upshot: Buchanan received a total of 3,424 votes in the county, or 0.79% of the total. Statewide, Pat won a mere 0.34% of the vote, and Palm Beach, a haven for retired liberal Jewish voters, was an unlikely hotbed of support for the ultra-conservative commentator with a penchant for anti-Semitic rhetoric.

That wouldn't stop Team Bush from arguing precisely that. "Palm Beach County is a Pat Buchanan stronghold," Ari Fleischer would quickly proclaim to explain the discrepancy (in the first of many seemingly delusional pronouncements). When questioned about this claim, Jim McConnell, Buchanan's Florida coordinator, told Jake Tapper of *Salon*, "That's nonsense." He estimated the number of Buchanan supporters in the county at no more than 500. McConnell explained the Buchanan campaign did no advertising in the county, as "the percentage of people down there who would be receptive to our message is much smaller than in other parts of the state." On the suspiciously high totals, he declared: "Do I believe that these people inadvertently cast their votes for Pat Buchanan? Yes, I do. We have to believe that based on the vote totals elsewhere." How many legitimate votes did he believe Pat received in the area? "I think 1,000 would be generous." This jibes with the statistical evidence.

Showing more integrity than Dubya, Pat Buchanan stated on the *Today* show, "I don't want any votes that I did not receive and I don't want to win any votes by mistake."

Of course, some of the Buchanan voters were likely confused Shrub fans as well. So let's give him the benefit of the doubt, and assume (generously) that a quarter of the 2,400 votes above Buchanan's (generous) 1000 were actually for him. That still would give Gore a net total of 1,800 votes, than enough to switch Florida's Electoral Votes to Al and push him into the White House.

But that is only part of the math. As it turned out, the faulty design lead to 6,607 discarded ballots, "overvotes" by voters who chose both Buchanan and Gore. There were also 1,631 overvotes for Bush and Buchanan (less than a quarter of the Pat-Al total) for a net difference of slightly fewer than 5,000 votes. Adding to that the 2,908 overvotes for Gore and Socialist David McReynolds (whose name appeared below Gore's on the opposite page) gives nearly 7,900 votes that probably should have gone to Gore, but did not.

That Al Gore lost thousands of votes—and thus the White House—over a ballot design glitch should outrage anyone who believes in fundamental democratic rights, but the American press treated it as an acceptable snafu. And yet, this was only the beginning of the deception surrounding the 2000 Florida election.

The most comprehensive investigation of the 2000 Florida election was by journalist Greg Palast, an American who, ironically enough, was working in Britain for the UK *Guardian*, the *London Observer*, and the BBC at the time. While most of the American press was downplaying the Jews-for-Buchanan fiasco, Palast rolled up his sleeves and researched an even more sordid scandal.

In the months before the election, Katherine Harris ordered 57,700 voters purged from the voter registries, claiming they were felons with no right to vote. The purge list, however, was inaccurate. For example, on one of the scrub lists, Palast uncovered 325 names with conviction dates in the future. Office clerks in the Secretary of State's office were told to blank out the dates of these time-travelers before they sent the lists to county election supervisors. The compiled purge lists had over 4,000 blank conviction dates.

Even without the Back-to-the-Future felons, the making of the list was a bogus enterprise. Suffixes such as "Jr." and "Sr." and middle names or initials were removed from the matching criteria in compiling the names to validate the list. Partial matches of first or last names (the first four letters) counted as a match, even in reverse order: for example, an "Anderson Christian" could wipe out a "Chris Anders." Meanwhile, DBT ChoicePoint, the private firm hired to compile the list, didn't bother to match address histories, though they had the information. Though DBT had 1,200 databases and four billion records to check the list against, none were checked. Only four criteria were used for verification: the partial name match, date of birth, gender, and race.

Why did race make the short list? Looking at the evidence, David Bositis, a voting demographics expert from the Washington's Center for Political and Economic Studies, declared it an "obvious technique to discriminate against Black voters." 46 percent of convicted felons are African Americans: therefore, a list of felons with a racial classification would have a near majority of blacks on it. Bositis concluded that the program "must have had a partisan motivation."

African Americans have an interesting voting pattern when it comes to presidential elections. In the 20 years since Reagan and Bush Sr. took over the White House, they have as a group come to distrust the Republican Party. As a result, over 90% of African Americans vote for the Democratic ticket (it was 93% in Florida 2000). In setting the criteria for the final purge list, the Secretary of State's office had hunted down the black vote, removing voters who would have damaged the election hopes of Jeb's brother.

How flawed was the list? At first, DBT ChoicePoint boasted to Palast that it was "85 percent correct." If this is true, that would still have been enough to alter the outcome of the election. However, Leon County officials chose to independently verify the list, and could only confirm 34 out of 694 on the list. Using these sample data and statistics, Palast concluded that the list was in error over 90% of the time.

To be fair to DBT, they were merely following the instructions of Katherine Harris's office. Under oath, ChoicePoint VP James Lee revealed that the state of Florida, not DBT, gave directions for compiling the list that the company warned would cause eligible voters to be erroneously included. Kat Harris, simultaneously in charge of both voter rolls and Shrub's Florida election campaign, ignored their warnings. Not that ChoicePoint, a company with tight ties to the GOP, complained too loudly on receiving an inflated multi-million dollar contract for intentionally shoddy work.

(Because of the controversy, DBT have left the business of ensuring voting integrity. Their replacement? Arthur Andersen, the upstanding accounting firm that vouched for Enron's books.)

Not all names on the list were removed from the voter rolls; a few counties rejected the scrub list. One notable example was Madison County. Linda Howell, the county election supervisor, had a personal reason to suspect the lists were flawed: she was erroneously included on them. In other areas, voters could appeal their inclusion, though some counties didn't bother to inform those affected of their loss of voting rights. ("I don't think that it's up to U.S. to tell them they're a convicted felon," explained Etta Rosado of Volusia County, which neither confirmed the information nor informed people they had been dropped from voter rolls.) Palast and the BBC concluded that at least 22,000 votes for Al Gore were lost through the voter purge operation.

Palast also discovered that at least 50,000 Floridians were illegally disenfranchised from voting by Governor Jeb Bush's office. These citizens, convicted felons from other states who never lost their voting rights, were denied their civil rights in defiance of court rulings. As 80% of all registered voters cast ballots, and 90% of the targeted demographic (out-of-state ex-cons) vote Democrat, Jeb's operation cost Al Gore at least 30,000 votes.

As a high percentage of these voters were African-American, the program was another racially targeted hatchet job inspired (at the very least) by political pragmatism. De facto Jim Crow didn't end there. Counties with a high percentage of black voters tend to be poorer; they had older voting equipment with much higher error rates. In some cases, the quality of the equipment wasn't even the factor. Accuvote is a machine that ensures paper ballot errors are corrected before the voter is through. In Leon, a primarily white county, the machinery reduced spoiled ballots to one in 500. Nearby Gadsden, a black-majority county, had the same machinery, but, for some reason, the reject mechanism wasn't activated, and one in eight ballots was spoiled. And these examples pale beside shocking news reports of white Highway Patrol officers setting up intimidating checkpoints near voting sites in a heavily black district of Broward County.

Writer Dave McGowan noted on his website other curious reports. In Volusia County, a precinct originally reported to the state that Bush had received 2,813 votes—in a county with 412 total ballots cast. Incredibly, Gore's vote total was even more suspicious: it was reported as −16,022, thus reducing his statewide vote total. At least in this case, the error (described as a "computer glitch" in *USA Today*) was discovered and corrected, but it calls into question the accuracy of the entire vote-counting process. In another Volusia County incident, sheriff's deputies investigated why an election worker left the ballot collection area with two uninspected bags. The *Washington Post* reported with a straight face that he was "merely taking home dirty laundry." The *UK Times* reported that as many as 17,000 ballots in primarily black areas were pre-punched for rival candidates, thus disqualifying the ballot when opponents were selected (which may have something to do with the abnormal number of rejected ballots in mostly African-American areas). All these mainstream news reports are disturbing but have yet to be thoroughly investigated. Even without these examples, the 2000 Florida election results would outsleaze any swampland swindle.

You'd think that all the evidence cited would've had supported compelling arguments that something was fishy in Florida. And yet the Gore campaign (to its great shame) ignored all the evidence. Evidently the Gore lawyers believed it was a loser bet, as if issues such as evidence of voter disenfranchisement and fraud are technicalities in a presidential election. Instead, they argued that, even with the Jews for Buchanan and the twin voter ethnic-cleansing programs of Jeb and Kat, Al Gore would have won the election if the ballots has been counted right.

This argument by the Gore campaign also met with obstruction by Team Bush, the office of Katherine Harris, and the U.S. Supreme Court (see Reason #25). Meanwhile, important facts were ignored while terms such as "hanging chad" and "dimpled ballots" became part of mainstream currency and the Bush campaign moaned about "recount after recount." The will of the Florida public was rejected in December 2000 for the highest of offices, and this led to an invalid election result. At the very least, there could have been a revote in Florida, either in Palm Beach County or statewide. This is a normal way to settle legitimately disputed elections, with a precedent in presidential elections: because of faulty voting machines, a revote was held in one Maryland county for the 1972 election, eight days after election. The revote was included in the state's final totals and certified by Congress. If Dubya truly desired to restore dignity to the presidency, he would have demanded no less himself.

None of this was meant to be. The end result is a national disgrace: a phony election illegitimately putting into office a sorry excuse for a man. The theft of the presidency is a fundamental betrayal of democracy. For this reason alone, Bush deserves to be rejected in 2004, to restore basic legitimacy to a government that is supposed to be of the people, by the people, and for the people.

Sources:

2000 Presidential General Election Results. Federal Election Commission, December 2001 ⟨http://www.fec.gov/pubrec/2000presgeresults.htm⟩.

Alterman, Eric. "For The Good Of The Nation, Let The Revoting Begin." *Common Dreams*, 10 November 2000 ⟨http://www.commondreams.org/views/111000-106.htm⟩.

Cowan, Rich. "13 Myths About The Results Of The 2000 Election." *Albion Monitor*, 14 November 2000 ⟨http://www.monitor.net/monitor/0011a/election2000myth.html⟩.

"The GOP's Popular-Vote Hypocrisy." *The Consortium*, 10 November 2000 ⟨http://www.consortiumnews.com/2000/111000a.html⟩.

"Gore's Florida 'Victory.'" *The Consortium*, 22 November 2000 ⟨http://www.consortiumnews.com/2000/112200a.html⟩.

Harris, Jeff. "A Statistical Analysis of the Florida Vote." *Online Journalism Review*, 4 April 2002 ⟨http://www.ojr.org/ojr/ethics/1017962655.php⟩.

Kick, Russ. "The Fix Is In." alterNewswire, December 2000 ⟨http://www.mindpollen.com/fix.htm⟩.

Lawsky, David. "Gore Supporters Say Ballots Cost Him Their Vote." Reuters, 21 November 2000 ⟨http://www.reuters.com⟩.

McGowan, Dave. "The Unelectable Son, Part II." The Center for an Informed America, 15 November 2000 ⟨http://davesweb.cnchost.com/votescam2.htm⟩.

Meyer, Philip. "Glitch Led to 'Bush Wins' Call." *USA Today*, 29 November 2000 ⟨http://www.unc.edu/~pmeyer/usat29nov2000.html⟩.

"Newspaper: Butterfly Ballot Cost Gore White House." CNN, 11 March 2000 ⟨http://www.cnn.com/2001/ALLPOLITICS/03/11/palmbeach.recount⟩.

Palast, Greg. *The Best Democracy Money Can Buy*. New York: Plume, 2003.

"Pat Buchanan Says His Palm Beach Votes Belong to Gore." Yahoo News, 9 November 2000 ⟨http://dailynews.yahoo.com/h/nm/20001109/pl/election_buchanan_dc_1.html⟩.

Seeley, John. "Early and Often." *L.A. Weekly*, 17–23 November 2000 ⟨http://www.laweekly.com/ink/00/52/politics-seeley.php⟩.

Tapper, Jake. "Buchanan Camp: Bush Claims Are 'Nonsense.'" *Salon*, 10 November 2000 ⟨http://dir.salon.com/politics/feature/2000/11/10/buchanan/index.html⟩.

Tapper, Jake. *Down and Dirty: The Plot to Steal the Presidency*. New York: Little Brown & Company, 2001.

"'What If' Scenarios Add Spark to Election." NewsMax.com, 2 November 2000 ⟨http://www.newsmax.com/articles/?a=2000/11/1/232310⟩.

2

→ 9/11: HE KNEW

September 11 was the defining moment of Shrub's illegal reign. Bush and his cohorts acknowledge this with creepy delight, as they shamelessly exploit the deaths of over 3,000 Americans for political profit at every opportunity. Dubya's most noted accomplishment is holding office during the worst national security failure in U.S. history. It indicates a pathology of American society that the public's respect for Bush and his supposed mandate both come from his most obvious fuck-up.

The question remains about 9/11: what kind of fuck-up was it? Were Shrub and his cohorts totally unprepared for the terrorist attacks, because the CIA (which was run by George Tenet, a Clinton leftover, as Bush apologists like to point out) and other intelligence agencies dropped the ball on collecting and presenting data? Or was the Bush Team handed ample information that was met with a disastrous nonchalance?

From the start, the Bush administration insisted that it had been impossible to conceive of using hijacked planes to attack U.S. targets. That's false, since a 1999 CIA report described precisely that possibility. There have also been at least two previous attempts by terrorists to use planes as bombs: one in 1994, in a plot to destroy the Eiffel Tower, and the other in 1986, in a plan to blow up a plane over Tel Aviv. The 1993 World Trade Center bomber Ramzi Yousef also was known to have entertained a fantasy of hijacking 11 planes and blowing them up over the Pacific Ocean. Bush could be expected to have heard about the failed September 12, 1994 kamikaze attack on the White House by a lone nut.

Further, twice in recent years authorities have put security measures in place to deter plane-as-missile attacks: 1996, during the Summer Olympics in Atlanta, and—less than two months before 9/11—in Genoa, Italy, during the July 2001 G8 summit.

Despite these facts, for eight months, the Dubya gang was given a free ride by the establishment press on this central question, as they pushed for (and received) huge increases in defense spending and police powers to combat the Osama menace. By May 2002, however, there was a shift in perception even among mainstream news sources, as revelations made clear where the finger should be pointed. On May 16, 2002, one outlet went so far as to choose "9/11 Bombshell: Bush Knew" as its front-page headline. This was met with outrage by Bush spokesman Ari Fleischer, who declared the headline "irresponsible" and "a poster child for bad journalism." Which reckless left-wing outfit chose the headline—was it *The Village Voice*, perhaps? *Mother Jones*? *The Socialist Worker*?

Actually, it was the *New York Post*, which rivals the *Washington Times* and the *Wall Street Journal* as the top right-wing cheerleader for the Shrub gang. (Little surprise, as the *Post* is owned by Rupert Murdoch, the media baron behind "Fair and Balanced" FOX News.)

What forced even the most devoted of Bush apologists to publish such a damning headline? The revelation that Dubya had been personally warned on August 6, 2001 (during his month-long slackathon in Crawford) of an Osama bin Laden terror network plot involving the hijacking of passenger airliners. The heading for the briefing: "Bin Laden determined to strike in the U.S."

For eight months, Bush had insisted that, had he known al Qaeda was planning an attack, he "would have done everything in power to protect the American people." He had also said to Tom Brokaw in January 2002, "It's hard to envision a plot so devious as the one that they pulled off on 9/11. Never did we realize that the enemy was so well-organized."

Here's some more evidence, known to authorities, that should have suggested something devious was in the works:

→ In a May 2001 briefing, CIA officials informed Bush of signs of increased activity by al Qaeda, and that bin Laden's terrorist group might try to hijack U.S. airliners. (Source: *USA Today*.)

→ On June 22, the FAA renewed warnings to airlines about terrorism. Four more warnings were provided in the next two months, including one about the use of disguised weapons. (Source: CNN.)

→ On June 26, U.S. intelligence sources reported to the White House a spike in communications about possible terrorist attacks. The State Department issued a worldwide alert to operate with caution, and closed the U.S. embassies in Senegal and Bahrain to the public. (Source: *Time*.)

→ On June 28, a written intelligence summary for National Security Adviser Condoleezza Rice said: "It is highly likely that a significant al Qaeda attack is in the near future, within several weeks." CIA Director Tenet "repeated this so often that people got tired of hearing it," according to a senior political appointee. (Source: *The Washington Post*.)

→ On July 5, Richard Clarke, the government's top counterterrorism official, bluntly stated in a White House meeting of high ranking officials: "Something really spectacular is going to happen here, and it's going to happen soon." All counterterrorism agencies (including the FAA, Coast Guard, FBI, Secret Service, and INS) were told to cancel vacations and nonessential travel. (Source: *The Washington Post*.)

→ In late July, the White House instructed Attorney General John Ashcroft to stop flying on commercial airplanes. In an unprecedented step, he used expensive charter jets (paid for by taxpayers at over $1,600 an hour) even for personal fishing trips. (Source: CBS News, in a pre-September 11 story.)

→ On September 10, a group of top Pentagon officials suddenly canceled travel plans for the next morning, apparently because of security concerns. (Source: *Newsweek*.)

There were also two other widely reported revelations that cast doubt on the Bush Team's claims of ignorance:

→ In July 2001, a classified memo written by a Phoenix FBI agent urged an investigation of a number of Middle Eastern men enrolled in American flight schools, citing bin Laden as someone who could organize such flight training.

→ In mid-August, FBI and immigration officials in Minnesota arrested Zacarias Moussaoui, a French-Moroccan, on immigration charges after he was reported to be acting suspiciously while training at a flight school. The suspicions seem reasonable: he had paid $6,800 in cash, asked for training on large jets despite his limited experience, and asked to learn how to fly but not how to land. An agent stated that Moussaoui "could fly something into the World Trade Center," and the Minnesota team warned the Secret Service before September 11 that a terror team could hijack a plane and "hit the nation's capital."

For the anthology *Everything You Know Is Wrong*, editor Russ Kick presented evidence of foreknowledge in his article "September 11, 2001: No Surprise." Here are some selections:

→ In 1994, Marvin J. Cetron wrote in *The Futurist*, "Targets such as the World Trade Center not only provide the requisite casualties, but, because of their symbolic nature, provide more bang for the buck. . . (Coming down the Potomac) you could make a right turn and take out the Pentagon."

→ The CIA had alleged lead hijacker Mohamed Atta under surveillance from January to May 2000.

→ In June, 2001, Osama bin Laden had stated (and it was publicly reported) that he was preparing a "hard hit" against U.S. interests across the globe.

→ On September 7, 2001, the State Department issued a "worldwide caution" that said: "American citizens may be the target of a terrorist threat from extremist groups with links to Osama bin Laden's al Qaeda organization." Former Secretary of State George Schultz said that he was "startled" by the memo, and that the State Department would only issue this warning "because they had some sort of intelligence. They had some sort of rumbling of something. . . [S]omething was cooking."

→ Florida Governor and Dubya's election swindle-helping brother Jeb called up the state National Guard on September 7, 2001 by an executive order that made reference to "the potential massive damage to life and property that may result from an act of terrorism. . ."

→ Author Salman Rushdie (*The Satanic Verses*) was grounded a week before the attacks from flights, after the FAA told his publisher that U.S. intelligence had warned of "something out there."

→ San Francisco Mayor Willie Brown was scheduled to fly to New York on the morning of September 11. Late on the night before, he received a call warning him to be very careful about flying. Brown has yet to reveal who gave him the warning.

→ In mid-2000, the following web domain names were registered: "attackontwintowers.com," "nycterroriststrike.com," "pearlharborinmanhattan.com," "terroristattack2001.com," "worldtradetowerattack.com," and "wterroristattack2001.com."

→ Two weeks before the attacks, Saddam Hussein put his military on the highest state of alert. The last time he had done that was during Gulf War I over a decade earlier. He hid in his network of bunkers and moved his wives from their palatial Baghdad homes.

→ Israeli, Russian, and Philippine intelligence had given U.S. authorities strong warning about terrorist attacks not long before 9/11.

→ According to German intelligence, U.S., the UK, and Israel intelligence all knew about a plot to hijack jetliners and crash them into U.S. landmarks three months before the September attacks, thanks to the global communications snooping system known as Echelon.

Reviewing the evidence, Kick concluded: "At the very least, the success of the 9/11 attacks reveals gross incompetence, criminal negligence, and general stupidity on the part of intelligence and other aspects of the government. Remember, this is truly the most charitable interpretation that can be given, and a fuller accounting of the facts reveals an even more unwholesome scenario: Some parties in the government knew what was about to happen but failed to act."

These are strong words, but backed up by disturbing facts. The evidence demands a thorough investigation, something that should be an immediate given with an event as calamitous as 9/11. Oddly, the Bush Team stonewalled from the beginning, blocking any investigation until after the November 2002 midterm elections, claiming that it would distract from the "war on terrorism" (never mind that World War II didn't stall an investigation of Pearl Harbor).

Their first choice to head the commission was Henry Kissinger, the consummate political establishment insider. Choosing him to head an "independent" investigation was so ludicrous that even the mainstream press, which normally fawns on Dr. K, mocked his appointment. Under a cloud of controversy and massive conflicts of interest, Kissinger withdrew from the investigation. His replacement, the former Republican Governor of New Jersey Thomas Kean, would charge that the Bush Team intimidated witnesses, blocked access to key documents, and engaged in a pattern of obstructing the investigation. Meanwhile, a July 2003 report by the Congressional committee investigation includes 15 pages detailing areas in which information was denied, limited, or delayed by the Bush administration.

Some paranoid conspiracy theorists may conclude from the above information that there is some sort of diabolical plot going on involving 9/11 and Team Shrub. While there may something to these theories, it is not necessary to indict Dubya and his accomplices. After all, Bush, during his losing bid to be elected president, touted himself as the "CEO president" who would run the country as would a corporate head honcho. Any CEO with a screw-up on his record near the magnitude of 9/11 would be toast. In that spirit, it would be downright ridiculous to elect a man president who was ultimately responsible for such a miserable failure.

Sources:

"9/11: Bush Knew." *BuzzFlash*, September 2003
‹http://www.buzzflash.com/perspectives/911bush.html›.

Ackerman, Seth. "Who Knew?" *In These Times*, 3 September 2003
‹http://www.inthesetimes.com/comments.php?id=340_0_1_0_C›.

Buncombe, Andrew. "Bush Told in August of Specific Threat to U.S.." *The UK Independent*, 19 May 2002 ‹http://news.independent.co.uk/world/americas/story.jsp?story=296628›.

"Bush Asks Daschle to Limit Sept. 11 Probes." CNN, 29 January 2002
‹http://www.cnn.com/2002/ALLPOLITICS/01/29/inv.terror.probe/›.

"Bush Briefed on Hijacking Threat before September 11." CNN, 15 May 2002
‹http://www.cnn.com/2002/U.S./05/15/bush.sept.11›.

"Bush Names Kissinger to Head 9/11 Probe." CNN, 29 November 2002
‹http://www.cnn.com/2002/ALLPOLITICS/11/27/intelligence.probe›.

Davis, Patty, and Lewandowski, Beth. "FAA Says It Cautioned Airlines of Hijack Threat before Attacks." CNN, 17 May 2002 ‹http://www.cnn.com/2002/TRAVEL/NEWS/05/16/airlines.warning›.

Elliot, Michael. "How the U.S. Missed the Clues." *Time*, 27 May 2002
‹http://www.time.com/time/magazine/story/0,9171,1101020527-238609-1,00.html›.

Farrell, Maureen. "The Attack Has Been Spectacular." *BuzzFlash*, 1 July 2003
⟨http://www.buzzflash.com/farrell/03/07/01.html⟩.

Gellman, Barton. "Before Sept. 11, Unshared Clues and Unshaped Policy." *Washington Post*, 17 May 2002: A01.

Goldberg, Michelle. "The Bush 9/11 Spin Machine" *Salon*, 16 May 2002
⟨http://archive.salon.com/politics/feature/2002/05/16/spin/index.html⟩.

Haag, John. "'Access Denied to Joint Inquiry on 9-11 by Bush Administration." *BuzzFlash*, 29 July 2003 ⟨http://www.buzzflash.com/contributors/03/07/29_denied.html⟩.

Report of the Joint Inquiry into the Terrorist Attacks of September 11, 2001. The House Permanent Select Committee on Intelligence and the Senate Select Committee on Intelligence. FindLaw, 24 July 2003 ⟨http://news.findlaw.com/nytimes/docs/911rpt/index.html⟩.

Isikoff, Michael, and Hosenball, Mark. "Full Disclosure?" *Newsweek*, 24 September 2003 ⟨http://www.msnbc.com/news/971399.asp?ocl=c1⟩.

Kaplan, Fred. "Critics Mock Choice of Kissinger for Inquiry." *The Sydney Morning Herald*, 29 November 2002 ⟨http://www.smh.com.au/articles/2002/11/28/1038386260108.html⟩.

Kick, Russ. "September 11, 2001: No Surprise." In his *Everything You Know Is Wrong*. New York: The Disinformation Company Ltd., 2002.

"Kissinger Resigns as Head of 9/11 Commission." CNN, 13 December 2002
⟨http://www.cnn.com/2002/ALLPOLITICS/12/13/kissinger.resigns/⟩.

Limbacher, Carl, and NewsMax.com staff. "Fleischer Blasts *Post* over Headline." Newsmax.com, 17 May 2002 ⟨http://www.newsmax.com/showinside.shtml?a=2002/5/17/154042⟩.

Martin, David. "What Bush Knew Before Sept. 11." CBS News, 17 May 2002
⟨http://www.cbsnews.com/stories/2002/05/16/attack/main509294.shtml⟩.

Sanderson, Bill. "Bush Had Hijack Warning." *The New York Post*, 16 May 2002: 2.

Solomon, John. "1999 Report Warned of Suicide Hijack." *Common Dreams*, 17 May 2002
⟨http://www.commondreams.org/headlines02/0517-06.htm⟩.

"Special 9.11 Edition: The Mainstream Catches Up." Bushwatch.com, 20 May 2002
⟨http://www.bushwatch.com/9.11special.htm⟩.

Stewart, Jim. "Ashcroft Flying High." CBS News, 26 July 2001
⟨http://www.cbsnews.com/stories/2001/07/26/national/printable303601.shtml⟩.

"Terror Warnings: Who Knew What When?" BBC News Online, 17 May 2002
⟨http://news.bbc.co.uk/2/low/americas/1992852.stm⟩.

Thomas, Evan, and Hosenball, Mark. "Bush: 'We're at War.'" *Newsweek*, 24 September 2001
⟨http://www.msnbc.com/news/629606.asp⟩.

"Timeline: Signs of Possible Terrorism and the Government's Response." *USA Today*, 4 June 2002 ⟨http://www.usatoday.com/news/sept11/index/missed-clues-timeline.htm⟩.

Vann, Bill. "September 11: After Two Years, Cover-up Begins to Unravel." World Socialist Web Site, 11 September 2003 ⟨http://www.wsws.org/articles/2003/sep2003/s11-s11.shtml⟩.

"Wrestling for the Truth of 9/11." *The New York Times*, 9 July 2003
⟨http://www.nytimes.com/2003/07/09/opinion/09WED1.html⟩.

3

→ WHERE'S OSAMA?

"The most important thing is for U.S. to find Osama bin Laden. It is our number one priority and we will not rest until we find him!"

—George W. Bush, September 13, 2001

"I don't know where he [Osama bin Laden] is . . . I just don't spend that much time on him really, to be honest with you. . . I truly am not that concerned about him."

—George W. Bush, March 13, 2002

Source:

Knight, Rebecca. "Never Give Up!" *BuzzFlash*, 17 June 2002 ‹http://www.buzzflash.com/southern/2002/06/17_southern.html›.

—→ **OSAMAGATE**

One partial explanation for the 9/11 intelligence breakdown has received mainstream reporting and acceptance: that the Bush Team hampered pre-September 11 investigation of Osama and his assets for political and economic reasons. Namely, an investigation of bin Laden's terror network would have offended the Saudi Arabian kingdom, Afghanistan's Taliban, and—surprise, surprise—oil interests.

One man likely to have been a proponent of this theory is John O'Neill, an FBI Deputy Director and head of New York City's anti-terrorism unit. O'Neill had been the top U.S. investigator of Osama bin Laden and al Qaeda for six years, having investigated the bombings of the U.S. African embassies and the USS *Cole* in Yemen.

Two weeks before September 11, he left his FBI post. Jean-Charles Brisard and Guillaume Dasquie (two French intelligence analysts and authors of *Forbidden Truth*) claim that he resigned to protest the placement of U.S. oil interests over bringing Osama and al Qaeda to justice. (This may be a self-serving claim by the controversial O'Neill, who left a marginalized figure. Still, his pariah status underscores his belief that his investigations were politically unpopular and unwelcome.) According to Brisard, O'Neill declared: "The main obstacles to investigating terrorism were U.S. oil corporate interests and the role played by Saudi Arabia in it."

From February to August 2001, the Bush administration was in secret diplomacy with the Islamic fundamentalist Taliban, who ruled Afghanistan. The purpose: a proposed Central Asian oil pipeline that would run through their country from a gigantic Caspian Sea reserve (more on this below). Indeed, less than four months before September 11, the U.S. pledged $43 million in assistance to Afghanistan, raising the total aid for the year to $124 million and making the U.S. the largest humanitarian donor to the nation. The Taliban were financially tied to bin Laden, who was living in defiance on their turf. The Bush Team blocked investigations of bin Laden and terrorism during these negotiations.

The kid glove treatment of those tied to al Qaeda and bin Laden didn't begin there: an entire network of Saudi businesses and charities financed the terror organization. According to Brisard, Saudi Arabia has transferred $500 million to al Qaeda over the past decade. It continues to finance bin Laden's terror network after the 9/11 attacks. Brisard concludes, "One must question the real ability and willingness of the kingdom to exercise any control over the use of religious money in and outside of the country."

Although officially bin Laden was in exile from Saudi Arabia since 1994, until 1998 he was able to use Saudi financial structures and had known contacts with Saudi officials. This should be no surprise: the repressive Saudi regime has maintained power, despite widespread discontent, by placating Islamic fundamentalists. As a result, it was a strong supporter (along with bin Laden) of the Taliban.

The FBI was fully aware of the situation. However, as Saudi Arabia is one of America's top suppliers of oil (and one of the U.S. defense industry's biggest clients), any investigation of these financial and political arrangements has long been viewed as politically taboo. Untouchability has extended to the bin Laden family—with the exception of supposed family black sheep Osama—a $12 billion virtual arm of the Saudi kingdom.

After the bombing on the USS *Cole* in October 2000, a Pentagon investigation concluded in January 2001 that al Qaeda had carried out the attack. The Clinton Administration did not respond because the investigation was completed during transition, and they didn't want to appear to be "wagging the dog" during the election to help Gore (as some charged about the August 1998 attacks on Sudan and Afghanistan during the Peckergate scandal). However, as Clinton White House senior advisor Sidney Blumenthal pointed out in a BuzzFlash interview, they "briefed the incoming Bush team of the imminent and urgent threat from al Qaeda. But the Bush people brushed this aside, downplaying terrorism as they played up missile defense in space. They ignored the warnings of Richard Clarke, who remained head of counterterrorism at the National Security Council, and took no action against Al Qaeda. . . It was the Bush administration that was presented the evidence about Al Qaeda's role in the attack on the USS *Cole*, not the Clinton administration. But George W. Bush did absolutely nothing—absolutely nothing."

John O'Neill intimately understood many of these details, and would have likely been a powerful critic of the Shrubian policy that undermined investigation into Osama and company before 9/11. But, in a morbid fortuity for the Bush Team, O'Neill died in the September 11 attacks, having just begun his new job as head of security in the World Trade Center.

The obstruction continued after September 11. In the immediate aftermath of 9/11, U.S. airspace was highly restricted. Despite this, planes flew around the country gathering about 140 privileged Saudi Arabians, including several relatives of Osama bin Laden, who were spirited out of the country by September 19. Some bin Laden family members were driven or flown under FBI supervision to a secret assembly point in Texas. Dale Watson, the FBI's former head of counter-terrorism, said, "they were not subject to serious interrogations." According to former White House counterterrorism chief Richard Clarke, the Bush administration approved of the operation.

Though there is no official confirmation, the Saudi ambassador to the United States, Prince Bandar bin Sultan, is believed to have organized the operation. (Prince Bandar met with George W. Bush on Sept. 13, 2001.) Prince Bandar had donated millions to bin Laden's favorite quasi-charity, the International Islamic Relief Organization. Up to $150,000 in donations made by his wife, Princess Haifa bin Faisal (the daughter of the late King Faisal), wound up in the hands of two of the alleged 9/11 hijackers. In the eight weeks following 9/11, the FBI detained over 1,000 suspects and potential witnesses, yet a group of people who arguably deserved the greatest suspicion were given the most lenient treatment.

In 2003, a 28-page chapter from the Congressional report focused on the ties between the 9/11 hijackers and agents of the Saudi government. Congressional sources claim that the Bush administration delayed the report for months over details surrounding Saudi involvement with al Qaeda.

Despite the stonewalling, a $116 trillion lawsuit has been filed by the families of the 9/11 victims against Saudi officials, banks, charities, and other defendants, claiming that they financed al Qaeda. Besides Osama bin Laden and the Taliban, defendants include Prince Sultan bin Abdul Aziz (Saudi Arabia's third-ranking leader, holding the titles of Deputy Prime Minister, Minister of Defense, Aviation Inspector, and Inspector General), Prince Turki al-Faisal (Saudi Arabia's Department of General Intelligence Chief from 1977 to 2001), Prince Mohammed al-Faisal, the Muslim World League, the Benevolence International Foundation, Al Haramain Islamic Foundation, the Faisal Islamic Bank, and the Saudi bin Laden Group (owned by bin Laden's brothers). Also named were Khalid bin Salim bin Mahfouz and Mohammed Hussein al Amoudi. Their families own Delta Oil, Unocal's partner in the proposed Afghan oil pipeline project. Mahfouz, a powerful banker, is a brother-in-law of Osama.

Add to all this the fact that 15 of the 19 alleged September 11 hijackers were Saudi citizens, and one can't help but wonder, along with filmmaker-writer Michael Moore, "Dear 'Mr. President,' who attacked the United States on September 11th—a guy on dialysis from a cave in Afghanistan, or our friends, the Saudi Arabians?"

It's a very good question—one that won't be answered as long as we have someone controlling the White House so closely tied to oil interests. These ties promoted an intelligence vacuum that helped lead to 9/11 and continues to hinder any real investigation of what happened.

Sources:

"$116 Trillion Lawsuit Filed by 9/11 Families." CNN, 16 August 2002 ‹http://www.cnn.com/2002/LAW/08/15/attacks.suit›.

"Bin Ladens Evacuated from U.S. After 9-11." WorldNetDaily.com, 4 September 2003 ‹http://www.worldnetdaily.com/news/printer-friendly.asp?ARTICLE_ID=34405›.

Blumenthal, Sidney. *The Clinton Wars*. New York: Farrar Straus & Giroux, 2003.

Brisard, Jean-Charles, and Dasquie, Guillaume. *Forbidden Truth: U.S.-Taliban Secret Oil Diplomacy, and the Failed Hunt for Bin Laden*. New York: Nation Books, 2002.

Burleigh, Nina. "Bush, Oil and the Taliban." *Salon*, 8 February 2002 ‹http://www.salon.com/politics/feature/2002/02/08/forbidden›.

Chossudovsky, Michel. "New Chairman of 9/11 Commission Had Business Ties with Osama's Brother in Law." Centre for Research on Globalisation, 27 December 2002 ‹http://globalresearch.ca/articles/CHO212A.html›.

Godoy, Julio. "U.S. Policy Towards Taliban Influenced by Oil—Authors." *Common Dreams*, 15 November 2001 ‹ http://www.commondreams.org/headlines01/1115-06.htm›.

Kolker, Robert. "O'Neill Versus Osama." *New York Magazine*, 17 December 2001 ‹http://www.newyorkmetro.com/nymetro/news/sept11/features/5513/›.

Lynne, Diana. "Saudis Still Financing al-Qaida." WorldNetDaily.com, 27 February 2003 ‹http://www.worldnetdaily.com/news/article.asp?ARTICLE_ID=31265›.

"The Man Who Knew." *Frontline*, 3 October 2002 ‹http://www.pbs.org/wgbh/pages/frontline/shows/knew/etc/synopsis.html›.

Mikkelson, Barbara. "Rumors of War (Flight of Fancy)." Urban Legends Reference Pages, 6 September 2003 ‹http://www.snopes.com/rumors/flight.htm›.

Moore, Michael. *Dude, Where's My Country?* New York: Warner Books, 2003.

Palast, Greg. *The Best Democracy Money Can Buy*. New York: Plume, 2003.

Phillips, Peter, and Project Censored. *Censored 2003*. New York: Seven Stories Press, 2002.

"Sept. 11 Families Sue Saudis, Sudan." CBS News, 16 August 2002 ‹http://www.cbsnews.com/stories/2002/08/15/attack/main518849.shtml›.

Tyler, Patrick E. "Fearing Harm, Bin Laden Kin Fled from U.S." *The New York Times*, 30 September 2001: A1.

"The Weekly Standard vs. BuzzFlash.com and Sidney Blumenthal: Part III." *BuzzFlash*, 9 September 2003 ‹http://www.buzzflash.com/editorial/03/09/09.html›.

Weiss, Murray. *The Man Who Warned America: The Life and Death of John O'Neill, the FBI's Embattled Counterterror Warrior*. New York: HarperCollins Publishers, 2003.

"Who's Who of the Defendants in the Sept. 11 Lawsuit." *The Charleston Post and Courier*, 22 June 2003 ‹http://www.charleston.net/stories/062203/911_22sidedef.shtml›.

5

→ LIARGATE

In 1998, impeachment proceedings were launched against President Bill Clinton, and his removal from office was narrowly averted. While the purpose of this book is not to defend Clinton, it is important to note that the main reason for the impeachment was that Clinton had lied about his personal sexual relations in a private lawsuit. This, we were told by GOP mouthpieces, was reason enough to warrant dumping a man from the office he was elected to: after all, rule of law was at stake.

By those standards, what should be done to a man who lied about the reasons for going to war and committed fraud in promoting a war that has cost billions of dollars and (so far) hundreds of lives of American soldiers?

On January 28, 2003, Bush declared in his State of the Union speech, "The British government has learned that Saddam Hussein recently sought significant quantities of uranium from Africa." This claim, central to the allegation that Iraq under Hussein was developing a nuclear arsenal, and thus was a clear and present danger to American security, led to war less than two months later.

Retroactive revision by the Bushistas notwithstanding, this wasn't a trivial statement. In the hysteria leading up to the war against Iraq, demands for evidence beyond this allegation of Iraqi malfeasance were dismissed as creating unnecessary and dangerous delay, on grounds that "the first sign of a smoking gun may be a mushroom cloud."

But the CIA had already investigated and discredited the Nigerian uranium tale. In fact, when asked to repeat many of the claims Bush made in the SOTU, Secretary of State Colin Powell, before he went in front of the United Nations on February 5, deleted much of the material provided, and—according to *U.S. News & World Report*—declared, "I'm not reading this. This is bullshit."

This was publicly revealed on July 6, when Joseph Wilson published an op-ed piece in the *New York Times*. The CIA had dispatched Wilson, an acting ambassador to Iraq before the first Gulf War, to Niger in February 2002 to investigate the allegation. Finding no credible evidence, he concluded that it was probably a crock. Because of this, the CIA had the claim removed from at least two speeches: Shrub's October 2002 address on the Iraqi threat, and a speech by U.N. Ambassador John Negroponte. The CIA protested its inclusion in the SOTU address but, in a compromise with the insistent White House, signed off, conditional upon the claim's being attributed to the British. (The British claim was based on forgeries that, according to International Atomic Energy Agency director general Mohamed El Baradei, "are so bad that I cannot imagine that they came from a serious intelligence agency.")

The mainstream press and political establishment ignored the implications of the revelation until Florida Senator Bob Graham spoke out on July 17, 2003. Graham, then a presidential candidate from the more conservative wing of the Democratic Party, declared that Dubya's SOTU claim was bogus: "This is a case in which someone has committed actions that took America to war, put American men and women's lives at risk, and they continue to be at risk. If the standard that was set by the House of Representatives relative to Bill Clinton is the new standard for impeachment, then this clearly comes within that standard." He would add ten days later that, in comparison to Clinton's lies about blowjobs, "the actions of this president [sic] are much more serious in terms of dereliction of duty for the president of the United States."

With all due respect to Senator Graham, no shit. Indeed, the best defense for Bush is that everyone should have known he was lying. Jim McDermott, a congressman from California, had a clue when he warned in September 2002, during a visit to Iraq, "I think the president would mislead the American people."

(Twerpish conservative pundit George Will denounced McDermott over this. Will ranted, "McDermott's accusation that the president—presumably with Cheney, Powell, Rumsfeld, Rice and others as accomplices—would use deceit to satisfy his craving to send young Americans into an unnecessary war is a slander." He added, "Saddam Hussein finds American collaborators among senior congressional Democrats." FOX News blowhard Bill O'Reilly would go further and fume that McDermott was "giving aid and comfort to Saddam while he was in Baghdad." Both have yet to apologize.)

In its attempt to spin away the revelation, the White House first argued that the claim that Saddam had sought uranium in Africa was technically not a lie, since it had been attributed to British intelligence. They added that it took up a mere 16 words of the entire address. This might remind some people of quibbling over the meaning of "is."

Semantic subtleties aside, here are some other falsehoods from the SOTU speech:

→ "Our intelligence officials estimate that Saddam Hussein had the materials to produce as much as 500 tons of sarin, mustard and VX nerve agent. U.S. intelligence indicates that Saddam Hussein had upwards of 30,000 munitions capable of delivering chemical agents. We have also discovered through intelligence that Iraq has a growing fleet of manned and unmanned aerial vehicles that could be used to disperse chemical or biological weapons across broad areas." (None of this has been found. Total words: 71.)

→ "Evidence from intelligence sources, secret communications and statements by people now in custody reveal that Saddam Hussein aids and protects terrorists, including members of Al Qaeda." (No evidence linking Saddam to al Qaeda has turned up. Total words: 26.)

→ "Our intelligence sources tell U.S. that he [Saddam] has attempted to purchase high-strength aluminum tubes suitable for nuclear weapons production." (That these tubes were unsuitable for nuclear weapons production was known months before the war. Total words: 20.)

The Bush Team, in a familiar pattern of passing the buck, tried to lay the controversy at the CIA and George Tenet's feet. Tenet would publicly apologize for allowing the inclusion of the sentence in the speech, which he did not write and to which his agency had objected. The Bush administration would then declare that they had "moved on" and that the "case is closed" on the issue, pretending the scandal was the CIA's and not theirs.

Unfortunately for Shrub, while the media may let political operations steal presidential elections, the CIA doesn't roll over when made the scapegoat. The pathetic attempt to blame Tenet was quickly dismissed as unconvincing, and a half-assed investigation continues.

According to Jason Leopold of Online Journal, a Pentagon committee led by Paul Wolfowitz, the Deputy Secretary of Defense, inserted the fraudulent claims into the speech. This was leaked to Leopold by a CIA official and four senators, who spoke in anonymity under threat of criminal charges for revealing secret information. Wolfowitz, the neoconservative architect of "Operation Iraqi Freedom," headed the Office of Special Plans. Its official job was to gather intelligence on the Iraqi menace not uncovered by the CIA and FBI. In reality, that meant manufacturing evidence, often with the help of the shady (to put it politely) Iraqi defector Ahmad Chalabi. Chalabi heads the Iraqi National Congress, a group of Iraqi exiles backed by the Bush Team.

But the ultimate blame for the SOTU lies falls much higher than Wolfowitz and company. After all, George W. Bush had a major role in it, according to the White House website, which depicts him wearing glasses as he "reviews the text," "rewrites portions of the address" after "sketching notes in the margin of speech drafts," and finally "gives his speechwriting team a few points after revising the State of the Union Address in the Oval Office."

To be fair, since the Bush Team is a gang of pathological liars, and the picture of Bush as rhetorician is incredible, this is presumably itself a lie, aimed at imparting to Shrub some gravitas. But even if the ungrammatical Dubya had nothing to do with writing the speech, he was behind its sentiments. Bush wanted war with Iraq, at any cost of lives and resources, and badly enough to lie to get it. His twisted ends and deceitful means make him unfit for the White House.

Sources:

Alterman, Eric . "'Lyndon B. Bush'?" *The Nation*, 4 August 2003 ‹http://www.thenation.com/doc.mhtml%3Fi=20030804&s=alterman›.

Green, Perri. "The Rest of Your Words, Mr. Bush, Are Also a Problem." *BuzzFlash*, 14 July 2003 ‹http://www.buzzflash.com/contributors/03/07/14_sotu.html›.

Hersh, Seymour M. "Selective Intelligence: Donald Rumsfeld Has His Own Special Sources. Are They Reliable?" *Common Dreams*, 6 May 2003 ‹http://www.commondreams.org/views03/0506-06.htm›.

Leopold, Jason. "Tenet Tells Senators Wolfowitz Committee Gave White House Dubious Intelligence." *Online Journal*, 21 July 2003 ‹http://www.onlinejournal.com/Special_Reports/072103Leopold/072103leopold.html›.

Leopold, Jason. "Wolfowitz Committee Instructed White House to use Iraq/Uranium Reference in State of the Union Speech" *Online Journal*, 16 July 2003 ‹http://www.onlinejournal.com/Special_Reports/07-16-03Leopold/07-16-03leopold.html›.

Pincus, Walter. "Bush Faced Dwindling Data on Iraq Nuclear Bid." *The Washington Post*, 16 July 2003: A01.

Solomon, Norman. "Media's War Boosters Unlikely to Voice Regret." *AlterNet*, 16 July 2003 ‹http://www.alternet.org/story.html?StoryID=16429›.

"State of the Union: Behind the Scenes." The White House, 2003 ‹http://www.whitehouse.gov/stateoftheunion/preparation/index.html›.

Wilson, Joseph C. IV. "What I Didn't Find in Africa." *Common Dreams*, 6 July 2003 ‹http://www.commondreams.org/views03/0706-02.htm›.

6

→ **LEAKGATE**

"Even though I'm a tranquil guy now at this stage of my life, I have nothing but contempt and anger for those who betray the trust by exposing the name of our sources. They are, in my view, the most insidious of traitors."

—George "Poppy" Bush, at the dedication of the George Bush Center for Intelligence.

Sometimes Shrub and his cohorts can't leave a good scandal well enough alone. That is how Liargate morphed into Leakgate. Remember Joseph Wilson? The Bush administration certainly does, after his exposing their case for war on Iraq as a fraud. Eight days after the *New York Times* published Wilson's exposé, right-wing mouthpiece Robert Novak (of *Crossfire* fame) outed Wilson's wife, Valerie Plame, as a CIA operative working on weapons of mass destruction. According to Novak, "two senior administration officials" leaked the information. According to the *Washington Post*, two White House officials called at least six D.C. journalists and disclosed the occupation of Wilson's wife before Novak's article was printed. The primary purpose of the leak was to discredit Wilson, implying that he had received his CIA mission through nepotism. In the process, however, the leakers blew the cover of a CIA agent.

Such a leak violates two federal laws, and carries a penalty of ten years of jail time. Plame was working under "non-official cover" as an energy analyst, meaning that she had little or no protection from the U.S. government. The cost for training an agent such as Plame runs in the millions of dollars, and may include the creation of CIA front companies. In this case, the front was Brewster-Jennings & Associates, which has employed other CIA officers. All of them would be exposed as working for Langley, and anyone associated with Plame or the other agents would now be under suspicion. Presumably, Plame did some of her WMD work in "Axis of Evil" nations Iran and North Korea, where government forces have few qualms about executing suspected enemies of the state. That makes it likely that people have died over this dirty trick. Former CIA officer Jim Marcinkowski declared: "This is not just another leak. This is an unprecedented exposing of an agent's identity."

Oddly, Bush apologists, who not four months before had frothed over the Dixie Chicks' treasonous criticism of Bush in concert, were suddenly downplaying the implications of the scandal. The apologies ignore that the Wilson-Plame affair is Kim Philby meets Watergate, the kind of stuff that topples governments.

Who leaked the information? The likeliest suspect is Karl Rove, Shrub's chief political advisor, surrogate brain, and master of dirty tricks. Whatever he did before the Novak article was published, Wilson insists that afterward Rove contacted numerous journalists and declared that Plame was now "fair game." Another usual suspect among journalists is Lewis Libby, Dick Cheney's chief of staff.

Whoever did it, Bush has shown little interest in finding the culprits. Novak knows who gave him the information, yet Shrub has yet to publicly pressure him to reveal his sources in the interest of national security. The Bush Team has so far resisted an independent investigation, claiming that the Justice Department can do the job by itself. Even so, Dubya declared with a smile that the leakers might not be found. According to Bush, "I have no idea whether we'll find out who the leaker is. I'd like to. I want to know the truth." His smirk gave the lie to his words.

The truth is, we won't get to the bottom of this until a serious investigation is performed, by those not tied to the corrupt and illegal Bush regime. For the sake of national security, that requires someone in the White House besides Shrub.

Sources:

Allen, Mike. "Bush Aides Say They'll Cooperate With Probe into Intelligence Leak." *The Washington Post*, 29 September 2003: A01.

Boehlert, Eric. "Suspicion Centers on Lewis Libby." *Salon*, 3 October 2003 <http://www.salon.com/news/feature/2003/10/03/libby/index_np.html>.

"CIA Seeks Probe of White House." MSNBC, 26 September 2003 <www.msnbc.com/news/937524.asp>.

Conason, Joe. "Agent's 'Outing' a National Outrage." *The New York Observer*, 6 October 2003: 5.

"Getting Personal: Ambassador Says White House Adviser Told Press His Wife Was 'Fair Game.'" ABC News, 1 October 2003 ‹http://abcnews.go.com/sections/nightline/U.S./CIAleak031001.html›.

Henican, Ellis. "Hunt for Leaker Lacks Inspiration." *Common Dreams*, 8 October 2003 ‹http://www.commondreams.org/views03/1008-04.htm›.

Meyer, Dick. "George W. Nixon." CBS News, 24 July 2003 ‹http://www.cbsnews.com/stories/2003/07/24/opinion/meyer/main564891.shtml›.

Mikkelsen, Randall. "Bush Says Leaker May Not Be Found in CIA-Iraq Probe." Yahoo News, 7 October 2003 ‹http://story.news.yahoo.com/news?tmpl=story&u=/nm/20031007/U.S._nm/bush_leak_dc_15›.

Morley, Jefferson. "The Leak and Its Consequences." *The Washington Post*, 1 October 2003 ‹http://www.washingtonpost.com/ac2/wp-dyn/A24144-2003Sep30?language=printer›.

Noah, Timothy. "Did Rove Blow a Spook's Cover?" *Slate*, 16 September 2003 ‹http://slate.msn.com/id/2088471›.

Novak, Robert. "Mission to Niger." Townhall.com, 14 July 2003 ‹http://www.townhall.com/columnists/robertnovak/rn20030714.shtml›.

Scahill, Jeremy, and Goodman, Amy. "Does a Felon Rove the White House?" *AlterNet*, 30 September 2003 ‹http://www.alternet.org/story.html?StoryID=16867›.

Strobel, Warren P. "CIA Identity Leak Far Worse Than Reported." Knight Ridder Newspapers, 11 October 2003 ‹http://www.realcities.com/mld/krwashington/6984705.htm›.

7

→ "BRING 'EM ON!"

On July 2, 2003, with casualties of U.S. soldiers in Iraq mounting two months after their mission was supposedly accomplished, Bush blustered, "There are some who feel like that the conditions are such that they can attack us there. My answer is bring 'em on."

The quote, on the surface, was a charming bit of machismo, perfectly suited for an action hero, worthy of John Wayne, Eastwood, Stallone or (at least in his pre-Governator days) Schwarzenegger before a face-off with a master enemy and his gang.

But there's a gap in the analogy: the Duke, Clint, Sly, or Arnold would only use that line to dare somebody to go after himself, not soldiers under his command. To challenge an enemy to attack others is as far from heroic as one can get. Even Jean-Claude Van Damme knows that much.

When informed of the comment, New Jersey Senator Frank Lautenberg called it "irresponsible and inciteful," and added, "I am shaking my head in disbelief. When I served in the Army in Europe during World War II, I never heard any military commander—let alone the commander in chief—invite enemies to attack U.S. troops." Once again, Shrub violates as none have before.

Since his taunt, daily attacks on U.S. troops have continued unabated. As of Friday, Jan. 2, 483 U.S. service members have died since the beginning of military operations in Iraq, according to the Defense Department. Of those, 330 died as a result of hostile action and 153 died of non-hostile causes, the department said."— AP. Bring 'em on, indeed.

Sources:

"'Bring 'Em On' Fetches Trouble." CBS News, 3 July 2003
<http://www.cbsnews.com/stories/2003/07/03/iraq/main561567.shtml>.

Ewens, Michael. "Casualties in Iraq." *Antiwar*, 14 October 2003
<http://www.antiwar.com/ewens/casualties.html>.

Ticker, Bruce S. "'Bring 'em On' . . . to Someone Else." *The Smirking Chimp*, 14 July 2003
<http://www.smirkingchimp.com/article.php?thold=1&mode=nested&order=0&sid=12225#72770>

8

→ SCREWING OUR TROOPS

The lead-up to "Operation Iraqi Freedom" included constant vili-
fication of anyone vocally opposed to the war by right-wing
mouthpieces, who declared that anti-war activists weren't "supporting our troops." The notion that those who oppose sending
American soldiers into harm's way over a questionable cause are
somehow showing a lack of support is funny.

The punchline is that, although the Bush Team has been
almost as cynically eager to exploit our troops for political gain as
to use the 3,000 who died on September 11, they have done more
to fuck with the lives of American soldiers than anybody in D.C.
since Vietnam.

"Bring 'em on!" and the casualty toll are merely the most
glaring examples of contempt for U.S. fighting men and women.
(Indeed, the callousness of Bush and his supporters was made
clear soon after the battle started: former Reagan and Poppy
Bush speechwriter Peggy Noonan, in a *Wall Street Journal* article
charmingly titled "We Can Take It"—"we" referring to American
soldiers and not pampered conservative blowhards—prattled, "In
a country as in an individual, the ability to withstand pain—the
ability to suffer—says a great deal about character. . . Can we still
take it? It won't be bad for U.S. to see that the answer is yes.")
Here are some other greatest hits of Shrub's brand of support for
our troops:

> → While troops are risking their lives, the wives and families
> of many soldiers are driven to welfare, food stamps, and char-
> ity handouts to survive low salaries relative to costs of living.
> As one military wife put it, "Military salaries are so low that
> they are almost impossible for a family to live on, leaving
> some women desperate, especially now when we also have
> the emotional turmoil of worrying if our men are safe in Iraq."
> Some deals aren't so charitable: in Oceanside, California, a

Main Street riddled with American flags and yellow ribbons also included "short-term loan" operations that would lend cash-strapped families up to $250 in exchange for a post-dated check—and a $44 fee.

→ As the *Christian Science Monitor* reported in July 2003, "Security threats, heat, harsh living conditions, and, for some soldiers, waiting and boredom have gradually eroded spirits." One Army officer described the troops' morale: "They vent to anyone who will listen. They write letters, they cry, they yell. Many of them walk around looking visibly tired and depressed. . . We feel like pawns. . ." Here are some quotes from their letters: "Most soldiers would empty their bank accounts just for a plane ticket home." "Make no mistake, the level of morale for most soldiers that I've seen has hit rock bottom." "The way we have been treated and the continuous lies told to our families back home has devastated U.S. all."

→ Soldiers have been jacked around, given departure dates and then detained in Iraq, month after month, all while sweltering in 120-degree temperatures and subsisting on as little as three liters per day of water. As one man put it, "Our morale is not high or even low. Our morale is nonexistent. We have been told twice that we were going home, and twice we have received a 'stop' movement to stay in Iraq. . . . Our men and women deserve to be treated like the heroes they are, not like farm animals." Sergeant Felipe Vega explained to ABC News his difficulty maintaining morale when the Army keeps changing the orders: "They turn around and slap you in the face." Another soldier said the situation "pretty much makes me lose faith in the Army. I mean, I don't really believe anything they tell me. If they told me we were leaving next week, I wouldn't believe them."

→ In what could amount to the biggest long-term screwing of American troops, some allege that soldiers who have died or become ill from pneumonia are victims of the side effects of anthrax and smallpox vaccines. As of August 2003, 100 soldiers have gotten pneumonia in Iraq and southwestern Asia. Two of them died, and 13 others became so ill they needed respirators. According to Moses Lacy, whose daughter died at the Mayo Clinic, "The common denominator is smallpox and anthrax vaccinations. These young people have given their lives to the military and they are getting a raw deal. The

Department of Defense is closing their eyes." Rachael Lacy became ill days after getting the vaccine on March 2. She was too ill to ever be deployed, and died April 4. Lacy is excluded from the investigation of the pneumonia outbreak, because she never was in Iraq, but her case is suggestive. Dr. Eric Pfeifer, the coroner who performed Lacy's autopsy, declared, "It's just very suspicious in my mind . . . that she's healthy, gets the vaccinations and then dies a couple weeks later." He listed "post-vaccine" problems on the death certificate. Senior Airman Michael Girard also is excluded from the investigation. He got his second anthrax shot before deployment on March 4, developed flu-like symptoms two days later, and by March 12 developed a rash on his left arm where he received the shot. The sickness evolved into bouts of bloody vomiting, leg, feet, and chest pains, constipation, headaches, stomach aches, insomnia, fatigue, and extremely high blood pressure. In one weekend he went to the emergency room four times. A nurse told him it might be pneumonia, a claim quickly reversed. According to Girard, "Everything that has been associated with this ever since I got sick has been like a coverup." He said he "was perfectly 100 percent healthy" before the vaccine: "I was in the gym for an hour to two hours per day. I was running. I was energetic." As Moses Lacy concluded, "Unless somebody breaks this story wide open, we are going to have a lot more deaths. I am afraid we are going to lose a lot because of this vaccine." Considering the history of deception by the Pentagon (Agent Orange and Gulf War Syndrome), his fear seems reasonable. Gulf War Syndrome II may explode very soon.

Meanwhile, here are some of the responses from Dubya and the GOP to the noble sacrifice of duty demonstrated by American troops:

→ While Bush and the Republicans pushed for tax cuts for the rich, they refused to push minor tax provisions that, according to the *Army Times*, "would be a boon to military homeowners, reservists who travel long distances for training and parents deployed to combat zones, among others."

→ The proposed 2004 defense budget would increase raises for some ranks, but also proposes capping raises for E-1s, E-2s and O-1s at 2%, well below the average raise of 4.1 %.

→ The GOP-controlled House of Representatives Budget Committee proposed slashing the Veterans Administration health care budget by $844 million, just as "Operation Iraqi Freedom" was starting. The House Republicans also proposed an additional $463 million cut the following year, and further cuts were planned for the next ten years.

→ Shrub's $9.2 billion military construction request for 2004 was a full $1.5 billion below the previous year's budget. Democratic Representative David Obey proposed restoring $1 billion by trimming the tax cut for people making $1 million by $5,200. His proposal was quickly shot down by Republicans.

→ The White House moaned that various pay-and-benefits incentives added to the 2004 defense budget by Congress would be wasteful and unnecessary—including a proposal to double from $6,000 the bereavement payment to families of troops who die on active duty.

Perhaps the most blatant example came when the DOD announced that it wanted to roll back recent increases in monthly imminent-danger pay and family-separation allowance for troops getting shot at in combat zones after October 1. Calling these payments budget-busters, the Pentagon claimed that they couldn't sustain the higher payments amid a host of other priorities. A White House spokesman referred questions about the proposal to the military.

This leads to a little fuzzy computation:

→ Number of soldiers in Afghanistan and Iraq, August 2003: 157,000

→ Total monthly increase the Pentagon declares is a "budget buster" $225

→ 157,000 times $225: $35,325,000

→ Monthly total times 12 for an annual figure: $423,900,000

The increase proposed on the allowance to those risking their lives in battle is less than a half billion dollars. The 2003 military budget (before extra "emergency" spending on Iraq war) is $400 billion.

Who the hell do they think they're trying to kid here?

Beneath the strained jingoism, anger is building among the troops. Retired Army Colonel David Hackworth, a man reputed to be the "Army's Most Decorated Soldier," has chronicled this. Hackworth, though conservative and hawkish, has a genuine empathy for the troops, having been wounded eight times. He has strong criticisms for the operation in Iraq, and has accurately described Secretary of Defense Donald Rumsfeld as "an arrogant asshole." Here are excerpts from messages he's received from troops:

→ "Soldiers get literally hundreds of flea or mosquito bites and they can't get cream or Benadryl to keep the damn things from itching. . . I am not talking about bringing in the steak and lobster every week. I am talking about basic health and safety issues that continue to be neglected by the Army."

→ "We did not receive a single piece of parts-support for our vehicles during the entire battle. . . not a single repair part has made it to our vehicles to date. . . I firmly believe that the conditions I just described contributed to the loss and injury of soldiers on the battlefield."

→ "We have done our job and have done it well, we have fulfilled our obligation to this operation, but we are still here and are still being mistreated and misled. When does it end? Do we continue to keep the liberators of Iraq here so they can continue to lose soldiers periodically to snipers and ambushes? My unit has been here since September and they have no light at the end of the tunnel. How many of my soldiers need to die before they realize that we have hit a wall?"

→ "The Army seems to have this NTC rotation mentality, which consists of fuck it live in the dirt and filth you only have to be here for a month. That works at NTC, but it seems no one has thought of how to sustain an Army in the field for weeks and months at a time. . . Our supply lines are clear. There is no excuse why basic health and safety issues and morale issues like mail cannot be addressed."

Some soldiers have become even more straightforward in their opinions. Referring to the deck of cards created by the U.S. government featuring Saddam Hussein and other wanted members of the Iraqi regime, one soldier quipped, "I've got my own 'Most Wanted' list. The aces in my deck are Paul Bremer, Donald Rumsfeld, George Bush and Paul Wolfowitz." When asked by ABC News what he'd say if Rumsfeld was in front of him, a soldier said: "I would ask him why we're still here, why we've been told so many times and it's changed." Another flatly declared, "I'd ask him for his resignation." Another soldier described the cause of the war in purely economic terms. "The main reason we're still here is to support Brown and Root," he said, referring to the company, owned by Halliburton (where Dick Cheney was CEO before stealing office), that has received fattened military contracts.

The comments by troops have received a strong response from the Bush Team. "It went all the way up to President Bush and back down again on top of us. At least six of us here will lose our careers." A White House operative "leaked" to Matt Drudge that ABC News correspondent Jeffrey Kofman is Canadian (and thus presumably French). Meanwhile, the Pentagon has launched a counteroffensive, sending out phony "letters from soldiers" to newspapers across the country informing people of U.S. military successes in Iraq. The hoax was uncovered when Gannett News Service discovered 11 identical letters supposedly written by different soldiers to different newspapers.

Despite these desperate attempts at spin, one result seems unavoidable: some 370,000 soldiers are deployed overseas from a total Army force of just over a million. Michael O'Hanlon, a military expert at the Brookings Institution, writes, "Hordes of active-duty troops and reservists may soon leave the service rather than subject themselves to a life continually on the road." With no end in sight to the wars in Iraq and Afghanistan, the U.S. military will likely soon face a major manpower shortage. The effects of Shrub's illegal occupation will reverberate for years: the first step in the recovery of real military defense would be getting someone in office who cares for the soldiers under his command.

Sources:

Benjamin, Mark. "Father of Dead Soldier Claims Army Coverup." *The Washington Times*, 7 August 2003 ‹http://www.washtimes.com/upi-breaking/20030807-043512-3755r.htm›.

Berkowitz, Bill. "Shafting, Not 'Supporting,' the Troops." WorkingForChange.com, 25 July 2003 ‹http://www.workingforchange.com/article.cfm?ItemID=15354›.

Collier, Robert. "Pentagon Retaliates Against GIs Who Spoke Out on TV." *The San Francisco Chronicle*, 18 July 2003: A1.

Epstein, Edward. "Pentagon Says Tough Duty Bonuses Are Budget-buster." *The San Francisco Chronicle*, 14 August 2003: A1.

Franklin, Jonathan. "The War According to David Hackworth." *Salon*, 4 August 2003 ‹http://www.salon.com/news/feature/2003/08/04/hackworth›.

"U.S. Soldiers' Wives Fight Bitter Battle of Their Own." *The Sydney Morning Herald*, 14 April 2003 ‹http://www.smh.com.au/articles/2003/04/13/1050172477656.html›.

King, Ledyard. "Hoaxed 'Good News From Iraq' Letters Exposed." Rense.com, 11 October 2003 ‹http://www.rense.com/general42/lett.htm›.

Kofman, Jeffrey. "A Big Letdown." ABC News, 15 July 2003 ‹http://abcnews.go.com/sections/wnt/World/iraq030716_2ndBrigade.html›.

Meyer, Dick. "George W. Nixon." CBS News, 24 July 2003 ‹http://www.cbsnews.com/stories/2003/07/24/opinion/meyer/main564891.shtml›.

Noonan, Peggy. "We Can Take It." PeggyNoonan.com, 31 March 2003 ‹http://www.peggynoonan.com/article.php?article=147›.

"Nothing but Lip Service." *Army Times*, 30 June 2003 ‹http://www.armytimes.com/print.php?f=0-ARMYPAPER-1954515.php›.

O'Brien, Barbara. "Bush Eats Barbecue. . . Soldiers Starve." DemocraticUnderground.com, 13 August 2003 ‹http://www.democraticunderground.com/articles/03/08/13_starve.html›.

"Reserves Wanting to Leave Mideast." *Augusta Chronicle*, 12 July 2003 ‹http://www.augustachronicle.com/stories/071203/met_021-6883.000.shtml›.

Steward, Charles R. "Republican Attack On U.S. Veterans." *Intervention Magazine*, 8 April 2003 ‹http://www.interventionmag.com/cms/modules.php?op=modload&name=News&file=article&sid=378›.

Tyson, Ann Scott. "Troop Morale in Iraq Hits 'Rock Bottom.'" *The Christian Science Monitor*, 7 July 2003 ‹http://www.csmonitor.com/2003/0707/p02s01-woiq.html›.

9

→ THE IRAQI QUAGMIRE

According to official counts:

Number of U.S. soldiers killed in Iraq since war began:
     550 (as of 2/25/04).

Number of U.S. soldiers officially wounded:
     3,119 (as of 2/25/04).

Estimate of Iraqi civilian casualties:
     10,000 (as of January 2004).

Proposed military commitment of U.S. ground troops for 2004:
     130,000.

Estimated costs in fiscal year 2003 (ending September 30) of the war:
     $79 billion.

Proposed costs in fiscal year 2004 (ending September 30) of the war:
     $87 billion.

Increase in fuel prices attributable to occupation:
     $100 million per day.

Sources:

Costello, Tom. "Washington at War over Iraq Costs." MSNBC, 8 September 2003 <http://stacks.msnbc.com/news/963452.asp>.

Ewens, Michael. "Casualties in Iraq." *Antiwar*, 14 October 2003 <http://www.antiwar.com/ewens/casualties.html>.

Francis, David R. "A Tally of U.S. Taxpayers' Tab for Iraq." *The Christian Science Monitor*, 25 August 2003 <http://www.csmonitor.com/2003/0825/p16s01-coop.html>.

10

➔ "VICTORY" IN IRAQ

When the numbers of casualties in "Operation Iraqi Freedom" are cited, only half the equation is mentioned (actually less than that, as the attempt to discount noncombat deaths and wounded coalition forces reveals). Rarely are any numbers reported of Iraqi military and civilian casualties.

The best estimate for the number of Iraqi civilian deaths comes from the website Iraq Body Count. That's because, as General Tommy Franks put it, "We don't do body counts." Originally, IBC put the total deaths among Iraqi civilians between five and ten thousand. They've since narrowed the number down to between 7,852 and 9,657. This seems to jibe with other reports; the *Los Angeles Times*, for example, reports that between 1,700 and 2,700 have been killed in or around Baghdad alone. Also, according to the IBC, over 20,000 Iraqis have been injured, based on data derived from over 300 published reports. Meanwhile, the *Sunday Times* of Australia cited military analysts in disagreement over how many Iraqi soldiers would die, with estimates ranging from 5,000 to over 10,000. As one analyst from the conservative Heritage Foundation put it, "These are extremely rubber numbers. It's difficult to verify, especially when you're dropping bombs on people and you don't go back and count bodies."

Whatever the number, NPR reporter Anne Garrels summed up the lack of information thus: "Rightly or wrongly, Iraqis believe their lives count for little in the eyes of the Americans, who dutifully tally the Americans killed, but give no numbers on Iraqis who were killed, whether they're guilty or innocent."

As for the estimated total costs of Iraqi reconstruction, they are projected to total $100 billion, including $16 billion for restoring water and $13 billion for electricity. There is talk of making some of this money loans rather than grants. While it may be financially wise, politically it's a nightmare: as Arizona

Senator John McCain put it, using oil revenue to repay loans "would confirm the propaganda of our enemies that this was a war for oil." It would also be an insult to the Iraqi people: charging them interest on payments to rebuild their country after the U.S. military has destroyed it.

The numbers add up to a lot of pissed-off Iraqis (and other Middle Easterners) hating the Great Satan over this. The Bush Team's reckless cruelty not only has created a quagmire; it also will create monsters. How many bin Ladens have been created by Shrub's clumsy attempts to reshape the world?

Sources:

Brahimi, Rym. "Uday, Qusay Win Sympathy in Death." CNN, 30 July 2003 <http://edition.cnn.com/2003/WORLD/meast/07/30/sprj.irq.bodies.brahimi>.

Ewens, Michael. "Casualties in Iraq." *Antiwar*, 14 October 2003 <http://www.antiwar.com/ewens/casualties.html>.

Ford, Peter. "Surveys Pointing to High Civilian Death Toll in Iraq." *The Christian Science Monitor*, 22 May 2003 <http://www.csmonitor.com/2003/0522/p01s02-woiq.html>.

Francis, David R. "A Tally of U.S. Taxpayers' Tab for Iraq." *The Christian Science Monitor*, 25 August 2003 <http://www.csmonitor.com/2003/0825/p16s01-coop.html>.

Iraq Body Count <http://www.iraqbodycount.net>.

"Iraqi Military Death Toll a Mystery." *Sunday Times*, 08 April 2003 <http://www.sundaytimes.news.com.au/printpage/0,5942,6256306,00.html>.

Jeffery, Simon. "War May Have Killed 10,000 Civilians, Researchers Say." *The Guardian*, 13 June 2003 <http://www.guardian.co.uk/Iraq/Story/0,2763,976392,00.html>.

"Many Deaths Left Out of Iraq Story." Fairness & Accuracy in Reporting, 20 August 2003 <http://www.fair.org/activism/iraq-casualties-networks.html>.

Stone, Andrea. "GOP Senators Join Push to Make Some Iraq Aid a Loan." *USA Today*, 1 October 2003 <http://www.usatoday.com/news/world/iraq/2003-10-01 iraqmoney_x.htm>.

11

→ **SHRUBONOMICS**

> **"This is an impressive crowd. The haves and the have-mores. Some call you the elite. I call you my base."**
>
> —George W. Bush, at a 2000 New York fundraiser

Historically, U.S. presidential elections are won and lost by the performance of the economy. What does it say about Bush, then, that it is almost a secondary issue in his basic lack of qualifications to ever be elected to the office, even though his track record is the worst of any candidate since the Great Depression? (This is no hyperbole; the last elected president to preside over a loss of jobs was Herbert Hoover.) During Bush's White House occupation, as of October 2003, 3.3 million jobs have been destroyed. That would be bad enough by itself, but it is compounded by a practically contemptuous view of balanced budgets and a fiddling banana-republic style of budget planning that inevitably leads to bankruptcy.

Though they have a lackadaisical attitude toward the calamities they have caused, it's clear that Shrub and Co. do have an economic agenda:

→ Lowering the taxes on the richest Americans and corporations;

→ Giving massive boondoggles to defense contractors, energy companies, and other corporate giants;

→ Consolidating more economic and political power in fewer and richer hands; and

→ Screwing everyone else.

So far, mission accomplished.

To some, Shrubonomics is the bastard child of Reaganomics. That would be unfair to Reagan: at least some innovative ideas were behind the so-called Reagan revolution (supply-side economics, monetarism, the Laffer curve, and other ideas of Milton Friedman and the other Chicago theorists). The theories behind the Reagan years didn't often pan out, but at least they were well thought-out and articulated (even if some of them were first written on cocktail napkins). And while the success of Reaganomics has long been overstated by right-wing ideologues, at least there were some positive effects, even if they were really due to Keynesian economics in disguise.

The Bush Team, meanwhile, can't claim a single economic success during its reign, and never propounded any convincing economic theories or ideas behind its policies. Bush and his advisors have spared themselves the trouble of even specious arguments, believing that if they repeated their mantra of cutting taxes again and again, the public wouldn't pick up on the swindle until it was too late. To the shame of the American public, this political bet appears to be correct.

One who wasn't fooled by the naked Emperor Dubya is Robert Solow, a 1987 Nobel Prize winner in economics and professor emeritus at the Massachusetts Institute of Technology. "The fiscal polices of this administration are systematically sacrificing the future of this nation," he bluntly declares. George Akerlof, a 2001 Nobel Prize winner and economist at UC Berkeley, calls the policies "the worst in over 200 years." Perhaps the most vocal critic of the Bush economic program is Paul Krugman, who in his book *The Great Unraveling* dismisses it as "bad economics wrapped in the flag."

The Bushistas seem to know all this. Perhaps this explains why, right after the 2000 election, Bush and Cheney stepped into a Chicken Little routine of warning that the economy was falling into recession. The cynical plan seems twofold: one, it helped push through the first of two radical tax cuts for the wealthy, and two, it allowed them to accelerate the economic downturn made inevitable by their warped policies, in turn allowing them (in their usual pass-the-buck style) to blame their fuck-up on Clinton. An economic recession did indeed follow: considering that macroeconomic outcomes can be heavily influenced by perceptions, their reckless recession talk probably was a contributing cause in addition to their policies.

Still, the American public can only be fooled for so long. Is it merely a coincidence that, after four years of Daddy Bush fumbling the economy and racking up a massive public debt, Clinton managed to bring record surpluses and create 22.5 million jobs? And is it merely a coincidence that this has been followed by even higher debt and job loss under Shrub? The economy that Dubya was handed was much better than any real president had inherited in modern history; his behavior since is reminiscent of a drunken frat boy given the keys to a Ferrari. At best, Shrubonomics is Reaganomics on crack. If the U.S. economy is ever to recover, we're going to need somebody else behind the wheel.

Sources:

The Dubya Report. "In Depth—Economic Policy"
‹http://www.thedubyareport.com/indepth_tax.html›.

Freeman, Robert. "Bush's Tax Cuts: A Form of National Insanity." *Counterpunch*, 30 May 2003 ‹http://www.counterpunch.org/freeman05302003.html›.

"George W. Bush: A Miserable Failure." 2003 ‹http://www.amiserablefailure.com›.

Hightower, Jim. *Thieves in High Places*. New York: Viking Penguin, 2003.

Krugman, Paul. *The Great Unraveling: Losing Our Way in the New Century*. New York: W.W. Norton & Company, 2003.

Krugman, Paul. "The Tax-Cut Con." *The New York Times*, 14 September 2003 ‹http://www.nytimes.com/2003/09/14/magazine/14TAXES.html.›

Meyerson, Harold. "Squandering Prosperity." *American Prospect*, 1 June 2003 ‹http://www.prospect.org/print/V14/6/meyerson-h.html›.

"Nobel Prize Winner Calls Bush Economic Policies 'Worst in 200 Years.'" AFL-CIO, 13 August 2003 ‹http://www.aflcio.org/yourjobeconomy/todayseconomy/ns08132003.cfm›.

Walsh, Joan. "Dubya's Mad-dog Economics." *Salon*, 16 March 2001 ‹http://archive.salon.com/politics/feature/2001/03/16/bush›.

12

→ IT'S STILL THE ECONOMY, STUPID

Here are some facts and figures that help clarify the picture.

Unemployment rate when Bill Clinton took office in 1993: 7.5%.

Unemployment rate when Bill Clinton left office in 2001: 4.0%, the lowest since 1969.

Unemployment rate as of September 2003: 6.1%, an increase of over 50%.

Unemployment rate, June 2003: 6.4%.

Number of jobs lost between the months of June and August 2003, when unemployment fell to 6.1%: 90,000.

How unemployment dropped 0.3% even though 90,000 jobs were lost: 566,000 frustrated jobless workers exited the labor force.

Number of jobs created during the Clinton years: 22.5 million.

Number of jobs created during the Clinton years in the private sector: 20.7 million.

Number of jobs created during the Dubya years (as of October 2003): −2.6 million.

Number of jobs created during the Dubya years in the private sector (as of October 2003): −3.3 million.

Total number of officially unemployed persons (as of October 2003): 9 million.

Total number of officially unemployed and unemployed "marginally attached" to the work force (as of October 2003): 10.5 million.

Total number of officially unemployed, unemployed "marginally attached" to the work force, and underemployed (as of October 2003): 15.5 million

Total number of officially unemployed, unemployed "marginally attached" to the work force and underemployed when Clinton left office: 10.6 million.

Net change in total officially unemployed, unemployed "marginally attached" to the work force, and underemployed during the Dubya years: 4.9 million.

Number of long-term (27 weeks or more) unemployed when Clinton left office: 0.7 million.

Number of long-term (27 weeks or more) unemployed as of September 2003: 2 million, over a 200% increase.

Number of Americans living in poverty, end of 2002: 34.6 million.

Net change in number living below poverty level, 2000–2002: 3 million.

Average annual change in median household income, 2000–2001 (inflation adjusted): –2.2%.

Average annual change in median household income, 2001–2002 (inflation adjusted): –1.7%.

Number of bankruptcies filed in year ending June 30, 2000: 1.276 million.

Number of bankruptcies filed in year ending June 30, 2003: 1.65 million.

Percentage increase in annual bankruptcies, 2000–2003: 29%.

Number of Americans without health insurance, end of 2000: 39.8 million.

Number of Americans without health insurance, end of 2002: 43.6 million.

Increase of Americans without health insurance: 3.8 million.

Number of Americans without health insurance at some point, 2001–2002: 74.7 million.

Sources:

"Bankruptcy Cases Continue to Break Federal Court Caseload Records." Administrative Office of the United States Courts, 18 August 2003 ‹http://www.uscourts.gov/Press_Releases/603b.pdf›.

Begala, Paul. *It's Still the Economy, Stupid: George W. Bush, The GOP's CEO*. New York: Simon & Schuster, 2002.

"Bush Defends Economic Policies." CNN/Money, 9 October 2003 ‹http://money.cnn.com/2003/10/09/news/economy/bush›.

"The Clinton Presidency: Historic Economic Growth." The Clinton White House, ‹http://clinton5.nara.gov/WH/Accomplishments/eightyears-03.html›.

"The Clinton-Gore Economic Record: The Lowest Unemployment Rate in 30 Years." The Clinton White House, 7 January 2000 ‹http://clinton4.nara.gov/WH/New/html/20000112_1.html›.

Connolly, Ceci. "Census Finds Many More Lack Health Insurance." *The Washington Post*, 30 September 2003: A01

"Democrats Attack Bush for Poverty Rise." *NewsMax*, 25 September 2002 ‹http://www.newsmax.com/archives/articles/2002/9/25/70340.shtml›.

Goldstein, Amy. "Bush Cites Stabilized Jobless Rate." *The Washington Post*, 4 October 2003: A07.

Gongloff, Mark. "Payrolls Slashed Again." CNN/Money, 5 September 2003 ‹http://money.cnn.com/2003/09/05/news/economy/jobs/index.htm?cnn=yes›.

"Information Please: 1992." *Fact Monster* ‹http://www.factmonster.com/year/1992.html›.

"Job Crisis in America." AFL-CIO, 2003 ‹http://www.aflcio.org/yourjobeconomy/jobs/jobcrisis.cfm›.

"Jobs & the Economy—The Bush Record." Fight for the Future 2003 ‹http://www.fightforthefuture.org/bushrecord/bush_jobs.cfm›.

Krugman, Paul. *The Great Unraveling: Losing Our Way in the New Century*. New York: W.W. Norton & Company, 2003.

"New Poll: Bush Trails Democratic Candidate." Democratic National Committee, 15 October 2003 ‹http://www.democrats.org/news/200310150003.html›.

"Nobel Prize Winner Calls Bush Economic Policies 'Worst in 200 Years.'" AFL-CIO, 13 August 2003 <http://www.aflcio.org/yourjobeconomy/todayseconomy/nso8132003.cfm>.

"Report Highlights Health Insurance Woes." *NewsMax*, 1 October 2002

Shields, Mark. "Let's Look at the Record. CNN, 9 December 2002 <http://www.cnn.com/2002/ALLPOLITICS/12/09/column.shields.opinion.clinton/index.html>.

Somerville, Glenn. "U.S. Posts First Job Gains in 8 Months." Yahoo News, 3 October 2003 <http://story.news.yahoo.com/news?tmpl=story&cid=564&ncid=564&e=10&u=/nm/2003100 3/ts_nm/economy_dc_23>.

"Uninsured Across America." Democratic National Committee, 2003 <http://www.democrats.org/specialreports/uninsured>.

Weisman, Jonathan. "U.S. Incomes Fell, Poverty Rose in 2002." *The Washington Post*, 27 September 2003: A01.

13

→ FUZZY MATH &
TAX-CUT VOODOO

During his failed 2000 election campaign, George W. Bush repeatedly referred to Al Gore's criticism of his tax-cut proposals as "fuzzy math." But everything Gore warned about the reckless foolishness in Shrub's plans has proven true. Three years later, it is clear that Bush is the one whose reasoning was fuzzy.

How fuzzy was it? First, ignore the $1.6 trillion tax cut of 2001, which managed to destroy the entire budget surplus and create no new jobs. Ignore the conclusion of Citizens for Tax Justice that 43% of the cut would wind up in the hands of the richest 1% of taxpayers, that those with an average income of $915,000 would get an average tax cut of $46,000 a year, and that the bottom 60% of taxpayers (income less than $39,000) would average $227 in savings (less than $5 a week).

Instead, focus on the $350 billion tax cut of 2003. Ignore the facts that 8 million taxpayers who make less than $75,000 a year would get no tax cut at all (including 6.6 million working people who earn $30,000 and under), that taxpayers earning over $1 million a year would receive an average tax cut of $93,500, and that two thirds of the tax savings would go to the ten percent who earn the most.

Never mind that the tax cut increased the child tax credit for the wealthy from $600 to $1,000, while adding no increase for the 6.5 million families, containing 12 million children (or one out of every six children), whose incomes range between $10,500 and $26,625. The costs of this credit would have been $3.5 billion (one percent of the total tax cut), deemed too hefty. Never mind that families earning less than $10,500 would receive no additional child tax credit.

(After all, pointing out these facts is merely stirring class warfare.)

Instead, focus on the main argument made for the tax cut by Bush and his mouthpieces, namely that it would create one million jobs.

Forget for a second that one million jobs isn't even 40% of the growth in jobs that the Clinton administration averaged per year. Forget as well that one million jobs is less than a third of the jobs destroyed so far during the Dubya years. Finally, forget that the claim, like nearly everything else Bush says, is complete bullshit, with no evidence to back it up (indeed, considering how the last Bush cut went, we should assume it will destroy jobs).

Even assuming, for once, that Bush isn't lying, and that the tax cut does deliver as promised, look at it as a simple math problem:

Number of jobs allegedly created by the tax cut: one million.

Total amount of the tax cut: $350 billion.

Total lost federal revenues per job created: $350,000.

If there were a federal program that spent $350,000 to create a job, it would be derided by conservatives (rightfully) as wasteful and bloated.

If Bush and his cronies are so interested in creating jobs, there are far more effective ways to do it, even according to their own numbers. Clearly, they are lying about their goals and motivations. As with the war against Iraq, their lies about something so important and with such great consequences are an outrage, and they should never again be trusted to control American economic policy.

Sources:

Berman, John, Hill, Dana, and Segan, Sascha. "Dueling Numbers, Factoids." ABC News, 4 October 2000 ‹http://abcnews.go.com/sections/politics/DailyNews/DEBATE001004.html›.

Firestone, David. "Tax Law Omits Child Credit in Low-Income Brackets." *Common Dreams*, 29 May 2003 ‹http://www.commondreams.org/headlines03/0529-05.htm›.

Freeman, Robert. "Bush's Tax Cuts: A Form of National Insanity?" *Counterpunch*, 30 May 2003 ‹http://www.counterpunch.org/freeman05302003.html›.

Gross, Daniel. "George Walker Hoover?" *Slate*, 30 April 2003 ‹http://slate.msn.com/id/2082321›.

Jackson, Derrick Z. "A Tax Cut For the Selfish." *Common Dreams*, 4 June 2003 ‹http://www.commondreams.org/views03/0604-09.htm›.

"Jobs & the Economy—The Bush Record." Fight for the Future, 2003 ‹http://www.fightforthefuture.org/bushrecord/bush_jobs.cfm›.

Sorensen, Harley. "Bush's Secret Jobs Plan". *Common Dreams*, 21 May 2003 ‹http://www.commondreams.org/views03/0521-09.htm›.

Weisbrot, Mark. "Tax Relief for the Prosperous Few." *AlterNet*, 13 February 2001 ‹http://www.alternet.org/story.html?StoryID=10471›.

14

➤ HE'S BANKRUPTING THE USA

In 1992, Bush's daddy left Bill Clinton with a then-record $290 billion deficit and fears of the U.S. tottering into bankruptcy. Clinton, after 12 years of reckless "conservative" economic policy under Reagan-Bush, was advised that the best cure for economic ails was responsible budget planning. He took the advice of his team, and the rest is history. With fiscal discipline, Clinton ended his term with a record $230 billion surplus, an astounding turnaround from the Reagan-Bush years. As predicted, the economy boomed, thanks to strengthened faith in its long-term viability. The national debt was projected to be gone by 2012, for the first time since 1835.

What has followed is even more astounding. The surplus has rapidly disappeared, and in 2003, Bush presided over a $374.2 billion deficit, smashing his poppa's record in the process. In other words, in less than three years, Dubya has managed to undo all of Clinton's eight years of progress, and come out over $80 billion worse than Clinton started. 2004 appears to be another record-breaking year for the Shrub team: White House budget director Joshua Bolten conceded that the gap for 2004 would likely exceed $500 billion, and that projection included cheery expectations of a strengthening economy. Bolten didn't seem too concerned, though, expecting the deficit to be halved by 2009 while Dubya plays the fiddle.

When Clinton left office, the projected ten-year surplus (assuming his sound policies were maintained) was $5.6 trillion. Estimates for the ten-year deficit are now $4 trillion (according to William Dudley, chief U.S. economist at Goldman Sachs) or $5 trillion (according to the respected bipartisan Concord Coalition). The total turnaround is mind-boggling $10 trillion dollars, or $1 trillion a year.

Charles Kolb, president of the business-backed Committee for Economic Development, warns, "If we do not reverse these trends we will produce in the next century the first generation of Americans who are less well off than their predecessors." Robert Bixby, executive director of the non-partisan Concord Coalition, states, "The coming decade is likely to rank as the most fiscally irresponsible in our nation's history." Bixby adds, "We're not talking about something that's going to go away when the economy recovers. Hard choices are going to have to be made on tax and spending policies."

Not only is Dubya avoiding hard choices, he is willfully making foolish, destructive ones. These words aren't chosen lightly: David Stockman, Ronald Reagan's budget director, concluded that the tax cuts under Reagan were a Trojan horse. It was a scam to funnel money to the wealthy and leave the nation in a fiscal crisis, so that the compelling solution would be to cut spending on government programs for the poor and middle class. Nothing appears to have changed with the junior Bush's strategy. Bush and his friends are willing to lead the U.S. straight into an iceberg, and they shouldn't be trusted.

Sources:

"$3.5 Trillion National Debt Gone by 2012?" *Newsmax*, 27 June 2000 ‹http://www.newsmax.com/articles/?a=2000/6/26/181034›.

Ahmann, Tim. "Groups Sound Warning on Large Budget Deficits." Yahoo News, 29 September 2003 ‹http://story.news.yahoo.com/news?tmpl=story&u=/nm/20030929/pl_nm/budget_warning_dc_1›.

Fram, Alan. "U.S. Deficit Hits $374.2B, Setting Record." Yahoo News, 20 October 2003 ‹http://story.news.yahoo.com/news?tmpl=story&u=/ap/20031021/ap_on_go_pr_wh/budget_deficit_9›.

Freeman, Robert. "Bush's Tax Cuts: A Form of National Insanity?" *Counterpunch*, 30 May 2003 ‹http://www.counterpunch.org/freeman05302003.html›.

Krugman, Paul. *The Great Unraveling: Losing Our Way in the New Century*. New York: W.W. Norton & Company, 2003.

Krugman, Paul. "Passing It Along." *The New York Times*, 18 July 2003: 17A.

Krugman, Paul. "The Tax-Cut Con." *The New York Times*, 14 September 2003 ‹http://www.nytimes.com/2003/09/14/magazine/14TAXES.html.›.

Nicholson, Jonathan. "U.S. Posts Record $374.22 Billion Budget Gap in 2003." Yahoo News, 20 October 2003 ‹http://story.news.yahoo.com/news?tmpl=story&cid=584&e=1&u= /nm/20031020/pl_ nm/economy_treasury_budget_dc›.

"President Clinton's Address." Online *NewsHour*, 27 January 2000
<http://www.pbs.org/newshour/bb/white_house/jan-june00/sotu1.html>.

Stockman, David A. *The Triumph of Politics: Why the Reagan Revolution Failed.*
Boston: G.K. Hall & Co., 1983.

Wallace, Kelly. "President Clinton Announces Another Record Budget Surplus." CNN,
27 September 2000 <http://www.cnn.com/2000/ALLPOLITICS/stories/09/27/
clinton.surplus>.

Walsh, Joan. "Plutocrats to the Rescue!" *Salon*, 15 February 2001
<http://archive.salon.com/politics/feature/2001/02/15/buffett/index.html>.

Walters, Joanna. "Reaganomics Are Back—But Don't Add Up." *The Observer*,
20 April 2003 <http://observer.guardian.co.uk/print/0,3858,4651614-102271,00.html>.

15

⟶ ENRONGATE

For 80 years, the standard for White House scandals involving big business and politics was Teapot Dome. In 1921, control of naval oil reserves at the Wyoming site (and another in Elk Hills, California) was transferred to the Department of the Interior by President Warren G. Harding. The reserves were then leased without competitive bidding to Harry Sinclair and Edward Doheny by Interior Secretary Albert B. Fall. A Senate investigation uncovered that Sinclair and Doheny both had "loaned" substantial amounts to Fall and lavished him with gifts. Due to the scandal, Harding (who was never alleged to be personally involved) saw his administration's reputation ruined, and is deemed by historians one of the worst presidents.

What, then, are we to make of Enrongate? The scandal surrounding Enron isn't merely about the bankruptcy of what was only shortly before (in terms of revenue) the seventh-largest U.S. corporation. As Watergate wasn't just about a second-rate burglary, Enrongate is about using political capital for private profit—a practice that surrounds the slimy Bush Team with a rotten stench.

On December 2, 2001, Enron (a Houston-based energy company) filed for bankruptcy. This was a stunning reversal of fortune, after a 2000–2001 gouging of the California energy market that resulted in the skyrocketing of the state's electricity prices. Cute names were later uncovered for strategies to illegally manipulate energy markets: "Fat Boy," "Death Star," "Get Shorty," "Ricochet," and "Load Shift." (See Reason #38.) That a company could fleece billions of dollars from California and still go belly-up indicates the voraciousness of Enron's executives' appetite for filthy lucre.

Enron had a tight relationship with Shrub, to put it mildly. As Charles Lewis, director of the Center for Public Integrity, put it, "Enron was the number one career patron for George W. Bush." Enron and its CEO-Chairman Ken Lay had given $2 million to

Bush's election efforts. A 2000 company memo "recommended" that low-level managers give $500 and senior executives at least $5,000 to the Bush campaign. During Dubya's presidential run, Enron lent him a corporate jet. Lay was listed by the Bush-Cheney campaign in 2000 as one of the "Pioneers" who raised at least $100,000, and Enron, Lay, and his wife each gave $100,000 for the inauguration gala. Bush affectionately referred to Lay as "Kenny Boy." *The New York Times* referred to Lay as a "shadow advisor to the president." But Shrub wasn't alone in playing butt-buddy with Enron. Indeed, the entire Bush Team is a Who's Who of compromised links to Enron:

→ Marc Racicot: The GOP Chairman was a lobbyist for Enron.

→ Robert Zoellick: Bush's U.S. Trade Representative was an Enron consultant on the advisory board.

→ Lawrence Lindsey: His Chief Economic Advisor was a board director at Enron.

→ James Baker: Florida recount chair served on the Enron board of directors.

→ Spencer Abraham: Energy Secretary also received campaign contributions from Enron, and used Lay as a prominent advisor.

→ John Ashcroft: The Attorney General has received $57,000 in campaign contributions from Enron and its employees. He was forced to recuse himself from the Enron criminal investigation because of conflict of interest.

→ Karl Rove: His chief political advisor owned up to $250,000 in Enron stock while he influenced the administration's energy policy, keeping Ken Lay personally updated by phone.

→ Dick Cheney: Texas oilman Cheney met with Enron executives four times during the formulation of Energy Policy in 2001.

→ George Herbert Walker "Poppy" Bush: His daddy is also a longtime friend of Ken Lay, having received campaign contributions and $50K for the George Bush Presidential Library Foundation.

→ Thomas White: High-ranking executive who headed Enron Energy Services, the division behind the looting of the California energy market, became Shrub's Army Secretary on May 31, 2001; he owned $50–100 million in Enron stock. Mention of his relationship with Enron was removed from his official bio.

→ Pat Wood III: The Federal Energy Regulatory Commission (FERC) Chairman was recommended by Lay. In his role as FERC head, blocked attempts to control the California energy crisis and allowed Enron to continue its swindle.

→ Harvey Pitt: Not to be outdone in the Conflict-Of-Interest Championship Sweepstakes, the Securities and Exchange Commissioner was the lawyer representing the big five accounting firms, including Arthur Andersen, Enron's firm. He had pushed for the slack regulation that helped create the Enron catastrophe in the first place. He too was hand-picked by Lay.

It looks like the *New York Times* had it backwards: Dubya was a shadow president for Lay.

Creative accounting made Enron look much better on paper than the reality. Funds secretly flowed into secret partnerships (with more cute names, such as "Raptor," "JEDI," "Chewco," and "LJM"). Unfortunately for Enron, all its political influence couldn't pay the piper. That didn't stop them from trying. Treasury Secretary Paul O'Neill received two phone calls from Lay as Enron collapsed, yet claims he said nothing about this to Bush. Commerce Secretary Donald Evans received phone calls from Lay in October 2001 about impending Enron doom: he claims he never informed Shrub of this fact, though he was Dubya's campaign manager in 2000.

Meanwhile, top Enron executives secretly sold their stock in Enron. Lay dumped over $16.1 million while giving speeches about the supposed great future of the company. Jeff Skilling, the former President and CEO of the company, managed to unload $15.5 million. Near the end, 500 executives also received $1,000–$5 million "bonuses" totaling $54.6 million. This was chump change for Enron: in the year leading to bankruptcy, they doled out $745 million in payments and stock awards to 144 senior executives: Lay received $150 million, Skilling $25 million,

Chief Financial Officer Andrew Fastow $10 million, and Bush Army Secretary White $17 million. Soon after the final bonus spree, they declared bankruptcy, and Lay laid off 4,200 workers, who were given minimal severance packages and immediately saw their health coverage and benefits disappear.

The Bush Team insists they did nothing wrong in all this, and didn't help Enron while it collapsed. They certainly helped Enron on the way up when it counted: Bush stopped the caps on electricity prices in California when Enron artificially manipulated supply for obscene profits. He also had the National Security Council organize a campaign against the Indian government, to help Enron sell a generating plant in Dabhol for $2.3 billion. (Pressure on India over the plant continued after September 11, when India's support was needed for the war on terror.) Politics is an unsentimental business; the Bush team's lack of support for Enron during its final gasp shows that helping Enron then would have been a political liability.

Pass-the-buck Bush after the bankruptcy predictably claimed that he barely knew Kenny-Boy; this lie even the most fawning Bushlicker couldn't buy. The money-making scam at Enron was the output of Shrub's policies, which were implemented under the advice of the company and its representatives. Considering the hype about Whitewater (a failed land deal Clinton was involved with a decade before his election), you'd think a thorough investigation of Enron would be in order. There has been none so far, and no prosecution of Lay and his top-echelon accomplices in the Enron larceny. As long as Dubya is in Washington, don't hold your breath waiting.

Sources:

"Behind the Enron Scandal." *Time*, 2002 ‹http://www.time.com/time/2002/enron›.

"Enron: After the Collapse." Online *NewsHour*
‹http://www.pbs.org/newshour/bb/business/enron›.

"Enron: Who's Who." BBC News, 2002
‹http://news.bbc.co.uk/hi/english/static/in_depth/business/2002/enron›.

"Enron Paid Hefty Bonuses before Bankruptcy." CNN, 10 February 2002
‹http://www.cnn.com/2002/LAW/02/09/enron.bonuses›.

"Enrongate." Bush Watch, 16 December 2001 ‹http://www.bushwatch.org/enron.htm›.

Gerstein, Josh. "Friends in High Places." ABC News, 10 December 2001
‹http://www.abcnews.go.com/sections/politics/DailyNews/enron011210.htm›.

Giardiello, Mario. "Why We Dare Call It Enrongate." *AlterNet*, 13 February 2002
‹http://www.alternet.org/story.html?StoryID=12412›.

Kay, Joseph. "Enron Execs Looted Company Prior to Bankruptcy." World Socialist Web Site,
22 June 2002 ‹http://www.wsws.org/articles/2002/jun2002/enro-j22.shtml›.

Kick, Russ. "The Incredible Shrinking Résumé of Thomas White." *The Village Voice*,
22–28 May 2002 ‹http://www.villagevoice.com/issues/0221/kick.php›.

Moore, Michael. "Enron Will Force Dubya's Resignation." AlterNet, 1 February 2002
‹http://www.alternet.org/story.html?StoryID=12330›.

Parry, Sam. "Bush Did Try to Save Enron." *AlterNet*, 3 June 2002
‹http://www.alternet.org/story.html?StoryID=13281›.

Payne, Phillip. "What Was Teapot Dome?" History News Network, 11 February 2002
‹http://hnn.U.S./articles/550.html›.

Press, Bill. "Enron Makes Whitewater Look Like Peanuts." CNN, 12 December 2001
‹http://www.cnn.com/2001/ALLPOLITICS/12/12/column.billpress/›.

Rothschild, Matthew. "Bush's Enron Cuff Links." *The Progressive*, 23 January 2002
‹http://www.progressive.org/webex/wx012302.html›.

"Special Report: Enron." *The Guardian Unlimited*,
‹http://www.guardian.co.uk/enron/0,11337,609866,00.html›.

"Teapot Dome." Infoplease.com ‹http://www.infoplease.com/ce6/history/A0848032.html›.

"We Demand a Special Prosecutor for Enrongate!" Democrats.com
‹http://democrats.com/elandslide/index.cfm?campaign=enron›.

16

→ **JOHN ASHCROFT IS WATCHING**

"To those who pit Americans against immigrants and citizens against non-citizens, to those who scare peace-loving people with phantoms of lost liberty, my message is this: your tactics only aid terrorists, for they erode our national unity and diminish our resolve. They give ammunition to America's enemies, and pause to America's friends."

—Attorney General John Ashcroft

Americans value nothing more than freedom. From the Declaration of Independence to the Bill of Rights, from Thomas Jefferson to Thomas Paine, we prize the blessing of liberty above all else. This is why Bush and his friends are the greatest enemy to basic American values this side of Osama.

Consider the PATRIOT Act, passed in the frenzy following September 11. The USA PATRIOT Act (a charming acronym for "Uniting and Strengthening America by Providing Appropriate Tools Required to Intercept and Obstruct Terrorism") is the most stunning attack on basic Constitutional rights at least since the infamous Alien and Sedition Acts of 1798. Among its most insidious elements:

> → Grants government authorities the power to require book-stores and libraries to list the names of books bought or borrowed. Other third-party-held documents that can be demanded include financial, travel, video rental, phone, medical, and church records. The subpoenas require no probable cause, provided the government certifies to a FISA

(Foreign Intelligence Surveillance Act) judge that the search protects against terrorism. The judge has no authority to reject this application, making his or her involvement essentially a rubber stamp. The target of a search needn't be a terror suspect, as long as the government's purpose purports to be an authorized investigation "to protect against international terrorism." Once the information is requested, a gag order automatically prohibits those facing the demand from talking about it to anyone else.

→ Allows personal records to be seized by the government if a "national security" letter is issued. The administrative subpoenas require no probable cause, court order or review, or judicial oversight. Among the records that can be subpoenaed are telephone and email logs, credit reports, and other financial and bank records, provided they would be "relevant" to an ongoing terrorism investigation. Those who turn over records are under a gag order against disclosing the demand.

→ Permits law enforcement agencies to circumvent Fourth Amendment requirement of probable cause when conducting FISA-stamped wiretaps and searches. If the feds say they have as a "significant purpose" the gathering of foreign intelligence, probable cause of criminal activity is discarded as a requirement.

→ Removes the probable-cause requirement in criminal cases of warrants for "pen registers" (which uncover phone numbers dialed from a subject's telephone) and "trap-and-trace" devices (which record originating phone numbers of all incoming calls). The government need only claim that the information likely to be obtained is "relevant" to an ongoing investigation of international terrorism.

→ Includes the "Carnivore" Internet surveillance program in pen registers and trap-and-trace, meaning that email can be surveilled to identify the investigated subject's correspondents. Email addresses are not easily separated from email contents, but the FBI claims it should be trusted to do so.

→ Authorizes roving wiretaps—i.e., taps specific persons rather than a single phone or computer. If the government decides to tap a computer at a public library, every communication by every user in the library can be intercepted.

→ Allows "Sneak and Peek" warrants—i.e., secret searches of home and property without prior notice. In other words, authorities can break into a residence when no one is home, look around, take pictures, and even seize property, all without informing the people living there. The only justification law enforcement needs is that notice might "seriously jeopardize an investigation or unduly delay a trial."

→ Mixes foreign intelligence–gathering with domestic criminal investigation, allowing the sharing of information between criminal and intelligence operations—including the FBI, CIA, NSA, INS, Secret Service, and Department of Defense. Law enforcement agencies may now share with intelligence agencies sensitive information gathered during a criminal investigation, opening the door to a resurgence of domestic spying by the CIA and other intelligence agencies.

→ Creates a new category of crime called "domestic terrorism," penalizing activities that "involve acts dangerous to human life that are a violation of the criminal laws of the United States," if the actor's intent is to "influence the policy of a government by intimidation or coercion." Ironically, this has alienated right-wing groups and fundamentalist Christians from the Act (groups that had previously been strong supporters of their fellow traveler Ashcroft), as it could be used to prosecute anti-abortion activists.

→ Disregards attorney-client privilege to authorize government surveillance of previously confidential discussions.

There doesn't seem to be anything patriotic about the PATRIOT Act, which mocks the First, Fourth, Fifth, Sixth, and Eighth Amendments. So far, over 150 communities, including several major cities and three states, have passed resolutions denouncing it as an assault on civil liberties.

When the package of laws was introduced five days after 9/11, Attorney General John Aschroft demanded that it be passed immediately. The bill became law 40 days later. Democratic Party leaders would whine that they were "forced" to approve the bill by intense political pressure. It passed 98-1 in the Senate (with only Democrat Russ Feingold bravely opposing). Texan Ron Paul, one of only three Republicans to oppose the bill in the House of Representatives, has stated that the bill wasn't even printed before the vote on it, and only a handful of staffers even had the opportunity to look at it.

The PATRIOT has a sequel, the Domestic Security and Enhancement Act, that would expand government surveillance and detention powers even more. After insisting that no such bill was in the works, the Justice Department internally circulated a confidential 120-page summary and text of PATRIOT II in early January.

The act allows the government to:

→ Access a citizen's credit reports without a subpoena.

→ Subject citizens to secret surveillance by their own government on behalf of foreign countries, including dictatorships.

→ Wiretap anybody for 15 days, and snoop on anyone's Internet usage (including chat and email), all without obtaining a warrant.

→ Grant legal immunity to police officers carrying out illegal searches if they were following orders.

→ Abolish federal court "consent decrees" that limit police surveillance of non-criminal organizations and public events.

→ Impose the death penalty on 15 new offenses.

→ Ease restrictions on the use of secret evidence.

→ Collect DNA from anyone, without a court order, for a mammoth database of citizen DNA information.

→ Secretly detain citizens on suspicion of terrorist activities until they are actually charged with a crime.

→ Allows citizenship to be revoked, if persons contributed "material support" to organizations deemed by the government, even retroactively, to be "terrorist."

→ End many of the first Patriot's "sunset provisions" (i.e., stipulations that the expanded law enforcement powers would be rescinded in 2005).

The good news: when PATRIOT II was leaked to the press, widespread opposition to its contents from liberal and conservative groups made its passage doubtful for now. Not that this will stop the Bush Team from trying: this summer, John Ashcroft went on a tour of 18 cities to gather support for their attacks on civil liberties.

Another creepy plan was halted (for now): Operation TIPS (Terrorism Information and Prevention System) was an extensive snitching program worthy of the KGB and the East German Stasi. The idea was to recruit one million workers, including letter carriers, meter readers, cable technicians, and others with access to private homes, as informants to the DOJ about suspicious activity. Leading the opposition to TIPS was Dick Armey, who has since retired as House Majority Leader. Although the ultraconservative Republican from Texas was a staunch ally of Dubya, a program to create an American network of deputized secret police conflicted harshly with his limited-government views. His spokesman explained, "He felt the programs were not consistent with free society."

The setbacks of PATRIOT II, Operation TIPS, and Total Information Awareness (described later in this book) have done little to deter Shrub and Ashcroft from their plans to attack civil liberties. In the meantime, they have rounded up more than a thousand men, most of them Middle Eastern, some of them detained indefinitely and in secret.

To be fair, the creation of what author Jim Redden has termed "Snitch Culture" didn't begin with Bush and his pals: the rush to crush constitutional liberties has been underway since Reagan took office and tried to undo the reforms made in the wake of Watergate. Bush I and Clinton both moved the campaign forward, and the torch was merely passed to Shrub. But Bush, Ashcroft, and their team have pushed forward with a vengeance, exploiting September 11 for restrictions on civil liberties that exceed their predecessors' accomplishments. Indeed, 9/11 had little to do with the content of the law: it was an old wish-list resubmitted in the hysteria that followed the WTC-Pentagon attacks.

Would having someone besides Bush in the White House be a blessing for freedom in the USA? Most definitely. At the very least, Republicans would speak out against any proposals that would give a Democrat-controlled executive branch expanded police powers (one benefit of GOP obsession with Slick Willie during the Clinton years). Further, given what has happened over the last three years, a growing number of Democrats and Republicans have grown wary of giving the state too much policing power. With groups such as People for the American Way and ACLU on the left and the Cato Institute and Eagle Forum on the right opposed to the laws proposed and actions taken by the Bush Team, it's time to put someone in office who respects the rights of all Americans.

Sources:

"ACLU Says Justice Dept.'s PATRIOT Act Website Creates New Myths About Controversial Law." ACLU, 26 August 2003 ‹http://www.aclu.org/SafeandFree/SafeandFree.cfm?ID=13371&c=206›.

"Ashcroft: Critics of New Terror Measures Undermine Effort. CNN, 7 December 2001 ‹http://www.cnn.com/2001/U.S./12/06/inv.ashcroft.hearing/›.

"Ashcroft vs. Americans." *Common Dreams*, 17 July 2002 ‹http://www.commondreams.org/views02/0717-01.htm›.

"Attorney General John Ashcroft." People for the American Way, ‹http://www.pfaw.org/pfaw/general/default.aspx?oid=2355›.

Dauenhauer, Katrin. "Congress Has Second Thoughts On Patriot Act." *AlterNet*, 24 July 2003 ‹http://www.alternet.org/story.html?StoryID=16479›.

Hentoff, Nat. "Ashcroft's Master Plan to Spy on U.S.." *The Village Voice*, 2 August 2002 ‹http://www.villagevoice.com/issues/0232/hentoff.php›.

Hentoff, Nat. "Big John Wants Your Reading List." *The Village Voice*, 22 February 2002 ‹http://www.villagevoice.com/issues/0209/hentoff.php›.

Hentoff, Nat. "John Ashcroft v. the Constitution." *The Village Voice*, 26 November 2001 ‹http://www.villagevoice.com/issues/0148/hentoff.php›.

Hentoff, Nat. "The Once and Former Rule of Law." *The Village Voice*, 3 June 2003 ‹http://www.villagevoice.com/issues/0328/hentoff.php›.

Kick, Russ. "Website for Operation TIPS Quietly Changes." *The Memory Hole*, 2002 ‹http://www.thememoryhole.org/policestate/tips-changes.htm›.

Lewis, Charles and Mayle, Adam. "Son of the Patriot Act." *AlterNet*, 7 February 2003 ‹http://www.alternet.org/story.html?StoryID=15138›.

Lithwick, Dahlia and Turner, Julia. "A Guide to the Patriot Act." *Slate*, 8–11 September 2003 ‹http://slate.msn.com/id/2087984›.

Moore, Michael. "Patriot Act: What It Is." MichaelMoore.com ‹http://www.michaelmoore.com/takeaction/issues/patriotact.php›.

"Patriot Act Abuses Seen." CBS News, 21 July 2003 ‹http://www.cbsnews.com/stories/2003/07/21/attack/main564189.shtml›.

Redden, Jim. *Snitch Culture*. Feral House, 2001.

Rothschild, Matthew. "A Grave Assault on the Constitution." *Common Dreams*, 15 November 2001 ‹http://www.commondreams.org/views01/1116-06.htm›.

Scheeres, Julia. "Feds' Spying Plan Fades to Black." *Wired* News, 4 December 2002 ‹http://www.wired.com/news/politics/0,1283,56701,00.html›.

Singel, Ryan. "A Chilly Response to 'Patriot II.'" *Wired* News, 12 February 2003 ‹http://www.wired.com/news/politics/0,1283,57636,00.html.›

Teather, David. "Civil Libertarians Prepare to Fight Bush Over Tougher Anti-terror Laws." *The Guardian*, 15 September 2003 ‹http://www.guardian.co.uk/international/story/0,3604,1041971,00.html›.

Trager, Jonathan. "Ron Paul: September 11 Is Grave Threat to American Liberties." LP News Online, August 2002 ‹http://www.lp.org/lpnews/0208/paul.html›.

"USA PATRIOT Act." ACLU ‹http://www.aclu.org/SafeandFree/SafeandFree.cfm?ID=12126&c=207›.

"USA PATRIOT Act as Passed by Congress." Electronic Frontier Foundation, 25 October 2001 ‹http://www.eff.org/Privacy/Surveillance/Terrorism/hr3162.php›.

Van Bergen, Jennifer. "Repeal the usA Patriot Act." *Truthout*, 1–6 April 2002 ‹http://www.truthout.org/docs_02/04.02A.JVB.Patriot.htm›.

Welch, Matt. "Get Ready for PATRIOT II." *AlterNet*, 2 April 2003 ‹http://www.alternet.org/story.html?StoryID=15541›.

17

➔ HE'S A COWARD

On May 1, 2003, when George W. Bush strutted onto the deck of the USS *Lincoln* in a Navy flight suit to declare "Mission Accomplished" in Iraq (a gloat since proven premature), much was made in the mainstream press of how heroic he looked playing Top Gun. With his trademark shit-eating smirk, he declared that he had flown the Navy S-3B marked with "George W. Bush Commander-in-Chief" on the window. This may be technically true, as he allegedly took the controls of the plane for a few seconds—like a little boy in the cockpit of an airplane. There was an intent to distort here—to imply that he flew the plane and landed it himself. Adding to the obfuscation were press report reminders that he had flown in the Air National Guard of Texas after his time at Harvard Business School.

You have to hand it to the Bush Team for spinning young Shrub's wartime cowardice into the right stuff. In 1968, with the Vietnam War killing thousands of young men, he had just graduated from Yale and was set to join the unlucky lottery for the draft to join the war his daddy (then a Congressman) favored. The junior Bush applied for the Texas National Guard, a group of weekend warriors that offered a safe way out of the death trap. Unfortunately, he got 25/100 on his test, only one point above "too-dumb-to-fly" status. Despite his deficiency in brains, he leaped over thousands of other candidates (some of whom would die in Vietnam) and was awarded a coveted slot. How did he get so lucky? Ben Barnes—then lieutenant governor of Texas—secretly advised James Rose of the Air Guard to find him a safe spot. Barnes only admitted to this in 1999, when forced to under oath. He claims, however, that it wasn't a favor to the Bush family, with whom he insists he had no contact. So evidently it was just a random act of kindness toward lucky ducky Dubya.

Now, there's nothing wrong with being opposed to war. And there's nothing wrong with being opposed to fighting in a war either—even if your reason is as simple as not wanting to die. War sucks, and there's no dishonor in wanting to avoid it. There is, however, something wrong with a man who is opposed to fighting in a war that his rich and well-connected family supports politically, but to which he voices no opposition, and then pulls those same oily strings to dodge. And there is something even worse about that same fellow later ordering troops into battle, risking their asses in a bullshit war for oil.

Despite this, Bush has gotten a free ride. Bill Clinton (who publicly opposed the war in the sixties) was ripped in press accounts over his Vietnam evasion: after the 2000 election, a Nexis search found 13,641 stories about Clinton's alleged dodging versus 49 about Bush's military record. Incredibly, one writer (the admittedly deranged Ann Coulter) wrote a screed proclaiming Shrub braver for his National Guard tour of duty—which she described as "fighter pilot" service—than Al Gore was for going to Vietnam. While in Saigon, Gore (according to Coulter) was a "Little Lord Fauntleroy" being served mint juleps while Bush risked his neck in Texas. Similar troop-support was given to John McCain during the 2000 campaign, when the Bush Team propagated rumors that McCain (a Vietnam POW) was left mentally unstable by his captivity and therefore couldn't be trusted in the Oval Office (charming, considering the source). Meanwhile, John Kerry (who won medals for bravery in Vietnam, though he later publicly denounced the war) has caught more flak over how he eats his cheese-steak sandwiches than Bush has over his scandalous flight from Vietnam.

But this is merely one example of outrageous chickenshittery. September 11? "Ain't my fault, Bill Clinton didn't stop Osama and weakened our military." The economy is in the tank? "Ain't my fault, it's Bill Clinton's and 9/11's." The case against Iraq was a fraud? "Ain't my fault the CIA signed off on British falsehoods." Enron? "I barely knew Kenny-Boy." When Harry Truman was President, he had a sign on his desk that said "The Buck Stops Here." The buck never stops with Dubya. Hell, he even tried to pass the buck on the whole "Mission Accomplished" fiasco. On October 28, he disavowed any connection to the premature sign, claiming it "was put up by the members of the USS *Abraham Lincoln*, saying that their mission was accomplished." He didn't explain why it took him six months to reveal this alleged fact. This brought outraged comments from General Wesley Clark, another man who didn't duck Nam: "This is wrong, this is irresponsible and this is not leadership. Politicizing the mission of those troops in the first place was bad theater, and diminished the office of Commander in Chief—but to now turn his comments on those very troops is outrageous." Outrageous, yes, but par for the course.

Apparently, the seeds were planted for Shrub's evasion of responsibility during the Vietnam years in more ways than one. After all, little Bush wasn't satisfied with merely getting out of Vietnam on a sweetheart deal. In 1972, four years into his six-year commitment, he failed to show for his annual flight physical. Indeed, there is no documentation that he showed up for anything in the final 17 months of his duty—and the National Guard doesn't skimp on paperwork. Despite the obscene amount of apparently AWOL time, he was never court-martialed (which would've opened up a political can of worms), and he was even let out of his commitment eight months early.

When will this snotty shit own up to anything? Apparently that won't happen until Americans kick his sorry ass out of D.C. at the earliest.

Sources:

Adams, Cecil. "Did George W. Bush Go AWOL During His Time in the National Guard?" *The Straight Dope*, 11 April 2003 ‹http://www.straightdope.com/columns/030411.html›.

The Angry Liberal. "'Top Gun-shy Bush': America's #1 Chicken Hawk Takes to the Skies." *BuzzFlash*, 5 May 2003 ‹http://www.buzzflash.com/theangryliberal/03/05/05.html›.

"Bush Disavows Mission Accomplished Banner." Yahoo News, 28 October 2003 ‹http://story.news.yahoo.com/news?tmpl=story&u=/ap/20031028/ap_on_go_pr_wh/bush_mission_accomplished_1›.

Clark, Wesley. "General Wesley Clark Responds to President Bush's 'Mission Accomplished' Remarks." General Wesley Clark for President, 28 October 2003 ‹http://clark04.com/press/release/047›.

"Commander in Chief Lands on USS Lincoln." CNN, 2 May 2003 ‹http://www.cnn.com/2003/ALLPOLITICS/05/01/bush.carrier.landing›.

Coulter, Ann. "Gore's 'Nam Flashbacks." TownHall.com, 30 October 2000 ‹http://www.townhall.com/columnists/anncoulter/ac20001030.shtml›.

"Finally, the Truth About Bush's Military Service Record." TomPaine.com, 27 September 2000 ‹http://www.tompaine.com/feature.cfm/ID/3671›.

Hatfield, J.H. *Fortunate Son: George W. Bush and the Making of an American President*. Brooklyn: Soft Skull Press, 2001.

Hicks, Sander. "Bush's Overseas Duty Deception." *BuzzFlash*, 5 March 2003 ‹http://www.buzzflash.com/contributors/03/03/05_bush.html›.

Milbank, Dana. "Steak Raises Stakes for Kerry in Philly." *The Washington Post*, 13 August 2003: A03.

Palast, Greg. *The Best Democracy Money Can Buy*. New York: Plume, 2003.

Schechner, Sam. "Top Gun." *Slate*, 2 May 2003 ‹http://slate.msn.com/id/2082471›.

Tapper, Jake. "The Brains Behind Bush." *Salon*, 21 January 2003 ‹http://www.salon.com/books/feature/2003/01/21/rove/index.html›.

"We Were Soldiers Once?" *Mother Jones*, 2003 ‹http://www.motherjones.com/news/outfront/2003/02/ma_217_01.html›.

➝ HE'S A WIMP

In many of the write-ups on Bush, much is made of his John Wayne-like swagger. Poppy Bush was haunted during both his presidential campaigns by his wimpy image. Granted, Bush Senior is a wimp, but he's head and shoulders above his man-child son. Was Gulf War II a pathetic attempt to erase the wimp stamp imprinted on daddy's head for leaving Saddam in power? The theory certainly explains a lot.

Take a look again at the cleverly staged May Day 2003 photo op. Watch as he prances around the aircraft carrier, sashaying his hips and winking at the troops. One can't help but think of his high school days at the prep school Andover, where he was head cheerleader during his senior year. In his smart flight suit, he plays the Navy pilot about as convincingly as the Village People play the biker or cop. A 12-inch George W. Bush action figure has emerged from the USS *Lincoln* charade. As casualties mount in the supposedly accomplished mission in Iraq, this doll in fighter-pilot drag sells as an "Elite Force Aviator"—a job Barbie's boyfriend Ken could do better.

Sources:

Conason, Joe. *Big Lies: The Right-Wing Propaganda Machine and How It Distorts the Truth.* New York: Thomas Dunne Books, 2003.

"Elite Force Aviator: George W. Bush—U.S. President and Naval Aviator—12" Action Figure." KBToys.com ‹http://www.kbtoys.com/genProduct.html/PID/2431939/ctid/17/place/aguc?_ts=n&ls =collect&_e=3f9f2&_v=3F9F294D784EaAA399FAD975&_ts=y›.

➝ HE'S A DUMBASS

"They misunderestimated me."
—George W. Bush

It is evident to all that George W. isn't the smartest man ever to run for president. Shrub's stupidity has led to some cheap shots. A widely circulated email claimed that his IQ was measured at 91 (the average is 100) by the Lovenstein Institute, making him the dumbest man to occupy the White House in over 70 years of measurements. The study asserted that he had a 6,500-word vocabulary, as opposed to an 11,000 average for the other elected presidents.

The email was a hoax: there is no Lovenstein Institute, as is easy to uncover. There were some other clues in the "report" that should've tipped people off: Bill Clinton is listed with the highest IQ of all at 182, exactly twice Double Digit Dubya's score. Still, the piece was so dismayingly plausible that it ran in the *London Guardian* as a legitimate story on July 19, 2001.

Another rip came from his inability to name the leaders of three out of four nations that were much in the news in 1999. When asked in an interview, he first replied, "Wait, wait, is this 50 Questions?" He then showed himself unable to name the leaders of Chechnya, India, or Pakistan. He did get Taiwan's correct, approximately, referring to President Lee Teng-hui as "Lee." Funny perhaps, but to be fair, being good at Jeopardy and Trivial Pursuit isn't the best measure of intelligence. Besides, many other candidates in 2000 (or 2004) probably wouldn't have been able to get those answers right.

So maybe his IQ isn't 91. For what it's worth, his college transcript reports that his SAT score was 1206 (566 in verbal, 640 in math) which, while not good enough to get him into Yale without a well-connected daddy, is impressive enough to suggest that he had the smarts to pay someone to take it for him. True, he did have a mere "gentleman's C" average in college, without a single A in four years (his highest score was a B+), but that is more likely to indicate laziness than stupidity. And why shouldn't he have been lazy? With his family connections, he was rewarded for his slack-off attitude with entrance into Harvard Business School, where he received a gentlemanly MBA.

Still, the proof of Bush's stupidity comes in the confused pudding of his off-the-cuff remarks, speeches, and press conferences. He looks pained when he has to respond to questions, as though he is fearful of being required to think. His speech is littered with malapropisms, gaffes, and incoherencies that betray illiteracy. (To some experts, they suggest dyslexia.)

Jacob Weisberg of *Slate* has collected some of Bush's miscues in three books. Some of his greatest hits:

→ "If I'm the one, when I put my hand on the Bible, when I put my hand on the Bible, that day when they swear us in, when I put my hand on the Bible, I will swear to not—to uphold the laws of the land." Toledo, Ohio, October 27, 2000.

→ "It's important for us to explain to our nation that life is important. It's not only life of babies, but it's life of children living in, you know, the dark dungeons of the Internet." Arlington Heights, Illinois, October 24, 2000.

→ "I don't want nations feeling like that they can bully ourselves and our allies. I want to have a ballistic defense system so that we can make the world more peaceful, and at the same time I want to reduce our own nuclear capacities to the level commiserate with keeping the peace." Des Moines, Iowa, October 23, 2000.

→ "Families is where our nation finds hope, where wings take dream." LaCrosse, Wisconsin, October 18, 2000.

→ "It's going to require numerous IRA agents." On Gore's tax plan, Greensboro, North Carolina, October 10, 2000.

→ "I think if you know what you believe, it makes it a lot easier to answer questions. I can't answer your question." Reynoldsburg, Ohio, October 4, 2000.

→ "We cannot let terrorists and rogue nations hold this nation hostile or hold our allies hostile." CNN online chat, August 30, 2000.

→ "The senator has got to understand if he's going to have— he can't have it both ways. He can't take the high horse and then claim the low road." To reporters in Florence, South Carolina, February 17, 2000.

Ironically, what should be viewed as an Achilles heel has been turned into a virtue by Shrub's spinmeisters. His ignorance and inarticulateness have been spun into proof that the Ivy Leaguer is in touch with "the common man." (That this is their view of the common man illuminates their contempt for the general public.) During the 2000 presidential debates, Gore was bashed by the media for his supposedly elitist mockery of Bush's inability to string together a complete sentence. Though by any honest measure, Gore kicked Bush's ass in all the debates, GOP whores construed them as a Dubya victories by factoring in a point-spread.

Another book about Bush's verbal stumblings is Mark Crispin Miller's *The Bush Dyslexicon*. He originally meant for the book to be humorous, but as he studied Shrub's miscues, mirth became outrage. He concludes that Bush's knuckledragging style reveals more willful ignorance than mental deficiency, and arises from his arrogance and contempt for others, his belief that the rules governing others don't apply to him. It's a short leap from such thinking to the belief that voters shouldn't decide elections.

Whether his undisputed intellectual limitations are due to a brain deficiency or to a form of psychopathy, this man has no business leading the United States of America.

Sources:

Adams, Cecil. "Who Was the Stupidest U.S. President? *The Straight Dope*, 22 June 2001 ‹http://www.straightdope.com/columns/010622.html›.

"Bush Fails Reporter's Pop Quiz on International Leaders." CNN, 5 November 1999 ‹http://www.cnn.com/ALLPOLITICS/stories/1999/11/05/bush.popquiz›.

"Bush I.Q." Bush Watch ‹http://www.bushwatch.com/bushiq.htm›.

Casey, Doug. "Dumb As a Post, or Just a Harvard Grad?" *WorldNetDaily*, 20 February 2003 ‹http://www.worldnetdaily.com/news/article.asp?ARTICLE_ID=31141›.

Forelle, Charles. "Grades of Bush '68 Surface in Magazine." *Yale Daily News*, 2 November 1999 ‹http://www.yaledailynews.com/article.asp?AID=2636›.

Miller, Mark Crispin. *The Bush Dyslexicon: Observations on a National Disorder*. New York: W.W. Norton & Company, 2002.

"Presidential IQ." Urban Legends Reference Pages, 5 September 2001 ‹http://www.snopes.com/inboxer/hoaxes/presiq.htm›.

Weisberg, Jacob. *George W. Bushisms: The Slate Book of The Accidental Wit and Wisdom of our 43rd President*. New York: Simon & Schuster, 2001.

Weisberg, Jacob. *More George W. Bushisms: More of Slate's Accidental Wit and Wisdom of Our 43rd President*. New York: Simon & Schuster, 2002.

Weisberg, Jacob. *Still More George W. Bushisms: "Neither in French nor in English nor in Mexican."* New York: Simon & Schuster, 2003.

Whyte, Murray. "Bush Anything But Moronic, According to Author." *Common Dreams*, 28 November 2002 ‹http://www.commondreams.org/headlines02/1128-02.htm›.

20

→ HE'S FULL OF SHIT

Never mind blowjobs or who invented the Internet—Bill Clinton and Al Gore, by any objective standard, have nothing on Bush when it comes to lying.

He lies about winning the election. He lies about September 11. He lies about the reasons for the war on Iraq, and the non-existent links between Saddam and Osama. He lies about the need for and benefits of a tax cut. He lies about being a "compassionate conservative." And these only begin to fill the sack of shit.

It runs in the company he keeps, a group of mouthpieces who have taken fabrication to new lows. The most infamous would have to be his former spokesman, Ari Fleischer, a man who was once laughed out of the White House Briefing Room because the usually fawning White House press couldn't swallow his absurdities. (He announced his resignation in late May 2003, just as the Iraqi lies began catching up to the Dubyaites.) To call them "spin doctors" is too flattering: spin, after all, implies that some truth is there, presented self-servingly. The Bush Team doesn't even bother to give lip service to reality.

Besides those previously mentioned, here are some the most infamous hits, as noted by BushWatch.com:

> → "I think what we need to do is convince people who live in the lands they live in to build the nations. Maybe I'm missing something here. I mean, we're going to have kind of a nation-building corps from America? Absolutely not." Shrub, October 11, 2000.

> → "President Bush has abandoned a pledge to invest $100 million a year in a program for rain forest conservation, according to the budget he released yesterday. Bush announced in a foreign policy speech last August that he planned to greatly expand the Tropical Forest Conservation

Act, which allows poor countries to restructure their debt in exchange for protecting the disappearing forests. 'Expanding the aims of the Tropical Forest Conservation Act, I will ask Congress to provide $100 million to support the exchange of debt relief for the protection of tropical forests,' Bush said in the speech, delivered in Miami on Aug. 25. But in the new federal budget, Bush has arranged for just $13 million for the program. Even that sum isn't new funding; instead, it is diverted from the Agency for International Development. 'They've zeroed it out,' said Debbie Reed, legislative affairs director for the National Environmental Trust. . ." *The Boston Globe*, April 10, 2001.

→ ". . .Bush looked at Cheney's proposal to drill for oil in Montana's Lewis and Clark National Forest and decided that it was a good idea, since the desire to drill for oil was the wish of the people of Montana. However, the people of Montana have gone on record as being against the drilling, and the group that supports drilling consists of oil companies from outside the state. . . The 1.8 million acres of the Lewis and Clark National Forest, which includes some 380,000 acres of the Bob Marshall Wilderness, could be redesignated by the Bush administration for drilling without coming up before Congress. All it would take, according to Cheney's task force, is repealing administrative protections that former controversial Lewis and Clark National Forest manager Gloria Flora spearheaded during the Clinton years. Such a change could be made by Norton. The rub, according to Jeff Juel of the Missoula-based Ecology Center, is that Flora's moves to preserve the Front included an extensive public commentary period, one that provided . . . overwhelming public support." *The Missoula Independent*, April 26, 2001.

→ "'I do support a national patients' bill of rights. As a matter of fact, I brought Republicans and Democrats together to do just that in the state of Texas, to get a patients' bill of rights through. . .' Texas, he added, was 'one of the first states that said you can sue an H.M.O. for denying you proper coverage. . .' Mr. Bush in 1995 vetoed the first version of the patients' rights bill that the Legislature sent him. . . two years later he let the section of the bill granting the right to sue go into effect without his signature." *The New York Times*, July 29, 2001.

→ "Recently Mr. Bush was asked about the decision of the Organization of Petroleum Exporting Countries to reduce output by a million barrels a day. . . . Mr. Bush was remarkably sympathetic to OPEC's cause; it seems that he feels the oil exporters' pain. 'It's very important for there to be stability in a marketplace. I've read some comments from the OPEC ministers who said this was just a matter to make sure the market remains stable and predictable,' he declared. Just in case you wonder whether this was really an endorsement of price-fixing, or whether Mr. Bush was just being polite, his spokesman, Ari Fleischer, left no doubt: 'The president thinks it's important to have stability, and stability can come in the form of low prices, stability can come in the form of moderate prices.' This is the same man who boasted during last year's campaign that he would force OPEC to 'open the spigot.' Did OPEC take Mr. Bush's remarks as a green light for further cuts? According to one oil analyst interviewed by Reuters, Mr. Bush's apparent expression of support for their efforts to keep prices high 'excited a lot of OPEC ministers.' Funny, isn't it? When California complains about high electricity prices, it gets a lecture about how you can't defy the laws of supply and demand. But when foreign producers collude to prevent prices from falling in the face of an oil glut, the administration not only signals its approval but endorses the old, discredited theory that cartels are in consumers' interest." Paul Krugman, *The New York Times*, August 4, 2001.

→ "When Bush was asked about [the Environmental Protection Agency's report] last week, he dismissively remarked: 'I read the report put out by the bureaucracy. . .' White House press secretary Ari Fleischer fessed up: President Bush didn't actually read that 268-page Environmental Protection Agency report on climate change, even if he said he did." AP, June 10, 2002.

→ "Bush often tells audiences that he promised during the 2000 presidential campaign that he would allow the federal budget to go into deficit in times of war, recession or national emergency, but he never imagined he would 'have a trifecta.' Nobody inside or outside the White House, however, had been able to produce evidence that Bush actually said this during the campaign. . . Now comes information that the three caveats were uttered before the 2000 campaign—by Bush's Democratic opponent, Vice President Al Gore." *The Washington Post*, July 2, 2002.

→ "Toward the bottom of last Friday's *Washington Post* story on the Woodward book by Mike Allen, the reader learns that Bush was 'preoccupied by public perceptions of the war, looking at polling data from Rove, now his senior adviser, even after pretending to have no interest.' How remarkable to be told so bluntly about this Bush obsession—after hearing so many blabbermouths on cable TV and in opinion columns insist that this president, unlike his predecessor, 'doesn't care about polls.'" Joe Conason, *Salon*, November 18, 2002.

→ "Mr. Bush's other foreign aid initiative, announced in his State of the Union address, is $10 billion in new money to fight AIDS in Africa and the Caribbean over five years. But his budget falls short of that promise. He is proposing only a $550 million increase over the global AIDS money in this year's spending bill now in Congress. Since the Global Fund to Fight AIDS, Tuberculosis and Malaria would be an effective channel for the aid, there is no excuse for the initiative's leisurely start. Mr. Bush's 2004 budget for the Global Fund, $200 million, actually cuts in half what Congress is likely to do in 2003. Mr. Bush has also found part of the money for his AIDS programs by cutting nearly $500 million from child health, including vaccine programs. Child survival is the biggest loser in the foreign aid budget—a scandalous way to finance AIDS initiatives. With the budget dominated by defense spending and huge tax cuts for the wealthy, the White House should not be forcing the babies of Africa to pay for their parents' AIDS drugs." *The New York Times*, February 17, 2003.

→ "President Bush proclaimed that a report by leading economists concluded that the economy would grow by 3.3 percent in 2003 if his tax cut proposals were adopted. No such report exists." Gordon Livingston, *The Baltimore Sun*, June 2, 2003.

Meanwhile, BushLies.net notes the following examples of deceit:

→ In the 2003 SOTU address, Bush vowed to expand AmeriCorps by 50 percent. Instead, funding for AmeriCorps has been cut by $100 million, forcing the program to cut volunteers from 2,400 to 575 and close 17 of its 20 programs.

→ An EPA assessment of Bush's "Clear Skies" plan concealed the fact that a proposal by Senator Carper (D–Del.) would provide greater long-term benefits at only slightly higher costs.

→ Before release of the EPA's 2003 Environmental Overview, the White House deleted a detailed chapter that found that global warming was due to human factors and that "climate changes have global consequences for human health and the environment."

→ A Labor Department report showing the real value of the minimum wage over time (which would show the workers losing ground under Bush, since there has been no increase since 1997) was removed from its website.

→ The Bureau of Labor Statistics' monthly Mass Layoff Statistics report was reduced by the administration in December 2002 to a footnote in the final report. After this was discovered by the *Washington Post*, the reports were reinstated.

→ A Council of Economic Advisors' forecast showing that the Bush "stimulus" plan would only create 170,000 jobs per year and be a "job killer" after 2007 was removed from its website.

→ In 2000 and 2001 Bush promised that Social Security funds would remain in a lockbox and that "we can proceed with tax relief without fear of budget deficits even if the economy softens" since his budget projections were "cautious and conservative."

→ Faced with growing deficits, Bush and Glenn Hubbard, chairman of the President's Council of Economic Advisors, now claim that deficits do not matter and have no impact on interest rates. As recently as 2002, Bush said, "I'm mindful of what overspending can mean to interest rates or expectations of interest rates." As for Hubbard, the 2002 edition of his textbook *Money, the Financial System and the Economy* not only states that higher deficits increase interest rates but also provides a formula to calculate the increase in interest rates per dollar increase in spending or tax cuts. In July 2003, interest rates on ten-year U.S. Treasuries jumped from 3.1% to almost 4%.

But perhaps the greatest example of the Bush Team's mendacity came in May 2003. A Treasury Department study projected an astounding $44.2 trillion long-term budgetary hole due to future health care and pension obligations. The report was shelved and suppressed. The report concluded that only five ways to avoid the shortfall existed: boosting individual and corporate taxes 69 percent, raising payroll taxes 95 percent, cutting non–Social Security and non-Medicare spending 56 percent, eliminating all other federal government spending, or some combination of these four measures.

The good news here: the report was a lie itself. It was commissioned by Bush's former Treasury Secretary John O'Neill, and the unstated purpose for the study was to create a state of panic that would promote plans to "privatize" some or all of Social Security. Its aim was to drum up fears of Social Security insolvency that would help promote this scheme. Unfortunately for the report, its release was ill-timed, during the heat of the debate over the 2003 tax cuts. It was politically unappealing to claim that the U.S. would be in the hole $44 trillion while claiming that a proposed $800 billion tax cut was fiscally responsible.

What does it say about the lies of Bush and his buddies that his biggest whoppers collide at such an inappropriate time? That's the problem for the pathological liar: it's hard to keep the whole story straight, because none of the little stories are constrained by reality. Even a loyal soldier like Colin Powell can't avoid calling it bullshit.

The lies of Bush and company are enabled by media half fawning over power and half in outright service of duplicity. As Al Franken has pointed out, media and politics have reached new lows in service of lying liars and the lies they tell. When will it stop? Change needs to begin at the top.

Sources:

Alterman, Eric. "Bush Lies, Media Swallows." *The Nation*, 11 November 2002 ‹http://www.alternet.org/story.html?StoryID=14518›.

"Ari Gets Laughed Out of the White House Briefing Room." *BuzzFlash*, 26 February 2003 ‹http://www.buzzflash.com/analysis/03/02/26_Ari.html›.

"Bush Lies." Bush Watch ‹http://www.bushwatch.com/bushlies.htm›.

BushLies.net ‹http://www.bushlies.net›.

Franken, Al. *Lies and the Lying Liars Who Tell Them: A Fair and Balanced Look at the Right*. New York: E P Dutton, 2003.

Gongloff, Mark. "The $44 Trillion Hole?" CNN/Money, 29 May 2003 ‹http://money.cnn.com/2003/05/29/news/economy/social_security_pain/›.

Lindorff, Dave. "Ari 'The Fabulist' Fleischer Quits the Scene." *Counterpunch*, 21 May 2003 ‹http://www.counterpunch.org/lindorff05212003.html›.

Malveaux, Suzanne, and McCaughan, Tim. "Treasury Denies Report that Deficit Paper Was 'Shelved.'" CNN, 29 May 2003 ‹http://money.cnn.com/2003/05/29/news/economy/social_security_pain›.

21

→ HE'S A PSYCHOPATHIC KILLER

Mark Crispin Miller, the *Dyslexicon* author who studied Bush's speech pathologies in detail, concluded that "Bush is a sociopathic personality . . . incapable of empathy. He has an inordinate sense of his own entitlement, and he's a very skilled manipulator." Miller would add, "He has no trouble speaking off the cuff when he's speaking punitively, when he's talking about violence, when he's talking about revenge. . . It's only when he leaps into the wild blue yonder of compassion, or idealism, or altruism, that he makes these hilarious mistakes." In other words, Bush's inarticulateness arises from darker inadequacies than did Dan Quayle misspelling "potato."

Case in point: in September 2002, Bush was handed a script containing the following saying: "fool me once, shame on you, fool me twice, shame on me." What he actually mouthed was this: "Fool me once, shame . . . shame on . . . you. [Long, uncomfortable pause.] Fool me—can't get fooled again!" The gaffe got quite a few laughs, but as Miller observes, "What's revealing about this is that Bush could not say, 'Shame on me' to save his life. That's a completely alien idea to him."

Is Miller reading too much into this? Take a look at the twisted smirk on Bush's face when he talks about warfare in Afghanistan and Iraq. Also revealing: while preparing to declare the start of war against Iraq, he pumped his fist and said, "Feels good." Or look at Donald "Redrum" Rumsfeld, his Secretary of Defense (who seems to be a caricature out of *Dr. Strangelove*). Rummy used the word "Kill" nine times during a 35 minute press conference, with disturbing glee. Consider the cruel treatment of Afghan POWs held at Guantanamo, Cuba in Camp X-Ray, who have been filmed dressed up in kinky gear more suited to an S&M fantasy out of Mapplethorpe than a military camp.

The first signs of something wrong in little Georgie came when he was a child. In a May 21, 2000 *New York Times* puff piece, Nicholas D. Kristof quoted Bush's childhood friend Terry Throckmorton: "'We were terrible to animals,' recalled Mr. Throckmorton, laughing. A dip behind the Bush home turned into a small lake after a good rain, and thousands of frogs would come out. 'Everybody would get BB guns and shoot them,' Mr. Throckmorton said. 'Or we'd put fire-crackers in the frogs and throw them and blow them up.'"

Cut to his years as governor of Texas, when he signed the death warrants of 154 prisoners in six years. In the entire history of the USA, no governor of any state has authorized more executions than Bush. Among the dead were Karla Faye Tucker, who became a born-again Christian on death row. He refused to commute her sentence, despite an appeal from Pat Robertson that would've made it polit-ically viable. He would later mock her plea for life in a *Talk* maga-zine interview: "Please, don't kill me," he whimpered, his lips pursed in parody. The interviewer, Tucker Carlson (the *Crossfire* con-servative and usually a political ally of Dubya) was so shocked by the warped gag that Bush stopped in mid-smirk (Carlson's descrip-tion of his facial expression) and took on a more serious veneer, suddenly realizing he was behaving inappropriately. Also among the snuffed: Gary Graham and David Wayne Spence, two men whose guilt is in serious doubt, and Betty Lou Beets, a 60-year-old grand-mother convicted of killing her chronically abusive husband. He did issue a solitary stay of execution to Ricky Nolen McGinn in June 2000, when questions about the accuracy of death penalty justice suddenly became a political issue for Mr. Compassionate Conservative. (Indeed, the *USA Today* article on the stay had this title: "Execution Stay Helps Compassionate Image.") McGinn was later lethally injected, on September 27, with little media attention.

Oddly, the only person whose death sentence he did commute was Henry Lee Lucas, one of the most notorious serial murderers-rapists-pedophiles-cannibals in U.S. history. (The movie *Henry: Portrait of a Serial Killer* was loosely based on his exploits.) Shrub's supposed reason: "Henry Lee Lucas is unquestionably guilty of other despicable crimes [for] which he has been sentenced to spend the rest of his life in prison. However, I believe there is enough doubt about this particular crime that the state of Texas should not impose its ultimate penalty by executing him." Though there were questions about the murder Lucas was set to be executed over (indeed, Lucas had originally confessed to over 600 murders, which seems highly unlikely), there are multiple murders he almost certainly did commit, and, as he claimed, in service of a well-financed Satanic cult. Further, as the Graham, Spence, and Beets cases show, there are other people of whose guilt Bush chose to ignore serious doubts. Why the sudden, atypically compassionate conservatism about Lucas?

Whatever the reason, Dubya has shown little concern for the other deaths he has caused or facilitated, whether of U.S. soldiers, Afghani and Iraqi people, or death-row inmates. And considering how his plans for the Middle East have backfired, he will likely become increasingly desperate. Desperate people with little compulsion over killing are a very dangerous lot: in *The Dead Zone*, Stephen King describes a future president who begins nuclear Armageddon because of his unbalanced, sociopathic nature. Of course, that was just a novel, and a far-fetched tale—in the prologue, the future president kicks a dog to death.

Sources:

Berlow, Alan. "The Hanging Governor." *Salon*, 11 May 2000
‹http://dir.salon.com/politics2000/feature/2000/05/11/bush/index.html›.

Carlson, Tucker. "Devil May Care." *Talk Magazine*, September 1999: 106.

"The Bin Laden Videotape: The Reactionary Politics of Terrorism." World Socialist Web Site, 18 December 2001 ‹http://www.wsws.org/articles/2001/dec2001/vid-d18.shtml›.

Conover, Bev. "Bush Isn't a Moron, He's a Cunning Sociopath." *Online Journal*, 5 December 2002. ‹http://www.onlinejournal.com/Commentary/Conover120502/conover120502.html›.

"Execution Stay Helps Compassionate Image." *USA Today*, 2 June 2000
‹http://www.usatoday.com/news/opinion/e1939.htm›.

"Henry Lee Lucas & Ottis Toole." Mayhem.net ‹http://www.mayhem.net/Crime/lucas.html›.

"McGinn Executed in Texas." CBS, 27 September 2000
‹http://www.cbsnews.com/stories/2000/09/27/national/main236710.shtml›.

McGowan, David. "All the President's Men." *You Are Being Lied To: The Disinformation Guide to Media Distortion, Historical Whitewashes and Cultural Myths*. New York: The Disinformation Company Ltd., 2001.

McGowan, David. "Texas Death Machine: George W. and Henry Lee." *Disinformation*, 28 December 2000 ‹http://www.disinfo.com/archive/pages/dossier/id419/pg1/›.

McGowan, David. "There's Something About Henry." Center for an Informed America, June 2000 ‹www.davesweb.cnchost.com/henry.htm›.

Miller, Mark Crispin. *The Bush Dyslexicon: Observations on a National Disorder*. New York: W.W. Norton & Company, 2002.

"Sinister Connections March 11–17." Conspire.com, 11 March 2001
‹http://www.conspire.com/2001_03_11_oldlinks.html›.

"Two Bodies Exhumed in Mexico." BBC News, 1 December, 1999
‹http://news.bbc.co.uk/1/hi/world/americas/544547.stm›.

Whyte, Murray. "Bush Anything But Moronic, According to Author." *Common Dreams*, 28 November 2002 ‹http://www.commondreams.org/headlines02/1128-02.htm›.

Zerbisias, Antonia. "TV Avoids Showing Deadly Side of War." *Common Dreams*, 22 March 2003 ‹http://www.commondreams.org/views03/0323-01.htm›.

22

➡ HE'S AN ENEMY OF THE PLANET

There's more than one way to skin a cat (or a frog), and more than one way to wipe out all human life on the earth. Rather than by nuclear bombs, we could destroy ourselves in an environmental holocaust. The policies of Bush and friends make this scenario increasingly plausible.

Massive distrust of Bush on this issue preceded the 2000 election. After all, pseudo-Texan Bush received more than $1.8 million in individual and PAC contributions from the oil and gas industry in 1999–2000. They kicked in an additional $2.2 million for his inauguration fund. From these same industries he and Dick Cheney have profited extensively; for example, Dick Cheney made over $36 million in 2000 as CEO of oil services company Halliburton.

The distrust was soon validated. Deb Callahan, president of the League of Conservation Voters, declared after the first 100 days, "The Bush White House is becoming the most environmentally hostile in history. When analyzed in its totality, President Bush's environmental record represents a backward step in American public policy and a cynical reminder of the powerful influence of big money and special interests in the process."

Here's a list of Bush's "Missions Accomplished" in the War Against Mother Nature in his first 100 days, as noted by the Center for Responsive Politics and Margot Higgins of the Environmental News Network:

→ Nullified several environmental policies passed in the final days of the Clinton administration.

→ Suspended rules approved by former President Bill Clinton to protect roadless areas in national forests.

→ Backed increased logging in national forests. (Bush received nearly $300,000 from the timber industry.)

→ Halved funding for research into renewable energy sources, such as solar and wind power.

→ Rejected a Clinton administration proposal to increase public access to information about the potential consequences of chemical plant accidents.

→ Issued an Interior Department proposal to emasculate updated environmental mining regulations.

→ Proposed a ban on private lawsuits that force the government to add plants and animals to the endangered species list.

→ Suspended rules approved by former president Bill Clinton for new limits on arsenic in drinking water.

→ Reversed his campaign pledge to reduce carbon dioxide emissionsus. The move would have prevented an estimated 30,000 deaths a year from respiratory illness.

→ Moved forward with plans for oil drilling in the Arctic National Wildlife Refuge, despite the facts that it will take at least ten years before any of the oil in the Refuge becomes available to American consumers, and that at current national demand, the Refuge will produce only six months' worth of oil. The oil will also be distributed on the world market, meaning the change in U.S. supply from the move will be minimal.

→ And the big one: the reversal on and withdrawal of the U.S. from the Kyoto treaty on global warming. Global warming is "the most dangerous and fearful challenge to humanity over the next 100 years," according to Britain's environment minister at the time, Michael Meacher. Australian Environment Minister Robert Hill said, "The Kyoto protocol wouldn't work without the United States. That would mean that the agreement of developed countries to cut greenhouse gases which was made in 1997 would have failed." Australian Senator Bob Brown said the decision was "a low point in world environment history."

One hundred days were just the beginning. Here are some other greatest hits of his reign of terror:

→ Directed government land managers to remove environmental and procedural obstacles to the development of oil and gas resources in the West.

→ As part of the National Defense Authorization Bill, promoted several anti-environment amendments to allow the military to ride roughshod over the federal Endangered Species Act and Marine Mammal Protection Act.

→ Is currently reviewing 23 million acres nationwide of lands eligible for wilderness protection, threatening millions of pristine acres with development.

→ California, Part One: filed an amicus brief in federal court in Fresno, siding with automakers and dealers in a suit against a California regulation requiring car manufacturers to sell "zero-emissions vehicles." Shrub received $1.3 million from the automotive industry.

→ California, Part Two: declared that the government must continue to study the greenhouse effect, after the state passed the first anti–greenhouse gas law to fight global warming. The auto industry plans to mount a legal challenge to that California law, too.

→ California, Part Three: fought for the extension of offshore oil drilling rights in California coastal waters near Santa Barbara. It is so widely unpopular in the Golden State that even Republican politicians vociferously oppose it. (California is a heavily Democratic state, and Dubya stands little chance of winning it in 2004.)

→ Deleted conclusions about the likely human contribution to global warming from a 2001 EPA report. Deleted a reference to a 1999 study showing that global temperatures had risen sharply in the previous decade, replacing it with a reference to a new study partly financed by the American Petroleum Institute.

→ The American Petroleum reference is not isolated: Bush has promoted industry-backed global warming doubters who, in tobacco-lobby style, claim the rise in global temperatures is not a real problem, is not caused by humans, and if it is happening at all, is actually good for the world.

→ The Montreal Protocol, a 1987 ban of manmade chemicals that were allowing more deadly ultraviolet rays to reach the earth, has been called the greatest environmental victory in history. The Bush Team is trying to delay or even reverse the healing of the ozone layer.

None of this should have been too surprising. Here are some dossiers of the people leading the Bush Team:

→ Secretary of Interior Gale Norton had previously led efforts to roll back endangered species protections and allowed mining company polluters to escape cleanup requirements and liability. She believes that corporations have a constitutional right to pollute.

→ Secretary of Energy Spencer Abraham, campaigning for Senate, argued for eliminating the Department of Energy, which he now runs, while also leading efforts to prevent increased fuel efficiency in vehicles.

→ Undersecretary for Energy Robert G. Card was CEO and president of a nuclear cleanup contractor that has been fined or penalized more than $725,000 for numerous worker safety, procurement, and other violations since 1996.

→ National Security Adviser Condoleezza Rice was a Chevron board member until January 15. Chevron has named an oil tanker in her honor.

→ Attorney General John Ashcroft has a history of blocking enforcement of environmental laws. He was the top recipient of Monsanto contributions during his losing reelection campaign for the U.S. Senate.

→ Secretary of Defense Donald Rumsfeld was president of Searle Pharmaceuticals, now owned by Monsanto.

→ Secretary of Agriculture Ann Veneman was on the board of directors of Calgene Pharmaceuticals, another Monsanto affiliate.

→ The HHS secretary Tommy Thompson was a good friend to Monsanto and other biotech firms. He received $50,000 from biotech companies for his election campaign.

How would Bush and his boys behave in the four years following 2004, knowing he was a political lame duck and didn't need to respond to political pressure? That's a question it would be unwise to answer by experiment.

Happy Earth Day, everybody.

Sources:

"Alarm After U.S. Abandons Environment Treaty." CNN, 29 March 2001 ‹http://www.cnn.com/2001/WORLD/asiapcf/auspac/03/28/kyoto.protocol›.

The Big Book of Bush. Sierra Club ‹http://www.sierraclub.org/bush/›.

"The Bush Administration's Air Pollution Plan." Natural Resources Defense Council, 5 September 2003 ‹http://www.nrdc.org/air/pollution/qbushplan.asp›.

"The Environment." *BushTimes*, 2003 ‹http://www.bushtimes.com/cgi-bin/iowa/news/?topic=2›.

Higgins, Margot. "100 Days of Bush: Disaster Zone for the Environment?" Environmental News Network, 30 April 2001 ‹http://www.enn.com/news/enn-stories/2001/04/04302001/bushover_43213.asp›.

Mieszkowski, Katharine. "Bush to California: Choke on This." *Salon*, 16 December 2002 ‹http://www.salon.com/tech/feature/2002/12/16/war_on_california/index.html›.

Mieszkowski, Katharine. "The Triumph of Fringe Science." *Salon*, 7 August 2003 ‹http://www.salon.com/tech/feature/2003/08/07/global_warming/index.html›.

"President Bush's First 100 Days: A Look at How the Special Interests Have Fared." Center for Responsive Politics, 26 April 2001 ‹http://www.opensecrets.org/bush/100days/environment.asp›.

Scherer, Glenn. "George Bush's War on Nature." *Salon*, 6 January 2003 ‹http://www.salon.com/news/feature/2003/01/06/nature/print.html›.

York, Anthony. "Kiss It Goodbye." *Salon*, 27 November 2002 ‹http://www.salon.com/politics/feature/2002/11/27/environment/index.html›.

23

→ HE'LL DESTROY OUR COURTS

One power of the president of the United States arguably exceeds all others: the power to appoint judges, especially to the Supreme Court. In exercising this power, the president exerts an influence on the country's direction that can long exceed his term of office. In his courtroom, a judge is virtually king, with only appeals (which are costly and unlikely to succeed) as a remedy. That said, the possibility of George Bush winning an election and appointing judges for four more years should put a chill in anyone disturbed by his scary agenda.

Here are profiles of Shrub's Top Ten Most Outrageous Judicial Nominees so far, ranked in terms of extremism and the sinister influence of the appointments:

10. Deborah Cook: Nominated to the Sixth Circuit Court of Appeals, a frequent dissenter on the Ohio Supreme Court. According to Ohio Citizen Action, her dissents "reveal a callousness toward the rights of ordinary citizens which offends any reasonable sense of justice." In one case, after she dissented from a ruling favorable to a disabled worker, the court majority criticized her opinion for its "lack of statutory support for its position," and termed it "confused," "pure fantasy," and "entirely without merit." In another case, she dissented from a ruling striking down a state law that made it virtually impossible for an employee to recover damages from an intentional tort committed by the employer. Strong opposition to her confirmation came from Ohio organizations concerned with protecting individual, civil, and consumer rights.

9. Jeffrey Sutton: Nominated to the 6th Circuit Court of Appeals, he's described even by one of his supporters as the "perfect kind of poster child for what Democrats see as prototypical George W. Bush judges." He has written in favor of declaring the Violence Against Women Act unconstitutional,

and strongly supported restricting federal protections against discrimination and injury based on disability, race, age, sex, and religion. More than 70 national organizations and over 375 regional, state, and local groups have opposed his confirmation.

8. Terrence Boyle: Nominated to the 4th Circuit, he is a North Carolina federal district court judge and former staffer of the retired Senator Jesse Helms. Civil rights groups have criticized his right-wing judicial activism and bad record in civil rights cases. He has been reversed twice by the Supreme Court, once in a unanimous ruling, for deciding that congressional redistricting in North Carolina improperly favored minority voters. He was also reversed when he refused to accept a settlement of a sex discrimination claim against a state agency, even though the agency had agreed.

7. Janice Rogers Brown: Nominated to the U.S. Court of Appeals for the District of Columbia, currently on the California Supreme Court. Was rated "unqualified" by the state bar's commission on judicial nominees, because of her lack of experience and tendency to inject personal views in her judicial opinions. Confirmed in 1996 after a contentious fight, she has authored many confrontational and harsh opinions—often in dissent—that would undermine civil rights, workers' rights, reproductive rights, and the environment.

6. James Leon Holmes: Nominated to the District Court for the Eastern District of Arkansas, this former president of Arkansas Right to Life once compared abortion to the Holocaust. He wrote that "concern for rape victims [with regard to abortion policy] is a red herring because conceptions from rape occur with approximately the same frequency as snowfall in Miami." He also wrote that "the wife is to subordinate herself to her husband" and that "the woman is to place herself under the authority of the man."

5. Miguel Estrada: Nominated to the District of Columbia Court of Appeals, a stepping-stone to the Supreme Court. A member of several right-wing activist groups, he is widely deemed to be a stealth candidate, the Latino Clarence Thomas. He dodged questions from the Senate Judiciary Committee and failed to provide records from his work in the Solicitor General's office. However, a former supervisor in the Solicitor General's office concluded that Estrada "lacks the

judgment" and is "too much of an ideologue to be an appeals court judge." Claimed under oath that he never personally considered *Roe v. Wade*—a curious lack of intellectual interest from a former Supreme Court clerk. Because of his lack of candor, Senate Republicans failed seven times to cut off debate on his nomination. An unconvincing campaign was launched to claim that their opposition was racially motivated, although opponents included the Puerto Rican Legal Defense and Education Fund and the Congressional Hispanic Caucus. Also opposed were the Congressional Black Caucus and many civil rights, labor, environmental, and women's organizations. He withdrew his name from consideration on September 4, 2003.

4. Carolyn Kuhl: Nominated for the powerful 9th Circuit Court of Appeals, currently a California Superior Court judge. The deputy solicitor general in Reagan's Justice Department, she has a long record of opposing reproductive rights, civil rights, and environmental protections. Under Uncle Ronnie, she wrote what a former Solicitor General called "the most aggressive memo" urging the Supreme Court to overturn *Roe v. Wade* as "flawed." Also supported tax breaks for Bob Jones University, despite its ban on interracial dating, a position protested in a letter signed by 200 of her colleagues. (By an 8-1 vote, the Supreme Court rejected Kuhl's position.) Urged the Supreme Court to overrule its precedent on "associational standing," which allows unions, environmental groups, and other associations to protect the rights of their members in court. The court rejected Kuhl's argument without dissent. She was reversed unanimously by the Court of Appeals after dismissing an invasion of privacy claim brought by a breast cancer patient whose doctor allowed a drug salesman in the examining room during an examination of the patient's breasts. Kuhl's nomination is opposed strongly by a coalition of unions, women's, environmental, civil rights, and other organizations.

3. William Pryor: Nominated to the 11th Circuit Court of Appeals, currently a "states' rights" advocate as Alabama's attorney general. As the state's top lawyer, he has authored or joined numerous briefs challenging the constitutionality of a host of federal employment protections, including the Americans with Disabilities Act, the Violence Against Women Act, the Family and Medical Leave Act, the Fair Labor

Standards Act, and the Age Discrimination in Employment Act. He has also urged Congress to eliminate a key provision of the Voting Rights Act, which protects the right to vote for African Americans and other minorities, and he opposed a Supreme Court ruling that tying prisoners to hitching posts was cruel and unusual. A vocal anti-choice activist, he called *Roe v. Wade* "the day seven members of our high court ripped the Constitution and ripped out the life of millions of unborn children." His nomination, opposed by more than 200 organizations, including unions, civil rights, environmental, women's, disability rights and other groups, is pending before the full Senate, where it is being filibustered by Senate Democrats.

2. Priscilla Owen: Nominated to the 5th Circuit Court of Appeals, she has a long career as a conservative judicial activist—including on the Texas Supreme Court under Bush. (Karl Rove received $228,000 for campaign services for her election to the court). She is one of the most frequent dissenters from an already-conservative court. In at least one such case, the Texas Legislature immediately passed legislation to overrule her position. She opposes reproductive rights; when Bush White House Counsel Alberto Gonzales was a justice alongside her in Texas, he wrote that her dissent on an abortion-related case constituted "an unconscionable act of judicial activism." (Gonzales criticized her positions on 11 cases.) Until nominated by Bush, she never voted to allow a minor to bypass parental notification. As a lawyer in private practice, her meal ticket was representing big oil companies, and she continues to favor big business. Opposed to environmental protections and consumers' interests, she favors employers and insurers. She has opposed the claims of injured and harassed workers, undermined the state workers' compensation system, and voted in favor of corporations that sold defective products. She was rejected by the Senate Judiciary Committee in 2002 but renominated by Bush in 2003. Her nomination is pending now before the full Senate, where it is being filibustered by Senate Democrats.

1. Charles Pickering: Nominated to the 5th Circuit Court of Appeals, he's a longtime opponent of civil rights. He authored an article in law school that described how laws that ban interracial marriage could be better enforced; his recommendations became Mississippi law. As a judge, he

pressured federal prosecutors to show leniency to a convicted cross-burner (which, besides being offensive, was clearly
unethical conduct). He voted to fund and had contact with the
infamously racist Sovereignty Commission, then lied about it
to the Senate Judiciary Committee. He has criticized the "one-
person, one-vote" principle and important provisions of the
Voting Rights Act, and ruled against the vast majority of people bringing job bias suits before him. None of this should be
surprising: he is strongly supported by Senate Majority Leader
Trent Lott. Has displayed hostility to Constitutional rights,
including the Miranda warning, and has been reversed 15
times for violating "well-settled principles of law." As a state
senator, Pickering opposed *Roe v. Wade* (indeed, fought for a
Constitutional amendment to ban abortion), and voted against
the Equal Rights Amendment. Was rejected by the Senate
Judiciary Committee in 2002 but renominated by Bush in 2003.

These are the worst, but they are consistent with the bulk of his
nominations, which reveal an extreme shift in the judiciary.

Five of these nominees are members of the Federalist Society,
which covertly wields great influence over our courts and promotes
an increasingly right-wing agenda. The Society's greatest champi-
ons are Antonin Scalia and Robert Bork, two of the scariest legal
minds of the last 50 years. Among its members on the Bush Team
are Attorney General John Ashcroft, Deputy Attorney General Larry
Thompson, Solicitor General Ted Olson, Deputy White House
Counsel Timothy Flanigan, DOE Secretary Spencer Abraham, Interior
Secretary Gale Norton, and Eugene Scalia (Antonin's boy). Another
member is the frothing bimbo right-wing mouthpiece Ann Coulter,
who summed up the Federalist Society philosophy on *Real Time*
with Bill Maher, when she explained that the U.S. is a nation of
both limited government and limited rights. The two claims spe-
ciously justify any goal of their overtly reactionary agenda. Within
the group, there is a contempt for basic civil rights and a lack of
recognition for any right to privacy.

Shrub and company have predictably whined about the supposed Democratic Party "obstructionism" in blocking judicial nominees via filibuster. According to Bush, "Today, we are facing a crisis in the Senate, and therefore a crisis in our judiciary. . . I believe
a fresh start is possible." His solution? Require the Senate to vote
within 180 days after a nominee is submitted, without filibusters.

Republican Senate Majority Leader Bill Frist supports this: "The need to reform is obvious and it is now urgent."

In fact, the Judicial Conference of the United States has labeled a number of judiciary vacancies as "emergencies"—but there's nothing new here. Judicial vacancies are at their lowest point in 13 years. Any crisis currently in the system is a leftover of the Clinton years, when Republicans blocked 35% of his judicial nominations (which weren't as ideological as Dubya's). During the Bush years, the Senate has confirmed over 140 nominees, and filibustered only two so far. So who's the obstructionist?

Of course, such a scenario is described even by Republicans as a "nuclear option." It would be so even if the Senate head making the ruling and the president making the nominations were legitimately elected. Whether they'll actually do this remains to be seen, but that it was even proposed reveals how little respect the Bush Team has for nearly 150 years of rule of law.

Sources:

"Approaching Judicial Armageddon?" People for the American Way, ‹http://www.pfaw.org/pfaw/general/default.aspx?oid=7532›.

"The Bush Record: One Extremist Nominee After Another." Democratic National Committee, ‹http://www.democrats.org/scotus/bushrecord.html›.

"Clinton, Conspiracism, and the Continuing Culture War." Political Research Associates ‹http://www.publiceye.org/conspire/clinton/Clintonculwar8-20.htm›.

Dean, John W. "The Ongoing Controversy Over Judicial Nominees: What Will It Mean if the GOP 'Goes Nuclear' On The Filibuster Rules?" *FindLaw*, 23 May 2003 ‹http://writ.news.findlaw.com/dean/20030523.html›.

"The Federalist Society: From Obscurity to Power." People for the American Way ‹http://www.pfaw.org/pfaw/general/default.aspx?oid=653›.

Risen, Clay. "If It Ain't Broke . . ." *Flak Magazine*, 29 May 2003 ‹http://flakmag.com/opinion/aintbroke.html›.

Smith, Dietz. "The Federalist Society." *The Rant*, 27 February 2003 ‹http://www.therant.info/archive/000530.html›.

"Stop the Bush Court-Packing Plan." AFL-CIO ‹http://www.aflcio.org/issuespolitics/factsheet_ns04242003.cfm›.

"Urge Senators to Stop Bush's Court-Packing Plan!" People for the American Way ‹http://www.pfaw.org/pfaw/general/default.aspx?oId=7681›.

24

➡️ THE SUPREME COURT

> Tim Russert: Which Supreme Court justice do you really respect?
> George W. Bush: Well, that's—Anthony [sic] Scalia is one.
> Russert: He is someone who wants to overturn *Roe vs. Wade*.
> Bush: Well, he's a—there's a lot of reasons why I like Judge Scalia.
>
> —NBC's *Meet the Press*, November 21, 1999

For over nine years, there hasn't been a Supreme Court vacancy—the longest period in nearly 200 years. Although a 2004 slot appears unlikely (as a general rule, Supreme Court nominations don't coincide with election years, when executive powers are up for grabs), both William H. Rehnquist and Sandra Day O'Connor look ready to have a fork put in them, and John Paul Stevens was born in 1920. Unforeseen tragedy could also always lead to vacancies.

The implications are enormous for all: Stevens is part of the court's moderately liberal wing, O'Connor a conservative, and Rehnquist one prong of the hard-right trident (along with Scalia and Thomas). Any opening can significantly alter the makeup of the court, depending on who is making the appointments.

George Bush has said that Scalia and Thomas are the models for his future picks. Presumably he's not referring to Long Dong Silver jokes at the water cooler. For those concerned about privacy, reproductive rights, civil rights enforcement, separation of church and state, civil liberties, the environment, workers' rights, and access to justice (not to mention legitimate presidential elections), this is a bad omen.

Sources:

"Courting Disaster." People for the American Way
‹http://www.pfaw.org/pfaw/general/default.aspx?oid=2756›.

"George W. Bush, Trent Lott and John Ashcroft: A Shared Philosophy." People for the American Way ‹http://www.pfaw.org/pfaw/general/default.aspx?oid=7284›.

"Supreme Court Watch." Democratic National Committee ‹http://www.democrats.org/scotus›.

25

——→ JEB, KAT, & THE SUPREMES

As Reason #1 revealed, the theft of the 2000 election was highly front-loaded. However, in the follow-up to the Election Day debacle, the Florida Secretary of State, the Supreme Court, and other right-wing partisans did all they could to evade democratic rule of law and justice. Such an operation reveals the GOP coup-masters' contempt for legitimate government.

As pointed out, the Gore Team argued that, despite the massive voter suppression operation of Jeb's operatives in Florida, Al Gore would still have won the election if a proper counting of ballots had been done. On this argument, the Gore Team was on solid legal foundation. According to Florida law, an election participant has the right to request a manual recount of votes. No surprise there: it has always been an accepted practice to use hand-counts in any close race, even by the system's own designers. In an interview with Jonathan Vankin of the *San Jose Metro*, Bob Swartz, founder of Cardamation (a leader in the computer punch card and card-reading machines business), explained about hand-counts: "If our goal is to get 100 percent accuracy, there's no question that's the way to achieve it."

The Bush Junta argued otherwise. In defiance of law and historical precedent, James Baker (an inside member of the posse for Shrub's daddy) claimed that hand-counts create "tremendous opportunities for human error and . . . mischief." He would also moan that hand-counts set election workers the "subjective" task to "divine the intent of the voter." This was hypocritical on two counts. First, while governor of Texas, Dubya himself signed a bill into law that approved the hand-count of ballots. Second, and perhaps more germane to the issue of Florida, Bush himself had received 561 extra votes (greater than his official margin of so-called victory) in seven different Republican-dominated counties, 143 from Volusia alone. When asked about the gains from hand-counts on separate occasions, Baker and Shrub spokeswoman Karen Hughes both abruptly ended their press conferences.

Besides being hypocritical, this argument was bullshit. As the Florida Supreme Court put it, "Although error cannot be completely eliminated in any tabulation of the ballots, our society has not yet gone so far as to place blind faith in machines. In almost all endeavors, including elections, humans routinely correct the errors of machines. For this very reason Florida law provides a human check on both the malfunction of tabulation equipment and error in failing to accurately count the ballots." Even the extremely partisan U.S. Supreme Court unanimously agreed "that punch card balloting machines can produce an unfortunate number of ballots which are not punched in a clean, complete way by the voter."

Why did Team Bush throw such a hissy-fit over the established routine of counting ballots? They feared that the votes were there, if counted in a certain manner. More to the point, if punch cards with dimpled ballots were counted in the vote totals, they feared Gore would win Florida, even with the widespread vote suppression.

How legitimate was the standard of counting dimpled ballots? The bill that Bush signed into law in Texas affirmed counting dimpled ballots as valid votes. The precedents cited by the Florida Supreme Court affirmed that this was the proper standard as well.

The courts were involved in the first place because Katherine Harris claimed that state law prohibited her from accepting amended returns after November 14, seven days after Election Day. The court dismissed her argument, pointing out that to punish voters because county canvassing boards had not met a statutory deadline was "unreasonable, unnecessary, and violates long-standing law." They would add, "Allowing the manual recounts to proceed in an expeditious manner, rather than imposing an arbitrary seven-day deadline, is consistent not only with the statutory scheme but with prior United States Supreme Court pronouncements."

The day after the ruling, Bush supporters staged a riot in front of the Dade County canvassing board, who were counting ballots as instructed by law. John Sweeney, a New York Congressman, urged this mob to "shut it down." Joe Geller, Dade County's Democratic chairman, was chased by the crowd and required police protection, and the throng pounded on the office doors of the elections supervisor. Several people were roughed up, and the frightened canvassing board reversed its decision to count the ballots. As reported by journalist Robert Parry in his Internet magazine *The Consortium*, the Brooks Brothers-clad rioters included at six people paid by the Bush recount committee, and at least three are now part of the White House staff. The recount committee also paid over $35K for an after-party celebration of the successful riot.

Meanwhile, Republicans in the Florida state legislature proposed to fill the state's 25 electoral college seats with supporters of Dubya rather than by vote of the people, even though such an unprecedented move would have provoked a constitutional crisis. Jeb Bush, who had previously promised to recuse himself from the electoral dispute involving his brother, declared that he would approve the use of these appointed electors.

Jeb didn't have to; the U.S. Supreme Court intervened and selected the winner. They did this after Bush, and not Gore, trotted his lawyers to federal court to intervene in the dispute. (This is why the infamous court decision was "Bush versus Gore" and not vice versa, as the plaintiff is listed first by custom.) In their first ruling, the Supremes claimed (5–4) that the Florida Court had changed the state Legislature's law after the election, and thus had ruled unconstitutionally. The Florida Court then issued another ruling, this time clarifying its basis in state law. The Supreme Court didn't dispute this: instead, they declared on December 12 that the Florida Court had erred by failing to "adopt adequate statewide standards for determining what is a legal vote" in the election. The Florida Court had cited state law, which declared the only legal standard for counting vote to be the "clear intent of the voter." This was deemed too vague by the U.S. Supremes, who ruled that the Court was required to specify what that meant. (Never mind that, had they done this, they likely would have been overruled for "changing state law" after the fact, effectively putting the Florida Supremes in a legal Catch-22.) They then (by a 5–4 vote) gave the Florida Court an impracticable deadline to rectify the matter. The fix was officially done.

(At the time of both rulings, three of the Supreme Court judges who ruled in favor of Bush had obvious ethical conflicts. Antonin Scalia's two sons were both lawyers working for Bush, Clarence Thomas's wife was collecting applications for people wanting to work for the Bush administration, and Sandra Day O'Connor was reported to have said about a likely Gore victory on Election Night after networks declared him the winner of Florida: "This is terrible." If one of those three had recused himself or herself, the Florida Supreme Court rulings would have stood.)

The irony here is that Bush might have won the recount, had it been done according to a certain scheme. For example, according to an examination of those ballots by a group of leading news organizations, had the recount been solely of undervotes in the four counties Gore contested, Gore would have lost by 225 votes; had it been an undervote count of the entire state, Gore would have lost by 430. This was widely reported in 2001, when the American press was desperate to legitimize Shrub in the post-9/11 hysteria. Less widely reported was that if overvotes had been included, a statewide count of all ballots would've deemed Gore the winner, no matter what criteria were used for deciding the "clear intent of the voter." In fact, Judge Terry Lewis (who was in charge of determining the rules of the recount) has indicated that he might have included legitimate overvotes in the vote totals, as there wouldn't have been any reason not to.

In any case, here is what members of the Supreme Court had to say about the *Bush v. Gore* ruling:

> "Chief Justice Rehnquist would 'disrupt' Florida's 'Republican regime.' The court should not allow its 'untested prophecy' that counting votes is 'impractical' to 'decide the presidency of the United States.'"
> —Justice Ruth Bader Ginsburg (Democrat appointed by Clinton)

> "Before this Court stayed the effort . . . the courts of Florida were ready to do their best to get that job done. There is no justification for denying the State the opportunity to try to count all the disputed ballots now."
> —Justice David Souter (Republican appointed by Bush)

> "There is no justification for the majority's remedy. . ."
> —Justice Steven Breyer (Democrat appointed by Clinton)

And here is the most telling quote of all:

> "Although we may never know with complete certainty the identity of the winner of this year's Presidential election, the identity of the loser is perfectly clear. It is the Nation's confidence in the judge as an impartial guardian of the rule of law."
> —Justice John Paul Stevens (Republican appointed by Ford)

Sources:

Campbell, Duncan. "Florida Republicans Hint at Electoral College Coup." *The Guardian*, 30 November 2000 ‹http://www.guardian.co.uk/international/story/0,3604,404847,00.html›.

Dickenson, Mollie. "Bush Gained Hand Recounts." *The Consortium*, 19 November 2000 ‹http://www.consortiumnews.com/2000/111900a.html›.

Dickenson, Mollie. "Does the System Still Work?" TomPaine.com, 14 November 2000 ‹http://www.tompaine.com/feature2.cfm/ID/3871›.

Dickenson, Mollie. "Supreme Court Intrigue." *The Consortium*, 11 December 2000 ‹http://www.consortiumnews.com/2000/121100a.html›.

"Election 2000." FindLaw ‹http://news.findlaw.com/legalnews/U.S./election/election2000.html›.

"Florida Supreme Court: Recount Results Count." CNN, 22 November 2000 ‹http://www.cnn.com/2000/ALLPOLITICS/stories/11/22/recount.ruling/›.

Harnden, Toby. "Bush Brother Will 'Defy the Courts' to Keep Gore Out." *The Daily Telegraph*, 1 December 2000 ‹http://www.telegraph.co.uk/news/main.jhtml?xml=/news/2000/12/01/wpres01.xml›.

Kick, Russ. "The Fix Is In." alterNewswire, December 2000 ‹http://www.mindpollen.com/fix.htm›.

Levine, Mark. "A Layman's Guide to *Bush V. Gore*." *Disinformation*, 29 May 2001 ‹http://www.disinfo.com/archive/pages/article/id677/pg1›.

"Mob Rule Wins for W." *The Consortium*, 24 November 2000 ‹http://www.consortiumnews.com/2000/112400a.html›.

Palast, Greg. *The Best Democracy Money Can Buy*. New York: Plume, 2003.

Parry, Robert. "Bush's Conspiracy to Riot." *The Consortium*, 5 August 2002 ‹http://www.consortiumnews.com/2002/080502a.html›.

Parry, Robert. "Gore's Victory." *The Consortium*, 12 November 2001 ‹http://www.consortiumnews.com/2001/111201a.html›.

Parry, Robert. "So Bush Did Steal the White House." *The Consortium*, 12 November 2001 ‹http://www.consortiumnews.com/2001/112101a.html›.

Parry, Robert. "W's Triumph of the Will." *The Consortium*, 27 November 2000 ‹http://www.consortiumnews.com/2000/112700a.html›.

"Ruling on Dimpled Ballots." ABC News, 22 November 2000 ‹http://abcnews.go.com/sections/politics/DailyNews/ELECTION_ballotruling001122.html›.

Tapper, Jake. *Down and Dirty: The Plot to Steal the Presidency*. New York: Little Brown & Company, 2001.

Vankin, Jonathan. "Call Me Hal." *Metro*, 21 December 2000 ‹http://www.metroactive.com/papers/metro/12.21.00/cover/election-0051.html›.

Vankin, Jonathan & Whalen, John. "Conspiracy Current Number 55: Time for a Revolt, er, Revote!" Conspire.com, 26 November 2000 ‹http://www.conspire.com/curren55.html›.

26

→ ELECTRONIC VOTING
ELECTION THEFT

**"It doesn't matter who casts the ballots.
What matters is who counts the ballots."**
—Joseph Stalin

Say what you will about the 2000 election; we have a paper trail proving that George W. Bush stole it. If a group of electronic voting companies get their way, in the future (including, frighteningly, in 2004) an election won't even have that.

Where to begin? Start in Nebraska: in 1996, Chuck Hagel, a Republican, won the race for the U.S. Senate, the first Republican Senate victory in the state in 24 years. *The Washington Post* declared that his "victory against an incumbent Democratic governor was the major Republican upset in the November election." His stunning victory included many largely black communities that had never before voted Republican, a turnabout made more remarkable by Hagel's right-wing political views. In 2002, he won by an astounding 83% of the vote.

Hagel is the former chairman and chief executive of ES&S, the company that made all the vote-counting equipment in the state of Nebraska during both elections. ES&S is a heavy contributor to the Republican Party. Hagel failed to disclose his relationship to and continuing ownership of the company on his FEC disclosure statements or to Senate ethics investigators.

How about Georgia? In 2002, Republican Saxby Chambliss upset incumbent Max Cleland by a 53–46% margin. Polls had showed Cleland leading 49–44%, understandable after Chambliss attacked the war hero (Cleland lost three limbs in a grenade explosion) for his supposed lack of patriotism. Republican Sonny Perdue also defeated incumbent Roy Barnes in the governor's race by a margin of 52–45%. The most recent poll had showed Perdue trailing by nine points.

In January 2003, a folder—illuminatingly named "rob-georgia"—was discovered at Diebold Election Systems, the company that built and programmed all of the Peach state's voting machines. There were three more folders inside it: one had instructions to place new files in the election management folder, the second had files which were to replace existing ones in the management folder, and the third instructed users to replace Windows with its contents and run a program. The Georgia Secretary of State's Office admits that a patch was administered to all 22,000 voting machines in the state before the election. Diebold is the main competitor of ES&S in the electronic voting field, and a heavy contributor to the Republican party.

Back in Florida, some voters who pressed the touch-screen button for Jeb's opponent in the 2002 election noticed something strange: their vote was registered for Bush. Meanwhile, in Texas, Jeff Wentworth for Senate, Carter Casteel for House, and Judge Danny Scheel all won their seats. Nothing necessarily suspicious about that, except that they all won with exactly 18,181 votes. All three are from Comal County, and both Wentworth and Casteel are Republicans, while Scheel is a conservative.

All of this is enough to make one ask, "What the fuck?" That two of the predominant electronic voting machine makers are heavily tied to the GOP is disturbing (as it would be if they were tied to the Democratic Party). There is usually no paper trail left by the machines, and they use proprietary source codes, meaning they're unavailable for inspection by the public or losing candidates.

Dan Spillane was a software engineer for VoteHere, an electronic machine company that employs former CIA director Robert Gates and Dick Cheney's former assistant as directors. After uncovering holes in their security system, he was fired, and he has filed a whistle-blower lawsuit. He describes their vote integrity program "very much like Arthur Andersen in the Enron case."

Speaking of Arthur Andersen, they've changed the name of Andersen Consulting to "Accenture" and incorporated offshore in Bermuda. Besides other schemes, Accenture has landed the fat contract for the new Pentagon online voting system in the 2004 presidential election to help American soldiers vote. Now that's supporting our troops.

Even without these shady examples, voting with no paper trail is a terrible idea. So is privatizing the power to count votes. Even if the companies involved in these activities aren't corrupt, their influence on political process would likely soon corrupt them. Electronic voting is a bad idea.

The good news? The controversy surrounding electronic voting (mainly due to brave isolated efforts by Beverly Harris of BlackBoxVoting.com and Internet magazines such as *Online Journal*) has slowly started receiving mainstream coverage and may become a serious political issue in the coming year. The bad news: in late October, a federal appeals court dismissed a suit over electronic voting machines, bizarrely justifying the machines by stating that "electoral fraud can never be completely eliminated no matter which type of ballot is used." Left unexplained by the judges was why it would then be okay to use a system that seems to maximize the potential for abuse and fraud.

In the meantime, Diebold CEO Walden O'Dell is a major fundraiser for the Bush re-election campaign. He recently wrote a letter declaring that he was "committed to helping Ohio deliver its electoral votes for the president next year." When a controversy ensued in the Buckeye State over his statement, he would unreassuringly explain that he wasn't talking about fixing the state's machines.

Sources:

Black Box Voting ‹http://www.blackboxvoting.com›.

BuzzFlash. "Will Electronic Voting Machines Steal the 2004 Election?" *AlterNet*, 1 October 2003 ‹http://www.alternet.org/story.html?StoryID=16874›.

Conover, Bev. "Computerized Voting Systems Cannot Be Made Secure." *Online Journal*, 20 October 2003 ‹http://www.onlinejournal.com/Commentary/102003Conover/102003conover.html›.

Hartmann, Thom. "If You Want To Win An Election, Just Control The Voting Machines." *Common Dreams*, 31 January 2003 ‹http://www.commondreams.org/views03/0131-01.htm›.

Hartmann, Thom. "Now Your Vote Is the Property of a Private Corporation." *Online Journal*, 13 March 2003 ‹http://www.onlinejournal.com/Commentary/031303Hartmann/031303hartmann.html›.

Hartmann, Thom. "The Theft of Your Vote Is Just a Chip Away." *AlterNet*, 30 July 2003 ‹http://www.alternet.org/story.html?StoryID=16474›.

Keating, Dan. "New Voting Systems Assailed." *The Washington Post*, 28 March 2003: A12.

Kravets, David. "Federal Appeals Court Dismisses Electronic Voting Machine Lawsuit." *SF Gate*, 29 October 2003 ‹http://www.sfgate.com/cgibin/article.cgi?f=/news/archive/2003/10/29/state0331EST0005.DTL›.

Landes, Lynn. "2002 Elections: Republican Voting Machines, Election Irregularities, and 'Way-off' Polling Results." *Online Journal*, 8 November 2002 ‹http://www.onlinejournal.com/Special_Reports/Landes111402/landes111402.html›.

Landes, Lynn. "Internet Voting: The End of Democracy?" *Online Journal*, 4 September 2003 ‹http://www.onlinejournal.com/Special_Reports/090403Landes/090403landes.html›.

Landes, Lynn. "Offshore Company Captures Online Military Vote." *Online Journal*, 21 July 2003 ‹http://www.onlinejournal.com/Special_Reports/072103Landes/072103landes.html›.

Landes, Lynn. "Voting Machines Violate Constitution." *Online Journal*, 15 April 2003 ‹http://www.onlinejournal.com/Commentary/041503Landes/041503landes.html›.

Leopold, Jason. "Electronic Voting Minus Paper Trails Makes It Easy to Rig Elections." *Online Journal*, 4 September 2003 ‹http://www.onlinejournal.com/Special_Reports/090403 Leopold /090403leopold.html›.

Levy, Steven. "Black Box Voting Blues." *Newsweek*, 3 November 2003 ‹http://www.msnbc.com/news/985033.asp›.

Palast, Greg. *The Best Democracy Money Can Buy*. New York: Plume, 2003.

Partridge, Ernest. "Are American Elections Fixed?" *Online Journal*, 3 April 2003 ‹http://www.onlinejournal.com/Commentary/040303Partridge/040303partridge.html›.

Punpirate. "Did Your Vote Count?" *Democratic Underground*, 15 February 2003 ‹http://www.democraticunderground.com/articles/03/02/15_vote.html›.

Vankin, Jonathan. "Call Me Hal." *Metro*, 21 December 2000 ‹http://www.metroactive.com/papers/metro/12.21.00/cover/election-0051.html›.

"Voting Machines: Vote Tampering in the 21st Century." WhoseFlorida.com, 2003 ‹http://www.whoseflorida.com/voting_machines.htm›.

"Voting Security." *The Progressive Populist*, 2003 ‹http://www.populist.com/voting.html›.

Zetter, Kim. "Did E-Vote Firm Patch Election?" *Wired*, 13 October 2003 ‹http://www.wired.com/news/politics/0,1283,60563,00.html›.

27

THE BUSH FAMILY BUSINESS PARTNERS: THE BIN LADENS

"Follow the money": when something as huge and tragic as September 11 happens, that saying should be taken to heart. What then is to be said of the suspicious business ties between George W. Bush (and his daddy) and the family of Osama bin Laden?

These connections aren't minor ones, either—they go back 25 years to the beginnings of his business career. In 1979, Dubya's first company, Arbusto Energy ("arbusto" is "shrub" in Spanish), obtained $50K of financing from Houston investor James Bath, a Bush family friend and a fellow member of the Texas Air Guard. In exchange, Bath received a 5% stake of little George's company. At the time, Bath had just been named the sole U.S. business representative for Salem bin Laden, one of Osama's brothers, who lived in Texas. It has not been proven that Salem was the actual financier of the Arbusto scheme, but Bath has claimed that at the time, he had no substantial money of his own. Strategically, it would make sense for a bin Laden to finance the son of a former CIA head to curry political favor.

Incredibly, a bin Laden brother may not be the most troubling connection Shrub has from his business association with Bath. Bath has major ties to the notorious Bank of Commerce and Credit International (BCCI), which looted $10 billion during the 1980s. BCCI was also a money-laundering operation for CIA covert operations, which Bath has claimed he joined in 1976 at the personal request of Poppy Bush. When Salem bin Laden conveniently died in a 1988 plane crash during the heat of the BCCI scandal, Saudi banker Khalid bin Mahfouz, a brother-in-law of Osama also involved in BCCI, inherited Salem's Houston interest. Bin Mahfouz was the banker for Sheik Abdullah Taha Bakhsh, who purchased a major stake in Harken Energy (Dubya's new company) in the mid-1980s. Bin Mahfouz allegedly financed the bin Laden terrorist network (see Reason #4—he is a defendant in the lawsuit).

Not to be outdone, Poppy Bush became a consultant for the Carlyle Group, one of the largest defense contractors. Carlyle represents the worst of crony capitalism, tied to political insiders from around the world. (Among others, Jim Baker is a Carlyle partner, and former Defense Secretary Frank Carlucci is Chairman.) Charles Lewis, executive director of the Center for Public Integrity, says, "Carlyle is as deeply wired into the current administration as they can possibly be. George Bush is getting money from private interests that have business before the government, while his son is president. And, in a really peculiar way, George W. Bush could, some day, benefit financially from his own administration's decisions, through his father's investments. The average American doesn't know that and, to me, that's a jaw-dropper." Something else the average American may not know is that a multimillion-dollar investor in Carlyle was the bin Laden family. Also unknown by Joe and Jane Sixpack: before becoming Texas governor in 1994, Shrub headed CaterAir, a Carlyle asset.

The 2001 annual meeting of Carlyle took place in the D.C. Ritz-Carlton on the morning of September 11. On one of the darkest days in U.S. history, the gathered were in the strange position of profiting handsomely from the tragedy. Unfortunately for the bin Ladens, political pressure forced them to (at least officially) cash out of the Carlyle Group. The possibility that the two biggest beneficiaries of the 9/11 tragedy could be the Bush and bin Laden families was unseemly. For one, Larry Klayman (head of Judicial Watch) was publicly outraged. (Though Judicial Watch is an unapologetically conservative group, specializing during the late nineties in lawsuits against the Clinton Administration, they have been admirably critical of Bush and Cheney in their many sleazy dealings.) Klayman declared, "This conflict of interest has now turned into a scandal. The idea of the President's father, an ex-president himself, doing business with a company under investigation by the FBI in the terror attacks of September 11 is horrible."

Isn't this a little unfair to the bin Ladens? After all, haven't they supposedly broken contact with the black sheep, Osama? That's a little hard to believe, after a video was uncovered showing Osama's mother, a sister, and two brothers with Osama at his son's wedding, just six and a half months before 9/11. Even without that, as Michael Moore put it in a public letter to Dubya, "If, after the terrorist attack on the Federal Building in Oklahoma City, it had been revealed that President Bill Clinton and his family had financial dealings with Timothy McVeigh's family, what do you think your Republican party and the media would have done with that one?"

Don't feel too bad for the bin Ladens: after all, the family is a major business partner of the Bechtel Group in Saudi Arabia. Thanks to Operation Iraqi Freedom, Bechtel was awarded a secret, closed-bid, open-ended Iraq contract that could ultimately be worth billions, a good portion of which will likely find its way into the bin Laden's bank account soon. It's all in the family.

Sources:

Beaty, Jonathan. *The Outlaw Bank: A Wild Ride into the Secret Heart of BCCI*. New York: Random House, 1993.

Brewton, Pete. *The Mafia, CIA, and George Bush*. New York: Shapolsky Publishers, 1992.

Briody, Dan. "Carlyle's Way." *Red Herring*, December 2001: 63.

"Bush Money." Bush Watch ‹http://www.bushwatch.com/bushmoney.htm›.

Farah, Joseph. "Coincidences and Capitalist Terrorists." WorldNetDaily, 20 September 2001 ‹http://www.worldnetdaily.com/news/printer-friendly.asp?ARTICLE_ID=24582›.

Floyd, Chris. "Group Therapy." *CounterPunch*, 12 May 2003 ‹http://www.counterpunch.org/floyd05122003.html›.

"Follow the Money: The Bush–bin Laden Connection." *Paranoia*, ‹http://www.paranoia-magazine.com/followmoney.html›.

"George W. Bush's Dubious Friends." Centre for Research on Globalisation, 1 October 2001 ‹http://www.globalresearch.ca/articles/INL110A.html›.

Gray, Geoffrey. "Bush Sr. Could Profit from War." *The Village Voice*, 11 October 2001 ‹http://www.villagevoice.com/issues/0141/gray.php›.

Hatfield, J.H. *Fortunate Son: George W. Bush and the Making of an American President*. Brooklyn: Soft Skull Press, 2001.

"Judicial Watch to File FOIA Lawsuit Today Over Carlyle Group Documents." Judicial Watch, 27 November 2001 ‹http://www.judicialwatch.org/archive/2001/printer_1082.shtml›.

Moore, Michael. *Dude, Where's My Country?* New York: Warner Books, 2003.

Ruppert, Michael C. "The Best Enemies Money Can Buy." *From the Wilderness*, 9 October 2001 ‹http://www.fromthewilderness.com/free/ww3/10_09_01_carlyle.html›.

Shorrock, Tim. "Crony Capitalism Goes Global." *The Nation*, 14 March 2002 ‹http://www.thenation.com/doc.mhtml?i=20020401&s=shorrock›.

28

→ **THE NORAD STAND-DOWN**

This list mostly avoids conspiracy theories, not so much because such theories aren't ever plausible as because they are unnecessary, given that most of the creepy schemes of the Bush Team are overt.

However, one mystery about September 11, 2001 is so disturbing, and so clearly a sign of something suspicious, that it would be irresponsible not to include it. That is the baffling sequence of failures of NORAD (North American Aerospace Defense Command) on that date.

For the most part, the 9/11 NORAD failure has been ignored by the mainstream media, and has been relegated to websites such as emperors-clothes.com and the underground film *AfterMath*. This is a shame, because the story demands serious public investigation.

On September 11, two F-15 fighter jets were in the air less than five minutes away from the Twin Towers when the first was hit—25 minutes after the plane, Flight 11, was known to be hijacked. Numerous air stations with combat-ready fighters were a few minutes of flying time from both NYC and D.C. There were well-established automatic procedures for intercepting aircraft that either were off-course or had lost communication. Yet none of the fighters were deployed.

The two in-flight fighters were patrolling off the coast of Long Island as ordered. Apparently, neither was informed about the North Tower strike, though the pilot reported seeing smoke over Manhattan. It was only after the second tower was hit at 9:03 that they were ordered to Manhattan for combat air patrol.

Two F-15s were scrambled at 8:52 a.m., 38 minutes after Flight 11 was hijacked and after it slammed into the WTC. But they were flown from Otis Air National Guard Base in Falmouth, Massachusetts, 153 miles away from the WTC. That shouldn't have stopped them from reaching Flight 175, since the F-15 has a top speed of 1875 mph. Instead, they only traveled 82 miles in the 11 minutes before the second plane smashed into the WTC. That comes out to a speed of 447 mph, less than a quarter of the plane's top speed. Apparently, the pilots weren't informed of the severity of the situation.

Minutes after the second WTC crash, military base commanders were calling NORAD to volunteer to scramble planes. The commander at Syracuse, New York said he could get a plane in the air armed with cannons in ten minutes. None of these planes were in the air until after the last hijacked plane crashed, over an hour later. Andrews Air Force Base is just ten miles from the Pentagon. On September 11, it had two squadrons of fighter jets with the job of protecting the skies over D.C. Not a single Andrews fighter took off until after the Pentagon was hit.

Instead, six minutes after the second attack on the WTC, NORAD ordered F-16s at Langley Air Force Base, Virginia, on battle stations alert. Yet the order to scramble didn't come until 18 minutes later, and they didn't take off until 9:30, another three minutes later. It took the F-16s 19 minutes to reach the Pentagon, 130 miles away. The speed comes to a leisurely 410 mph, slightly above one quarter of their 1,500 mph top speed. At 9:41 (eight minutes before the F-16s arrived), Flight 77 slammed into the Pentagon. It was first discovered to be off-course at 8:46, and NORAD was reportedly warned both at 9:16 and 9:24 a.m. that it was probably hijacked. In other words, even with a slothful half-hour response time in alerting NORAD, there was still 25 minutes to scramble planes to D.C. (Incidentally, on September 11, NORAD was in its semi-annual exercises called "Vigilant Guardian"—when forces are placed in the highest state of readiness.)

On September 16, Dick Cheney claimed on *Meet the Press* that presidential authorization was required to scramble fighter jets to intercept aircraft. This was not true: authorization was required only to shoot down a plane. According to FAA and DOD protocols in place at the time, if a plane deviates 15 degrees or two miles from course, the flight controllers hit a panic button. If NORAD hears of any difficulties in the skies, it is serious business. They scramble jet fighters to take off and intercept aircraft that are off course. This would not even have been unusual: fighters were scrambled 67 times between June and September 11, 2001. Redundant or backup scrambles, not done on 9/11, were also the norm.

A good case study: on October 25, 1999, golfer Payne Stewart's Lear jet went off course and drifted across the country for hours with no one controlling it, apparently after a rare pressurization failure. A series of military planes provided an emergency escort, after scrambling to his jet approximately 20 minutes after ground controllers lost contact. It supposedly took 18 minutes just to report the Flight 11 emergency to NORAD.

The Lear only failed to respond to communications, whereas the 9/11 jetliners also veered radically off course and switched off their transponders. Stewart's jet also was in the South, which has fewer air defense stations than the Northeast. Large passenger aircraft in crowded air corridors are more closely watched than small private aircraft. Finally, Stewart's jet went off course at 45,000 feet, 10,000 feet higher than jetliners fly. So why the hard-on for Payne Stewart, in contrast to the lackadaisical response on September 11?

Mindy Kleinberg, who lost her husband in the WTC attack, would like to know. Testifying before the National Commission on Terrorist Attacks on the United States, she asked: "On September 11 both the FAA and NORAD deviated from standard emergency operating procedures. Who were the people that delayed the notification? Have they been questioned?" She added, "NORAD had sufficient information that the plane that had hit the World Trade Center was hijacked. At the time, they also had knowledge that two other commercial airliners, in the air, were also hijacked. It would seem that a national emergency was in progress. Yet President Bush was allowed to enter a classroom full of young children and listen to the students read. Why didn't the Secret Service inform him of this national emergency?"

These are pressing questions that the Bush Team seems uninterested in answering. A joint statement issued by the Republican chairman Thomas Kean and Democratic vice chairman Lee Hamilton of the commission singled out the Pentagon for withholding information relating to NORAD. It appears that even Kean and Hamilton suspect that the Bush administration and the DOD have something to hide.

Perhaps there is a better explanation for the NORAD 9/11 lapses than an intentional stand-down of national air defense. It would be nice to hear one. Until there is real cooperation with the investigation of 9/11 by the Executive Branch, the questions will stay in the air.

Sources:

"Air Defense." 9-11 Research ‹http://911research.wtc7.net/planes/defense›.

Bykov, Illarion, and Israel, Jared. "Guilty For 9-11: Bush, Rumsfeld, Myers." *Emperor's Clothes*, 17 November 2001 ‹http://emperors-clothes.com/indict/indict-1.htm›.

Bykov, Illarion, and Israel, Jared. "Mr. Cheney's Cover-up." *Emperor's Clothes*, 21 November 2001 ‹http://emperors-clothes.com/indict/indict-2.htm›.

"Dan Rather's Excellent New Fact!" *Emperor's Clothes*, 3 January 2002 ‹http://emperors-clothes.com/indict/faq2.htm›.

Johnson, Glen, Zuckoff, Mitchell, and Brelis, Matthew. "Facing Terror Attack's Aftermath: Otis Fighter Jets Scrambled Too Late to Halt The Attacks." *The Boston Globe*, 15 September 2001: A1.

Johnson, Jeremy. "Family Members Demand Answers from 9/11 Commission." World Socialist Web Site, 9 April 2003 ‹http://www.wsws.org/articles/2003/apr2003/hear-a09.shtml›.

Lynn, Joyce. "Film—*AfterMath: Unanswered Questions from 9/11* Draws Overflow Crowd." *Online Journal*, 7 May 2003 ‹http://www.onlinejournal.com/Media/050703Lynn/050703lynn.html›.

"NORAD Stand-Down." 9-11 Research ‹http://911research.wtc7.net/planes/analysis/norad›.

Scott, William B. "Exercise Jump-Starts Response to Attacks." *Aviation Week and Space Technology*, 3 June 2002 ‹http://www.aviationnow.com/content/publication/awst/20020603/avi_stor.htm›.

Stand Down ‹http://www.standdown.net›.

Szamuely, George, Bykov, Illarion, and Israel, Jared. "9-11: Ho-Hum, Nothing Urgent." Emperor's Clothes, 9 January 2002 ‹http://emperors-clothes.com/indict/urgent.htm›.

Thompson, Paul. "The 9/11 Timeline 25-Page Summary." Wanttoknow.info ‹http://www.wanttoknow.info/9-11timeline25pg›.

29

→ **"ANOTHER PEARL HARBOR"**

In September 2000, two months before the 2000 Election and one year before 9/11, a right-wing think-tank, Project for the New American Century (PNAC), released a manifesto on "Rebuilding America's Defense." Members of the PNAC included Dick Cheney, Donald Rumsfeld, Deputy Defense Secretary Paul Wolfowitz, Richard Perle (formerly chairman of Shrub's Defense Policy Board and still a powerful military advisor), I. Lewis Libby (Cheney's chief of staff), William Kristol (editor of *The Weekly Standard*, published by FOX News media baron Rupert Murdoch), sermonizer on virtue and gambling addict William Bennett, and Jeb Bush.

Among the recommendations in the policy paper:

→ Develop a "bunker-buster" nuclear weapon system;

→ Develop a "Star Wars" missile defense system and strategic dominance of space;

→ Reposition permanently based forces to Southern Europe, Southeast Asia, and the Middle East;

→ Massively increase defense spending;

→ Have American forces capable of fighting and decisively winning multiple-theater, simultaneous major wars;

→ Fortify the U.S.'s ability to "perform the 'constabulary' duties associated with shaping the security environment in critical regions" (in other words, become an overt colonial power).

In a quote that should raise some eyebrows, "Rebuilding America's Defense" predicts that "advanced forms of biological warfare that can 'target' specific genotypes may transform biological warfare from the realm of terror to a politically useful tool." The report also specifically listed North Korea, Syria, and Iran as dangerous regimes, anticipating George W. Bush's identification of the "axis of evil."

This was bold stuff, and at the time unlikely to become national policy. The PNAC even admitted as much, leading to an even more disturbing line in the blueprint: "Further, the process of transformation, even if it brings revolutionary change, is likely to be a long one, absent some catastrophic and catalyzing event—like a new Pearl Harbor."

One year later, on September 11, the PNAC got its new Pearl Harbor. Since then, the dreamt-of radical change in U.S. military policy has become mainstream policy—all thanks to a massive tragedy due to failures on their watch. This has led some cynics to wonder if "a new Pearl Harbor" really meant "a new Reichstag."

Does this sound too Oliver Stone-esque for you? Consider that in *Body of Secrets*, author James Bamford recently uncovered Operation Northwoods, a 1962 plan to sell military action in Cuba by fabricating or committing acts of violence and blaming them on Fidel Castro. Among the Operation's nifty suggestions: shooting down a plane filled with college students, sinking an American ship ("casualty lists in U.S. newspapers would cause a helpful wave of national indignation"), and even rigging national hero John Glenn's rocket to explode. JFK would reject the modest proposal, a year before he became a victim of what some believe was a military-intelligence assassination plot. In any case, Northwoods appears to prove a 9/11 Reichstag at least wouldn't be outside the box.

Consider as well that on September 10, 2001, George Bush's public approval rating was rapidly falling, just as a *Newsweek* cover story revealed his claim to the Presidency as completely illegitimate. Thanks to 9/11, the *Newsweek* was quickly pulled off the magazine racks for a new special edition, and in the hysteria that followed, Shrub's popularity skyrocketed, at least temporarily.

One supporter of the Bushy knoll 9/11 theory is Michael Meacher, the UK environment minister from May 1997 to June 2003. (He resigned in protest against the Iraq war.) He told the

Guardian, "it is clear the U.S. authorities did little or nothing to pre-empt the events of 9/11. . . . Was this inaction simply the result of key people disregarding, or being ignorant of, the evidence? Or could U.S. air security operations have been deliberately stood down on September 11? If so, why, and on whose authority? . . . The 9/11 attacks allowed the U.S. to press the 'go' button for a strategy in accordance with the PNAC agenda which it would otherwise have been politically impossible to implement."

Sources:

Bamford, James. *Body of Secrets: Anatomy of the Ultra-Secret National Security Agency*. New York: Anchor, 2002.

Kaplan, David A. "Accidental President." *Newsweek*, 17 September 2001:28–34.

Meacher, Michael. "This War on Terrorism Is Bogus." *The Guardian*, 6 September 2003 ‹http://politics.guardian.co.uk/iraq/comment/0,12956,1036687,00.html›.

Phillips, Peter, & Project Censored. *Censored 2004*. New York: Seven Stories Press, 2003.

Pilger, John. *Hidden Agendas*, 12 December 2002 ‹http://pilger.carlton.com/print/124759›.

Pitt, William Rivers. "The Project for the New American Century." Information Clearing House, 25 February 2003 ‹http://www.informationclearinghouse.info/article1665.htm›.

The Project for the New American Century ‹http://www.newamericancentury.org›.

30

→ NEOCON GONE WILD!

The PNAC manifesto is the most influential statement of a movement with extraordinary and shadowy powers in decision-making within the Bush Team: the neoconservatives.

The history of the neocon movement begins in the 1960s and 1970s, when a small group of mostly Jewish liberal intellectuals became alienated from the left, in part over social issues but also over the left's dovish defense policies. During Reagan's presidency, most of these disaffected liberals became Republicans, thanks to his anti-Soviet position and massive military increases. Because they were former liberals, their ex-comrades called them "neoconservatives."

Neocons disagree with what was—until recently, at least—conventional conservative views on military policy. While Republicans overwhelmingly favor higher defense budgets, the realist faction of conservative thought (embraced by Colin Powell and Henry Kissinger) is wary of military conflict, prefers to work with international organizations to reach diplomatic goals (for practical, if not ethical, reasons), and, if the use of force is deemed necessary, prefers to use it overwhelmingly to end the conflict as quickly as possible. The realist camp is, for whatever its faults, the successful fusion of conservative isolationist tendencies and the pro-war ideas of the anti-communist set: advocacy of a defense so strong it rarely needs to be used.

The neocons are not so prudent. Much of their hawkishness derives from the philosophy of University of Chicago professor Leo Strauss, who was haunted (like many intellectuals) by the Nazi Holocaust. Strauss believed that the Nazi rise was due to weakness and indulgence in the Weimar Republic; his students became the leaders of the neocon movement. Neocons tend to favor establishment of the U.S. as the world's unchallenged superpower, unreserved support for Israel, and unilateral and preemptive American action against perceived threats.

During the Clinton years, neocons fell out of political favor. But after the takeover by Bush and especially after the frenzy that followed 9/11, they have become drunk on power.

On the morning of September 12, 2001, Rumsfeld declared in a cabinet meeting that Iraq should be "a principal target of the first round in the war against terrorism," although no evidence had linked Iraq to the terrorist attacks. Only the persuasive arguments of Colin Powell for picking on Afghanistan, a more legitimate (and easier) target, spared Iraq for 18 months. The eagerness to make war against Iraq can be understood by reading the PNAC blueprint: "While the unresolved conflict with Iraq provides the immediate justification, the need for a substantial American force presence in the Gulf transcends the issue of the regime of Saddam Hussein." In other words, the bogeyman of Saddam was the excuse to justify an imperialist occupation of the Middle East.

Cheney, Redrum, Wolfie, and Perle eventually got their wish for a war in Iraq, helped along by a pack of lies. Now, American soldiers are paying the price for the neocons' wet dreams in blood. The neocons imagined Iraq as phase one in a war for global domination. So far, it looks like a summer blockbuster, with sequels already planned, that has laid an opening weekend box-office egg.

As the quagmire persists, it should be clear why the neocon agenda so appealed to Shrub: to a man like him (or his daddy) of unconvincing machismo and limited intelligence, a war-loving policy is as natural and appealing as an affected swagger. But what attracted the neocons to their cause in the first place? After all, Perle and Wolfowitz can be accused of many things, but stupidity isn't one of them. They were apparently so busy studying political philosophy and military theory in college that they (like Dubya) couldn't spare any time to participate in the military. Without understanding the human element, they had no grasp of how war is for a soldier or for a civilian facing attack. It was all a theoretical game to them, only now the game is real. Apparently, their strategies worked better when they practiced them with their toy soldiers.

Sources:

"Empire Builders." *The Christian Science Monitor*, ‹http://www.csmonitor.com/specials/neocon›.

Heer, Jeet. "The Philosopher." *The Boston Globe*, 11 May 2003.

Lobe, Jim. "Neo-Cons." Inter Press Service 2003 ‹http://www.ipsnews.net/focus/neo-cons›.

Phillips, Peter, & Project Censored. *Censored 2004*. New York: Seven Stories Press, 2003.

Pilger, John. *Hidden Agendas*, 12 December 2002 ‹http://pilger.carlton.com/print/124759›.

Pitt, William Rivers. "The Project for the New American Century." Information Clearing House, 25 February 2003 ‹http://www.informationclearinghouse.info/article1665.htm›.

The Project for the New American Century ‹http://www.newamericancentury.org/›.

31

→ CHICKEN-HAWKS ON PARADE

Shrub, Wolfowitz, and Perle are not alone in their bravery with others' lives. Indeed, the roster of right-wing hacks in politics and media seems to be crammed with examples of the curious creature known as the chicken-hawk.

Here is a list of some of the better-known chicken-hawks, aside from Prince George: Elliott Abrams, Dick Armey, John Ashcroft, William Bennett (too busy gambling), Jeb Bush, Saxby Chambliss (who outrageously alleged that his Democratic opponent—war hero Max Cleland, who lost three limbs—was unpatriotic, based on his questioning the Iraq War), Richard Cheney (according to Dickie, he "had other priorities"), House Majority Leader Tom Delay (who explained that so many minority youths had volunteered that there was no room for patriotic white folks like himself), Jerry Falwell, Senate Majority Leader Bill Frist, Newt Gingrich, Phil Gramm (who avoided the draft with multiple student deferments), Sean Hannity, neocon leader Bill Kristol, Rush Limbaugh (he got a 4-F thanks to an "anal cyst"), former Senate Majority Leader Trent Lott (like Shrub, he was a football cheerleader instead), Bill O'Reilly (Mr. Blue Collar straight-talker studied in London for a year rather than go to 'Nam), Dan Quayle (avoided Vietnam service, thanks to a journalism slot in the Indiana National Guard), Ronnie's even wackier son Michael Reagan, Pat Robertson (claimed in his biography combat in Korea, but his Congressman dad got him reassigned to Japan), Clarence Thomas, Michael "Savage" Weiner, and George Will (who, granted, is clearly not up snuff to throw a baseball, much less a hand grenade).

It's enough to fill an entire deck of cards. In fact, a deck of Republican chicken-hawk cards does honor these brave promoters of wars for others to die in. A deck of prominent Republicans who fought in the military would be much harder to fill.

To his credit, Secretary of Defense Donald Rumsfeld did serve in the Navy as an aviator and flight instructor, albeit after the Korean War was over. He also bravely served as Reagan's Special Envoy to the Middle East in 1983–1984, when he met with Saddam Hussein twice and helped reestablish the U.S.'s diplomatic relations with the Butcher of Baghdad.

Other rare Republicans to serve include Colin Powell (whose intimate experience with the death of soldiers may explain his profound ambivalence toward war) and Senator John McCain (who was later savagely smeared by the Shrub Team during the 2000 campaign as likely to be mentally unstable because of having been a POW).

George W. Bush has yet to attend the funeral of a single soldier he has sent to die. And he selects and promotes people who are, like him, chicken-hawks, whose garrison-state ideas are grounded in wishes or fantasies rather than actual experience.

Sources:

"The Chickenhawk Database." *The New Hampshire Gazette*, ‹http://www.nhgazette.com/cgibin/NHGstore.cgi?user_action=list&category=%20NEWS%3B%20Chickenhawks›.

"The Deck of Republican Chickenhawks." ‹http://www.chickenhawkcards.com›.

Scheer, Christopher. "Bush Ignores Soldiers' Burials." *AlterNet*, 30 October 2003 ‹http://www.alternet.org/story.html?StoryID=17079›.

"Who Served in the Military?" AWOLBush.com ‹http://www.awolbush.com/whoserved.html›.

32

→ **"A CARPET OF GOLD OR A CARPET OF BOMBS"**

In December 1997, leaders of the Taliban visited Texas (where George W. Bush was governor) at the invitation of Unocal and other Lone Star state oil barons. Already the Taliban had earned a nasty reputation for repressive rule, with plans for turning Afghanistan into a land where Western culture's pleasures were taboo and women were denied basic human rights. During their four-day visit, they were "given VIP treatment" by the crude merchants, according to the *UK Telegraph*, driven by a chauffeur and staying in a five-star hotel.

Unsurprisingly, the Taliban were hypocrites, preaching a morality for the masses while flouting it in private. (Paging William Bennett.) Also unsurprisingly, beneath all the rhetoric about the War Against Terror in Afghanistan, a fundamental motivation for the conflict (as in Iraq) could be black gold. The oil actually is in the Caspian Sea region, not Afghanistan. The untapped oil and natural gas reserves in Central Asia are estimated to be worth $3 trillion, an amount that even energy companies don't sneeze at.

To get this oil, pipelines must be built, and the route most attractive to Unocal went straight through Afghanistan. (Two other countries that played integral roles in the battle for the Caspian sea are Chechnya and Kosovo—thus explaining the likely motivation behind the three great battles of industrialized nations and the Third World between the two Gulf Wars.) In terms of business, the Taliban's totalitarian style was viewed as a plus; authoritarian governments reduce the number of players involved in negotiations.

The deal-making between the Texas Tea Consortium and the Taliban accelerated right after Shrub took office. The $43 million in U.S. aid given to them U.S. in May 2001 may well have been to sweeten the pot. However, by summertime, the Taliban were balking at the proposed deal, which struck them as favoring the Western oil companies. (They probably also suspected that such an agreement would lead to open revolt against their unpopular regime.)

Faced with surprisingly uppity Taliban, the U.S. representatives told them, "accept our offer of a carpet of gold, or we bury you under a carpet of bombs," according to Jean-Charles Brisard, author of *Forbidden Truth*. The Taliban made their choice, and the U.S. planned an early October attack on Afghanistan, according to former Pakistani Foreign Secretary Niaz Naik, who claims he was told of the war plans in mid-July by U.S. officials. In other words, while September 11 supposedly changed everything, it didn't change any plans for the invasion of Afghanistan.

Could the serious threat made by U.S. oil negotiators have led to a pre-emptive attack on September 11? Perhaps something more sinister is going on here. After all, normally, in the lead-up to a planned war, a campaign of propaganda is waged to demonize the target and justify the commitment to war. Oddly, no such campaign was waged against Afghanistan before September 11 by the Bush administration. It's almost as if somebody on Team Dubya knew that such a propaganda campaign would be rendered unnecessary.

Sources:

Arney, George. "U.S. 'Planned Attack on Taleban.'" BBC News, 18 September 2001 ⟨http://news.bbc.co.uk/1/hi/world/south_asia/1550366.stm⟩.

Biggs, Brooke Shelby. "Pipe Dreams." *Mother Jones*, 12 October 2001 ⟨http://www.motherjones.com/web_exclusives/features/news/pipedreams.html⟩.

Brisard, Jean-Charles, and Dasquie, Guillaume. *Forbidden Truth: U.S.-Taliban Secret Oil Diplomacy and the Failed Hunt for Bin Laden*. New York: Nation Books, 2002.

Crogan, Jim. "New World Disorder: The Oil War." *LA Weekly*, 30 November–6 December 2001 ⟨http://www.laweekly.com/ink/02/02/new-crogan.php⟩.

Eutsey, Dwayne. "Soylent Green is Oil." *BuzzFlash*, 7 June 2002 ⟨http://www.buzzflash.com/contributors/2002/06/07_Soylent.html⟩.

Godoy, Julio. "U.S. Policy Towards Taliban Influenced by Oil—Authors." *Common Dreams*, 15 November 2001 ⟨http://www.commondreams.org/headlines01/1115-06.htm⟩.

Morgan, Dan, and Ottaway, David B. "Azerbaijan's Riches Alter the Chessboard." *The Washington Post*, 4 October 1998: A1.

Morgan, Dan, and Ottaway, David B. "Gas Pipeline Bounces between Agendas." *The Washington Post*, 5 October 1998: A1.

Morgan, Dan and Ottaway, David B. "Kazakh Field Stirs U.S.-Russian Rivalry." *The Washington Post*, 6 October 1998: A1.

Neville, Harry "Bush's Homeland Security Pipeline." *BuzzFlash*, 29 March 2002 ‹http://www.buzzflash.com/contributors/2002/03/29_Homeland_Security_Pipeline.html›.

Plessner, Gerald. "Did George W. Bush Do Business with the Taliban?" *Democratic Underground*, 15 January 2002 ‹http://www.democraticunderground.com/articles /02/01/15_taliban.html›.

Ridgeway, James. "The French Connection." *The Village Voice*, 2–8 January 2002 ‹http://www.villagevoice.com/issues/0201/ridgeway.php›.

"Taleban in Texas for Talks on Gas Pipeline." BBC News, 4 December 1997 ‹http://news.bbc.co.uk/1/hi/world/west_asia/37021.stm›.

"Transcript—CNN's American Morning with Paula Zahn." *Common Dreams*, 8 January 2002 ‹http://www.commondreams.org/headlines02/0108-04.htm›.

33

→ WHERE ARE THE TALIBAN?

Almost lost in all the coverage of the Iraq quagmire: the victory in Afghanistan isn't panning out either.

Within the first nine months of 2003, 36 U.S. soldiers had been killed in combat in Afghanistan. Further, Khan Mohammed, a senior Afghan commander in Kandahar, told the Associated Press in October 2003: "There is no doubt that the situation is getting worse." According to the AP, Taliban militants and al Qaeda forces have become more daring in their attacks.

A pamphlet carrying the signatures of four of the most wanted Taliban leaders (Mullah Akhtar Uman, Mullah Bradar, Mullah Abdur Rauf, and Hafiz Adur Rahim) was circulated in late October 2003. It declared: "We are determined that the Afghan masses will never accept foreign law and oppression and the U.S. rule will remain only on paper." Meanwhile, Mullah Omar (like Osama bin Laden) is still at large.

Some claim that Hamid Karzai (officially the leader of the post-Taliban Afghanistan) is actually little more than mayor of Kabul, and that his power is limited to the nation's capital. That may be an exaggeration, but there is some truth to it. The Afghan government is impoverished and impotent, barely keeping control by reliance on the threat of another U.S. war campaign. As the U.S. continues to fail in Iraq, that threat soon may mean little to the Taliban resistance. While Karzai himself appears to be fairly popular in his country, much of the power in Afghanistan is held by warlords who often aren't liked by the people they rule. Murders, rapes, and robberies have been commonplace under their rule. It is just this kind of situation that led to the Taliban gaining power in the first place; their authoritarian rule at least kept order and let people feel safer. Will the Taliban return to power? Perhaps, or maybe a charismatic warlord (such as Northern Alliance General Abdul Rashid Dostum) will take over, and will either turn to "ethnic cleansing" or develop a cult of personality à la Saddam Hussein. U.S. military intervention leading to something worse certainly is a problem with a history in the region.

Sources:

"Resurgent Taliban." Online *NewsHour*, 2 September 2003 ‹http://www.pbs.org/newshour/bb/middle_east/july-dec03/taliban_9-02.html›.

"Taliban Vow Attacks After Mullah Omar Meeting." *China Daily*, 25 September 2003 ‹http://www1.chinadaily.com.cn/en/doc/2003-09/25/content_267308.htm›.

"Taliban Warn U.S. to Quit Afghanistan." News.com.au, 31 October 2003 ‹http://www.news.com.au/common/story_page/0,4057,6930420%255E1702,00.html›.

"U.S. Military Denies Taliban Making a Comeback in Afghanistan." *USA Today*, 1 October 2003 ‹http://www.usatoday.com/news/world/2003-10-01-U.S.-afghan_x.htm›.

"We Felt Safer Under the Taliban, Say Kabul Residents." *Common Dreams*, 25 January 2002 ‹http://www.commondreams.org/headlines02/0125-01.htm›.

34

→ THE HOMELESS CRISIS

In New York City, more than 38,000 people were homeless in December 2002, an increase of 25% in one year. This is a record number in the 20 years records have been kept in the city, which includes the Reagan years, when the problem first began to explode. Of these people, more than 16,600 were children, or 44% of the total, and over 13,000 were adults with dependents. Perhaps most disturbing of all, 20% of homeless families had a working head of the household, compared with 10% in the eighties.

NYC isn't alone. Jay Shaft, editor at the Coalition For Free Thought in Media, reported that homelessness and poverty have risen in America by more than 35% since 2000. Los Angeles and Chicago had increases of 50% between January 2001 and summer 2003. In 2002, the U.S. Conference of Mayors reported that shelter requests exceeded shelter availability by 30%.

To be fair, the homeless crisis didn't disappear under Clinton. While Clintonomics did lead to a decrease in the number living in poverty of seven million (when he left, the poverty rate of 11.3% came close to 1973's record low of 11.1%), the cracks in the system remained under his reign. Further, 46% of the job growth since 1994 was in jobs that paid less than $16,000 a year, the vast majority with no health insurance.

Whatever the faults in dealing with the crisis under Bubba, Shrub has exacerbated it with his own cynical policies. A leading cause of homelessness is a lack of affordable housing, and Section 8 vouchers to help poor families obtain housing have dried up under Bush's reign. The U.S. Department of Housing and Urban Development (HUD) cut funds to housing agencies by 30% in fiscal year 2003 over "internal accounting errors."

Oddly, there's been little mention of this disturbing phenomenon in the media. FOX News, for one, has reported on it with a glib nonchalance. Robert Shaffer dismissed supposed increases in homelessness as a reporting fad, stating that, "with a Republican in the White House, homelessness is in vogue again after more than a decade when AIDS was the cause du jour. So has it become cool to care about the downtrodden? Have the homeless, once again, become hip?" Trendiness aside, Shaffer conceded that HUD reported a 25% increase between 1991 and 2002, and the National Coalition for the Homeless puts it closer to 50%. (Right-wing hack Steven Milloy described the numbers as "junk science" in another nifty Fox piece.) Granted, it's FOX News. But the contempt for the downtrodden by the reactionary outlet is matched by the indifference of supposedly liberal media outlets. It underscores the moneyed and out-of-touch media establishment's lack of connection with the working class and poor.

One news source that isn't ignoring the crisis is the World Socialist Web Site (which, to its credit, doesn't hide its agenda). Among the underreported items about homelessness, WSWS listed a disturbing number of freezing deaths of homeless people in winter. This includes 151 who died in Boston (among them a two-month-old baby).

Dismaying, but not too surprising. After all, the number of Americans living in poverty increased by 3.5 million between 2000 and 2002, to nearly 35 million people. The number of Americans suffering from hunger is also on the rise, and this isn't due to the Atkins Diet. The only other president to approach Dubya's dismal record on fighting poverty was his daddy. Under Poppy Bush, the number of the poor increased by six million. (Bush Junior should surpass that total in 2004.) "A kinder, gentler nation," "one thousand points of light," "compassionate conservatism," and "faith based initiatives" are all basically the same thing: sweet nothings to cover the abdication of basic duty. Like father, like son.

Sources:

"Homeless, Poor Freeze in U.S. Cold Wave." World Socialist Web Site, 5 February 2003 ‹http://www.wsws.org/articles/2003/feb2003/cold-f05.shtml›.

"How George Bush Is Losing Two Wars." *The New York Observer*, 21 July 2003: 4.

"Hunger, Homelessness On the Rise in Major U.S. Cities." *The U.S. Conference of Mayors*, 18 December 2002‹http://www.usmayors.org/uscm/news/press_releases/documents/hunger_121802.asp›.

Johnson, Jeremy, and Vann, Bill. "Record Numbers Swamp New York City's Homeless Shelters." World Socialist Web Site, 15 February 2003 ‹http://www.wsws.org/articles/2003/feb2003/home-f15.shtml›.

Milloy, Steven. "Homeless Data Based on Politics, Not Numbers." FOX News, 27 December 2001 ‹http://www.foxnews.com/story/0,2933,41706,00.html›.

Shaffer, Robert. "Homelessness Back in Vogue." FOX News, 7 January 2002 ‹http://www.foxnews.com/story/0,2933,42239,00.html›.

Thoreau, Jackson. "Poor Americans Continue to Multiply Under Bush." *Online Journal*, 29 September 2003 ‹http://www.onlinejournal.com/Commentary/092903Thoreau/092903thoreau.html›.

35

➞ THE CORPORATE CROOKS

In the summer of 2002, Enrongate wasn't the only corporate scandal in the news. Besides Enron and Arthur Andersen, the list is impressive: WorldCom (the largest bankruptcy in history, as CEO Bernie Ebbers left the company $30 billion in debt while personally "borrowing" over $400 million, with $7 billion in improperly reported earnings), Global Crossing (the fifth largest bankruptcy ever, as Chairman and founder Gary Winnick pocketed $734 million in stock value while saddling the corporation with $12.4 billion in debt), Tyco (the conglomerate had $80 billion in market value wiped out in a year, while CEO Dennis Kozlowski, who made $112.5 million in salary and compensation in 2001 and cashed out at over $258 million, was indicted for tax evasion), Adelphia Communications (John Rigas and family turned it into a personal piggy bank, bankrupting the company after taking loans worth $3 billion), Qwest (CEO Joseph Nacchio saddled the company with $26 billion of debt and overstated revenue of $1 billion, while director Phil Anschutz was the greediest executive of all, according to *Fortune*, having pocketed over $1.5 billion in stock sales), Merck (recorded $14 billion in revenue that was never collected), ImClone (CEO Sam Waksal was indicted on fraud, perjury, obstruction of justice, and conspiracy charges after allegedly attempting to sell company stock before the FDA announced that it wouldn't approve the firm's cancer drug, while Martha Stewart did manage to sell hers (due to a tip-off from her broker), AOL Time Warner (after combined-assets value tanked from $290 billion to under $85 billion, the company made a record quarterly write-down of $54 billion, revealed an SEC investigation of accounting procedures, and over-reported advertising revenue to keep stock prices up during merger), Kmart (debt reduced to junk status and stock value imploded as mass layoffs ensued—but not before an $11.5 million giveaway to the CEO), and Xerox (had to restate $6.4 billion in revenues and $2 billion in earnings since 1997). Other companies embroiled in business scandals involving investigations or lawsuits were GE, Vivendi Universal, Johnson & Johnson, Rite Aid, Sunbeam, Bristol Myers, ABB, Cendant, Computer Associates, Cornell Companies, Dollar General, Elan, HealthSouth, HPL Technologies, Lucent, MicroStrategy, Network Associates, Peregrine Systems, Phar-Mor, PNC Financial Services, Waste Management, and Dick Cheney's old company Halliburton (see Reason #36). Then there's AES, CMS Energy, Duke Energy, Dynegy, El Paso, Reliant Energy, and Williams, all of which have been implicated in the California energy price-rigging scandal with Enron. Last but not least, three Wall Street firms were neck deep into Enrongate themselves. Citigroup and JP Morgan Chase loaned Enron $5.3 billion, then attempted to disguise the loans as commodities transactions and derivative swaps to hide Enron's desperate cash-poverty, and Merrill Lynch (which also settled a conflict-of-interest lawsuit with the New York Attorney General's office for $100 million—in private emails, shares given a "buy" recommendation were described as a "piece of shit") ousted an analyst with skeptical views on Enron, after Enron blamed loss of a $750 million stock offering on his reports.

Of course, not all of this was the fault of Shrub. After all, a large portion of the fraud occurred during the Clinton years. However, much of the scandal of the late '90s can be credited to the so-called Newt Gingrich Revolution, when the GOP took over both houses of Congress in 1994. Both Clinton and his SEC Chairman Arthur Levitt took positions blocked by the Republicans in Congress that have been proven prophetic.

Levitt opposed the abusive uses of stock options that have enriched many to the detriment of their companies; the Newtoids defended it, and the practice stayed in place. The Private Securities and Litigation Reform Act of 1995, a "tort-reform" bill to curb shareholder lawsuits against companies and accountants, was made law despite SEC objections and a veto by President Clinton, who warned that it would close courthouse doors to investors with legitimate claims. Finally, Levitt saw conflict of interest in the practice of accounting firms involved in both hefty consulting deals with and audits of these same firms. The big five accounting firms (including Arthur Andersen) spent $23 million in lobbying to block his plans to stop the practice. After Congress threatened to cut SEC funding, Levitt backed down.

Compare Levitt with the SEC Chairman picked by Dubya, Harvey Pitt, the lawyer who represented Wall Street firms and the accounting industry during their battles with Levitt. Pitt's blunders continued: in the wake of the many accounting scandals, he announced the creation of the Public Company Accounting Oversight Board, supposedly to combat the menace. It was soon revealed that the appointed head, William Webster, was audit committee chairman of U.S. Technology, a company facing charges of fraud. Faced with the increasing liability of his fundamental lack of credibility as a regulator, he resigned in November 2002, the day after elections.

Fortunately for investors, the freefall of the stock market has reversed in the year-plus since. Still, there is a considerable lack of confidence in the integrity of the regulation, especially considering the sleazy ties of both Cheney and Shrub to financial chicanery themselves (see next two reasons). Worrisomely, in August 2003, the New York Stock Exchange revealed that it had paid chairman and chief executive Dick Grasso a nearly $140 million lump sum. The board of directors who gave him the jackpot were all handpicked by Grasso. The controversy over the scandal led to his resignation, as the Bush administration stayed quiet on the sidelines.

Meanwhile, most of the top dogs involved in bogus business practices have escaped prosecution. Indeed, the leader in securing corporate integrity no longer appears to be the SEC, but NY Attorney General Eliot Spitzer. "Kenny-Boy" Lay, Bernie Ebbers, and Gary Winnick (who gave Poppy Bush $80,000 in 1998) have strangely remained unprosecuted for their deeds. Compare their treatment to that of Martha Stewart (a Democratic Party donor), both legally and in the press. Perhaps it says something about the Bush Team that they could turn Martha Stewart into someone pitiable.

Sources:

"Bigger Than Enron." *Frontline*, 20 June 2002 ‹http://www.pbs.org/wgbh/pages/frontline/shows/regulation/etc/synopsis.html›.

"Corporate Ethics." Online *NewsHour*, ‹http://www.pbs.org/newshour/bb/business/ethics›.

"Corporate Ethics." *The Washington Post*
‹http://www.washingtonpost.com/wp-dyn/business/specials/corporateethics›.

"The Corporate Scandal Fact Sheet." Citizen Works, 2002
‹http://www.citizenworks.org/enron/corp-scandal.php›.

"In Depth: Corporate Scandals." BBC News, 17 February 2003
‹http://news.bbc.co.uk/1/hi/in_depth/business/2002/scandals›.

"Scandal Inc." CNN/Money ‹http://money.cnn.com/news/specials/corruption›.

36

→ HALLIBURTONGATE

Dick Cheney's opinion about all the corporate sleaziness would be interesting to hear. After all, he has experience as a CEO of a giant firm, Halliburton, and thus might be in a position to denounce the accounting mischief and other shenanigans. Unfortunately, his tongue might be tied by Halliburton's own tangled cons and schemes.

The SEC began investigating Halliburton in May 2002 for the overstatement of revenues from 1999 to 2001, after news organizations began reporting on its curious transactions. The total amount of the overstatements was $445 million. SEC Chairman Harvey Pitt reassuringly claimed that Cheney wouldn't receive any special treatment.

Cheney's response to all this was to hide in a bunker, as he did following September 11. During the summer of 2002, when the corporate scandals were peaking, Cheney press conferences were less common than videotaped pronouncements by Osama bin Laden. Aside from keeping his commitments to all-important fundraisers, Cheney was practically mum and invisible. Compare this to his high profile role in blaming the California energy crisis on the Golden State or taking the lead on *Meet the Press* to push for the White House's anti-terrorism campaign on September 16, 2001.

Meanwhile, Halliburton officials stressed that Cheney wasn't involved, which, even if true, would contravene Shrub's insistence that CEOs take personal responsibility for financial practices. Cheney had earlier been gleefully eager to take personal credit for his Halliburton reign as "a great success story," but suddenly clammed up when the story was of fraudulent practices.

One man unwilling to let Cheney off the hook was Larry Klayman, the head of Judicial Watch. Disgusted by the widespread deception, Klayman and his group filed a $200 million class-action lawsuit against the company and Cheney personally. Judicial Watch points to an interview in which current Halliburton CEO David Lesar declared, "The vice president was aware of who owed us money, and he helped us collect it." As Klayman would note, "It is now confirmed by Halliburton itself that Cheney had a 'hands on' role in the financial management of the company. Mr. Lesar's admissions reinforce the strength of our lawsuit."

To be fair to Halliburton, not all of its problems are due to phony accounting practices. Many of them can be blamed on the acquisition of Dresser Industries (a firm burdened with multi-billion-dollar asbestos lawsuits from worker exposure) for $7.7 billion. 10,000 jobs were lost because of the merger, and Dresser executives received golden parachutes (Cheney himself earned $26.4 million the same year as the massive layoffs). Dallas attorney John Wall (who represents the laid-off workers) told *USA Today*, "I never understood why they did that. They overpaid for Dresser, and all they did was buy a bunch of liabilities."

One possible explanation for the curious purchase is that Dresser Industries is the first firm that hired George "Poppy" Bush in 1948, after he graduated from Yale as a Skull and Bones member. On the Board of Directors then was Prescott Bush, Poppy Bush's daddy. The middle name of Poppy Bush's arguably even-dumber-than-Shrub son Neil is Mallon, in honor of Henry Neil Mallon, the head of Dresser at the time. That leads to the question whether Cheney knowingly acquired a negative asset to enrich old friends of the Bush family.

The combination of lousy business practices would shrink the value of Halliburton. When Cheney sold all his shares for his VP run, it was valued at $52 a share: two years later it had dropped over 75% to $12. (Besides the stock sale, Cheney would receive his own $33 million golden parachute from the firm as a "retirement" package.)

There's a happy ending for Halliburton to all this: thanks to "Operation Iraqi Freedom," it has won more than $1.7 billion in U.S. government projects through its subsidiary Brown and Root. It stands to make even more via no-bid contracts, and has beaten out the bin Laden–tied Bechtel Group as the top beneficiary of Dubya's adventures in Iraq.

In defense of the sweetheart deals generated for his old company by a war based on lies, Cheney declared, "Since I left Halliburton to become George Bush's vice president, I've severed all my ties with the company, gotten rid of all my financial interests. I have no financial interest in Halliburton of any kind and haven't had now, for over three years." Besides the fact that he still props up former business partners there, this was a lie, albeit a white lie. In 2001, Cheney received $205,298 in deferred salary from Halliburton, more than his salary for occupying the White House. (His total deferred salary will be over $800 grand.) He also holds over 400,000 stock options.

Meanwhile, U.S. soldiers are sweltering in 120-degree-plus temperatures. Some are directly involved in supporting Halliburton. Kellogg Brown and Root, a subsidiary, has won contracts to haul fuel, and soldiers are serving their time as armed escorts for the corporation. It's enough to make one wonder how low Bush Team can go in terms of sleazy business dealings.

Sources:

"Accounting Questions." Online *NewsHour*, 24 July 2002 ‹http://www.pbs.org/newshour/bb/business/july-dec02/halliburton_7-24.html›.

"The Corporate Scandal Fact Sheet." Citizen Works, 2002 ‹http://www.citizenworks.org/enron/corp-scandal.php›.

Dobbs, Michael. "Halliburton's Deals Greater Than Thought." *The Washington Post*, 28 August 2003: A01.

Edwards, Johnny. "Reserves Wanting to Leave Mideast." *The Augusta Chronicle*, 11 July 2003 ‹http://www.augustachronicle.com/stories/071203/met_021-6883.000.shtml›.

Floyd, Chris. "Thieves Like Us: Cheney's Backdoor to Halliburton." *CounterPunch*, 29 October 2003 ‹http://www.counterpunch.org/floyd10292003.html›.

"George H.W. Bush." Famous Texans ‹http://www.famoustexans.com/georgebush.htm›.

"Halliburton CEO Admits Cheney Knew of Alleged Fraudulent Accounting Policies." Judicial Watch, 15 July 2002 ‹http://www.judicialwatch.org/2151.shtml›.

Hightower, Jim. "Bush, Cheney, War and Halliburton." 1 April 2003 ‹http://www.jimhightower.com/air/read.asp?id=11063›.

Hindo, Brian. "What's Lighting Halliburton's Fire." *BusinessWeek*, 21 May 2003 ‹http://www.businessweek.com/technology/content/may2003/tc20030521_3251_tc055.htm›.

Jackson, Derrick Z. "Cheney's Conflict with the Truth." *The Boston Globe*, 19 September 2003 ‹http://www.boston.com/news/globe/editorial_opinion/oped/articles/2003/09/19/cheneys _conflict_with_the_truth›.

McNamee, Mike and Forest, Stephanie Anderson. "The Cheney Question." *BusinessWeek*, 12 July 2002 ‹http://www.businessweek.com/bwdaily/dnflash/jul2002/nf20020712_2785.htm›.

McQuillan, Laurence. "Investigations Pry into Cheney's Business." *USA Today*, 9 June 2002 ‹http://www.usatoday.com/news/washington/2002/06/10/cheney-usat.htm›.

Neal, Terry M. "Gadfly Klayman Chooses Consistency Over Predictability." *The Washington Post*, 16 July 2002 ‹http://www.washingtonpost.com/ac2/wpdyn?pagename=article&node =&contentId= A8394-2002Jul15&notFound=true›.

Ruppert, Michael C. "The Best Enemies Money Can Buy." *From the Wilderness*, 9 October 2001 ‹http://www.fromthewilderness.com/free/ww3/10_09_01_carlyle.html›.

Sandalow, Marc. "Cheney's Disappearing Act." *The San Francisco Chronicle*, 4 August 2002 ‹http://www.sfgate.com/cgi-bin/article.cgi?file=/c/a/2002/08/04/MN85660.DTL.›

37

→ **HARKENGATE**

Halliburton is not the worst tie the Bush Team has to the corporate business scandals. Don't underestimate the depths of a man who started in business with the bin Laden family.

In 1986, Spectrum 7, a failing energy company owned by George W. Bush and two partners, was bought for $2 million by Harken Energy. Asked why he bought the floundering company, Harken founder Phil Kendrick explained, "His name was George Bush." Shrub was put on Harken's board of directors and audit committee.

Unfortunately, Georgie's bad luck streak continued for Harken, which proceeded to lose large amounts of money. (Indeed, every energy company that Dubya worked for would fail miserably, adding to worries about a man who can't profit from oil in Texas despite the best connections.) But then, in 1989, Harken came up with a nifty scheme to hide some of its losses and prop up its stock value. It sold a subsidiary, Aloha Petroleum, to Harken investors, who borrowed the money from Harken itself. The trade hid $10 million in losses. The Aloha trade was a perfect example of the fraudulent activity at the center of usthe corporate scandals. The SEC declared the obviously full-of-shit transaction phony, and Harken was required to restate its earnings.

Before this ruling, Shrub sold two-thirds of his shares in the company, 212,000, at $4, for a total of $848,000, about four times the worth of Martha Stewart's sale that has her potentially redecorating a federal penitentiary. Six months later, the stock was trading at barely over $1 a share. He took nearly eight months to inform the SEC of the sale, which came only weeks before Harken filed a quarterly report revealing that it had lost $23 million, something Bush did know about. One week before his stock dump, Harken lawyers warned Bush and others they could face insider trading charges if they sold their shares.

Dubya sold them anyway, knowing that he was above the law. Although an internal SEC memorandum concluded that he broke the law, he was never charged with any crime. Surely this decision not to prosecute had nothing to with the fact that his daddy was president, the SEC chairman was a good pal and appointment of Poppa Bush, and the general counsel of the SEC was a former lawyer for Shrub who had negotiated his purchase of the Texas Rangers. The day after the Bush-controlled SEC decided not to press charges, the warning memo from Harken lawyers was received by the SEC.

Worst of all, most of this was publicly known before the 2000 election, yet was dismissed by corporate media more interested in Gore's claim of inventing the Internet. Indeed, the only reason Harkengate even became an issue again in 2002 was an exposé by the gutsy Paul Krugman in the *New York Times*; before his piece, Dubya's personal example of corporate fraud went unreported as the scandals multiplied.

To be fair to Shrub, he was merely following the example of his brothers. Neil was on the board of directors of Silverado Savings and Loan, one of the notorious failed S&Ls that cost American taxpayers $1 billion. In 1990, federal regulators filed a $200 million lawsuit against Neil Bush and others for "gross negligence." (The proceedings to close Silverado began on November 9, 1988, the day after Poppy Bush was elected president.) Neil never did face any jail time. Nor did brother Jeb, who bilked nearly $5 million from another failed S&L via a Florida real estate scam.

As the corporate scandals began to multiply, little Georgie tried to talk tough in July 2002, declaring he'd had it with these crooked CEOs and their crooked behavior. Yet, when asked about Harken and his own Enron-esque activity, Dubya suddenly became a moral relativist, claiming "sometimes things aren't exactly black-and-white when it comes to accounting procedures." Whatever the truth in this philosophy, it has no application to the Harken trades by Bush. Indeed, as Krugman noted, Shrub and Harken's activity looks almost like a textbook example of the bogus accounting that became commonplace in the late nineties.

So far, there has been, unsurprisingly, no new investigation of Harkengate. On *Crossfire*, the always colorful James Carville summed up the situation this way: "He thought he was exempt from the rules. He sold the stock and then he did not turn over the letter from the lawyers to the SEC until after the investigation was over. And I'm telling you that from the facts we know now, it appears we have someone guilty of insider trading sitting in the White House."

Sources:

Conason, Joe. "Did Those 'Boutique' Liberals Bail Out Bush?" *Salon*, 11 July 2002 ‹http://www.salon.com/news/col/cona/2002/07/11/bush›.

Kranish, Michael and Healy, Beth. "Board Was Told of Risks Before Bush Stock Sale." *Common Dreams*, 30 October 2002 ‹http://www.commondreams.org/headlines02/1030-06.htm›.

Krugman, Paul. "Everyone is Outraged." *The New York Times*, 2 July 2002: A21.

Krugman, Paul. "The Insider Game." *The New York Times*, 12 July 2002: A19.

Lindlaw, Scott. "Bush Corporate Record Examined." *The Washington Post*, 3 July 2002 ‹http://www.washingtonpost.com/wp-dyn/articles/A19419-2002Jul3.html›.

Royce, Knut. "Bush Violated Security Laws Four Times, SEC Report Says." *Public I*, 4 October 2000 ‹http://www.public-i.org/story_01_100400.htm›.

Scheim, David E. "Truth or Hustle: The Bush Record." Campaignwatch.org ‹http://www.campaignwatch.org/more1.htm›.

York, Anthony. "The Hypocrite in Chief." *Salon*, 2 July 2002 ‹http://www.salon.com/politics/feature/2002/07/02/bush›.

38

ENRON
& THE CALIFORNIA ENERGY SWINDLE

The bankruptcy of Enron was merely the second act in its 2001 tale of corruption. First came the electricity swindle of California, in which the most populous state of the nation (which constitutes a sixth of the U.S. economy) saw its huge budget surplus wiped out (turning quickly into hulking Shrubonomics debts) and suffered widespread blackouts, something normally associated with the Third World. This led to astronomical utility bills for residents of the Golden State.

How did it all happen? Media attempts to explain it otherwise aside, the real cause was state deregulation of the electricity market. The proof is in the differences within the state between the deregulated areas and the control sample. For example, Angelenos are hardly known for being stern power conservationists, and yet they were unaffected by the crisis. The reason: Los Angeles has a municipal-owned utility system, and thus was not part of the scheme. A study by Public Citizen concluded that peak power demand was lower in four of six key months during the crisis, which disproves power producers' claim that increased consumer demand was the culprit.

California Assembly Bill 1890 was presented to the public as a restructuring of the electricity market for their benefit. The vocal enthusiasm for the measure of Republican Governor Pete Wilson—arguably the most cynical politician ever to come from the Golden State—should have been an early warning sign. The measure changed the electricity marketplace radically, splitting the electricity business into one group of companies to generate power, and another to buy and deliver it. Utility companies were to sell off their power plants, and price caps on electricity (a turn-of-the-century Progressive era reform to prevent market manipulations and gouging) were eliminated, with caps on utility bills to follow when companies recouped expenses from failed plants. The theory behind the deregulation plan was that having multiple sellers and distributors of electricity would let a competitive marketplace develop, to the benefit of the consumers. It didn't quite turn out that way: the moves led to an energy oligopoly that secretly (and illegally) limited the supply of electricity to reap windfall profits. While utilities were paying $35 per megawatt hour in 2000 for electricity, the price climbed to $1,400 during the crisis.

What did Shrub do about the crisis? Not much, besides reverse the imposition of price caps in California, which Bill Clinton had ordered (belatedly) on December 20, 2002. Charitably, he offered to ease air pollution regulations on the state's power plants. He then joined the chorus of pundits who blamed supposedly leftist California policies on the crisis, and declared it a state problem, not a federal one. His administration also turned down a request by California to waive federal mandates requiring the use of corn-derived ethanol in clean-burn fuels. The decision, at odds with their supposed concern that environmental edicts could harm the economy, could lead to fuel shortages and sharper price increases. (Curiously, Archer Daniels Midland, a major campaign contributor, produces about half of the nation's ethanol, and Williams Energy Services of Texas and agribusiness giant Cargill produce about 5% each.) Bush fiddled while California blacked out, an unsurprisingly blasé tune for a state he soundly lost during the 2000 campaign and likely will lose again in 2004.

Bush-backer Enron was a major beneficiary of all this. Quarterly revenues for the firm rose 271% from a year earlier to $40.8 billion, and earnings from their wholesale energy business nearly tripled. After the bankruptcy of Enron, California officials uncovered the evidence of what they had suspected all along: the "crisis" was manufactured by power companies hoarding energy supplies to maximize profits. From 30% to 50% of power was off the market, rising to over 75% at key moments of the crisis. A memo written by Enron lawyers in December 2000 outlined practices alleged by California officials: phony congestion of electricity transmission and sham sales to artificially raise prices. According to Enron's own lawyers, "The net effect of these transactions is that Enron gets paid for moving energy to relieve congestion without actually moving any energy or relieving any congestion." Sean Gallagher, a lawyer for the California Public Utilities

Commission, declared, "To us, this is really the smoking-gun memo. It's Enron's own attorneys admitting that Enron is manipulating the California market." All told, the Foundation for Taxpayer and Consumer Rights concluded, the fraud cost $71 billion, which amounts to $2,200 for every Californian.

Another memo was uncovered, from Enron CEO Kenny-Boy Lay to Dick Cheney, that included recommendations on how to handle the California energy crisis. These became the talking points for Cheney the following day. At the time, Bush and company were notably snubbing California Democratic officials. As Senator Dianne Feinstein put it in the *Los Angeles Times*, "Throughout the crisis, I was not allowed a private interview with the president or vice president—even though such a talk may have helped California. Something is wrong when a senator representing 35 million Californians is not able to talk personally to the president or vice president in the midst of a crisis, but executives from a company that contributed millions of campaign dollars have complete access and significant influence." Something is also wrong when these same executives evade any prosecution for their blatant criminal acts, aided by Team Dubya's insouciance.

One official mystery of the Enron scandal remains: what happened to all the fucking money? Granted, Enron was neck-deep in fraudulent accounting, but $40 billion is still a lot of bucks. While much of the focus in the Enron scandal has been on using offshore accounts to hide company losses, less has been made of the secret partnerships to siphon profits. What are the names on the partnerships? Does it go higher than Kenny-Boy? Former Enron Vice Chairman and Chief Strategy Officer Clifford Baxter probably knew the names. Unfortunately, Baxter allegedly committed suicide before he could cooperate with any investigators, though he appeared quite willing to. Before his supposed suicide, Baxter feared for his life, and according to the *New York Times*, he considered hiring a bodyguard for protection. A business associate said, "This was practically the last person in the world you'd expect to commit suicide." Indeed, Baxter was already looking to be lionized as a hero in the Enron case. Curiously, four months later, the treasurer for El Paso (a fellow Texas energy company involved in the California scandal) allegedly committed suicide as well—another miraculous break for the Texas energy barons that Bush and his pals happily serve.

Sources:

"Army Chief Faces Enron Questions." CBS News, 22 July 2002 ‹http://www.cbsnews.com/stories/2002/07/22/politics/main515789.shtml›.

Attkisson, Sharyl. "Feds Probe Enron Role in Energy Crisis." CBS News, 13 February 2002 ‹http://www.cbsnews.com/stories/2002/02/13/national/main329304.shtml›.

Attkisson, Sharyl. "The Mysterious Death of An Enron Exec." CBS News, 10 April 2002 ‹http://www.cbsnews.com/stories/2002/04/10/eveningnews/main505845.shtml›.

"Blackout: The California Crisis." *Frontline*, 2001 ‹http://www.pbs.org/wgbh/pages/frontline/shows/blackout/california›.

"Bush Rejects California Energy Plea." BBC News, 30 May 2001 ‹http://news.bbc.co.uk/1/hi/world/americas/1358504.stm›.

"Energy 'Crisis' Was a $71 Billion Hoax." *Democratic Underground*, 21 January 2002 ‹http://www.democraticunderground.com/forum_archive_html/DCForumID38/1176.html›.

"Enron's California Memo: Smoking Gun?" *USA Today*, 7 May 2002 ‹http://www.usatoday.com/money/energy/enron/2002-05-07-enron-calif-memo.htm›.

Gonzales, Vince. "California Energy Crisis A Sham." CBS News, 17 September 2002 ‹http://www.cbsnews.com/stories/2002/09/17/eveningnews/main522332.shtml›.

"High Ranking El Paso Exec Dies in Apparent Suicide." *USA Today*, 3 June 2002 ‹http://www.usatoday.com/money/energy/2002-06-03-el-paso-suicide.htm›.

Noah, Timothy. "Dubya's Regrettable Bipartisanship." *Slate*. 12 June 2001 ‹http://slate.msn.com/id/1007836/›.

Palast, Greg. *The Best Democracy Money Can Buy*. New York: Plume, 2003.

Rappleye, Charles. "The Enron Rip-off." *LA Weekly*, 19–25 April 2002 ‹http://www.laweekly.com/ink/02/22/news-rappleye.php›.

Sterling, Robert. "The California Electricity Swindle." *Disinformation*, 1 February 2001 ‹http://www.disinfo.com/archive/pages/dossier/id825/pg1›.

York, Anthony. "Enron's California Smoking Gun." *Salon*, 16 January 2002 ‹http://www.salon.com/news/feature/2002/01/16/california_enron›.

York, Anthony. "From Enron to Cheney to California." *Salon*, 1 February 2002 ‹http://www.salon.com/politics/feature/2002/02/01/enron_memo›.

39
→ THE CHENEY ENERGY PROGRAM

It's not hard to believe that a gang of cretins who would exploit the blood of 3,000 Americans for cynical political gain would use a bogus energy crisis to push for a dishonest agenda, which is precisely what the Bush Team did. With the California electricity crisis still on people's minds, George W. Bush unveiled the energy plan of Dick Cheney's "Energy Task Force" in May 2001. With his smart-ass smirk barely concealed, Bush declared, "If we fail to act, we could face a darker future, a future that is unfortunately being previewed in rising prices at the gas pump and rolling blackouts in California."

Greg Palast called it "charitable" to describe the plan as a "scheme to pay off the president's oil company buddies, fry the planet, and smother Mother Earth in coal ash, petroleum pollutants and nuclear waste." The Cheney scam dismissed alternative energy sources and focused on promoting oil, gas, and nuclear power (sources in which Halliburton is heavily invested). Besides weakened environmental regulations and the potentially disastrous push for drilling in the Arctic Wildlife Refuge, Cheney called for a new power plant to be completed every week for 20 years— over a thousand.

Fortunately, the Cheney plan wasn't greeted well, at least by anyone with even nominal concerns for the environment. Jan Pronk, head of the U.N. Forum on Climate Change, said, "In terms of the possibility of forming an integrated policy, this is a disastrous development." It even received a thumbs-down from the Libertarian-leaning Cato Institute, which was particularly opposed to the proposal giving the Feds powers to seize private property— using eminent domain—and hand it to power companies for power lines. (How such a policy fits in with their self-proclaimed opposition to big government, market interference, and violations of property rights was left obscure by Bush-Cheney.)

Outrage soon turned into tough questions. How did the Energy Task Force come up with its recommendations? The General Accounting Office (GAO) wanted to know. Its head, David Walker, was a former Reagan appointee chosen to head the GAO by Trent Lott. He was an unlikely Bushista nemesis, but beyond his Republican ties, Walker is a man of integrity, and he requested that the White House reveal who was consulted by Cheney's clique and what was discussed. His request was rebuffed by Cheney, who claimed that the GAO (and therefore Congress) had no authority to seek the information. Walker filed suit, and told *USA Today*: "It's the piece of a bigger puzzle. The bigger puzzle is a desire by the administration to draw a different line in the sand on the separation of powers."

John Dean, Tricky Dick Nixon's former counsel, declared that "not since Richard Nixon stiffed the Congress during Watergate has a White House so openly, and arrogantly, defied Congress' investigative authority. Nor has any activity by the Bush Administration more strongly suggested they are hiding the incriminating information about their relationship with the now-moribund Enron, or other heavy-hitting campaign contributors from the energy business. . . If Vice President Cheney were to prevail in such a suit, the high Court will have decided that Congressional oversight of the Executive Branch is limited to only what the President and Vice President are willing to permit." Dean's conclusion: "The Vice President can only win if we have another Bush vs. Gore-like ruling."

In December 2002, a Bush vs. Gore-like ruling was issued. The suit was dismissed—by Judge John D. Bates, an ultra-conservative appointed by Bush after serving as Deputy for the Office of Independent Counsel Kenneth W. Starr.

Despite the partisan ruling against the GAO, another suit has moved forward, again by Larry Klayman and Judicial Watch. Klayman, like Walker, showed once again that his sense of ethics went deeper than his ideological fidelity. The Judicial Watch suit's progress has already revealed that the Task Force relied exclusively on energy companies for advice, many of them big GOP donors. Energy Secretary Spencer Abraham met more than 100 representatives of energy industry companies and corporate associations from January to May 2001, 18 of which contributed more than $16 million to the party since 1999. On the list: ChevronTexaco,

ExxonMobil, British Petroleum, Edison Electric Institute, the Nuclear Energy Institute, the National Association of Manufacturers, the Independent Petroleum Association of America, and, of course, Enron. No consumer groups or environmental groups were contacted. All of this was uncovered even though 15,000 documents from the Energy Department, 10,000 from the EPA, and the entire requests for the Department of Treasury and Commerce weren't released as ordered by court.

The case continues to be fought in court. However it ends up, the arrogance of Dick Cheney in his ludicrous legal arguments (following an equally ludicrous energy plan) is appalling. As John Dean summed it up, "He told the *Today Show* that he wants to 'protect the ability of the president and the vice president to get unvarnished advice from any source we want.' That sounds all too familiar to me. I worked for Richard Nixon."

Sources:

"Anger Over Bush Energy Plan." CNN, 18 May 2001
‹http://www.cnn.com/2001/WORLD/europe/05/18/bush.reaction›.

Dean, John W. "GAO v. Cheney Is Big-time Stalling." FindLaw, 1 February 2002
‹http://writ.news.findlaw.com/dean/20020201.html›.

Knight, Danielle. "USA: Documents Show Bush Energy Plan Fuelled by Industry."
CorpWatch, 28 March 2002 ‹http://www.corpwatch.org/news/PND.jsp?articleid=2173›.

Leopold, Jason. "Cheney's Cover Up: Nixon Redux." *CounterPunch*, 12 December 2002
‹http://www.counterpunch.org/leopold1212.html›.

Page, Susan. "GAO Chief, Cheney Barreling Toward Showdown." *USA Today*, 17 February
2002 ‹http://www.usatoday.com/news/washington/2002/02/18/usat-showdown.htm›.

Palast, Greg. *The Best Democracy Money Can Buy*. New York: Plume, 2003.

Palast, Greg. "Bush Energy Plan: Policy or Payback?" BBC News, 18 May 2001
‹http://news.bbc.co.uk/1/hi/world/americas/1336960.stm›.

Taylor, Jerry. "Just Say 'No' to the Energy Plan." The Cato Institute, 19 May 2001
‹http://www.cato.org/dailys/05-19-01.html›.

Whitmore, Thomas M. "Remove Judge John D. Bates from Walker v. Cheney."
PetitionOnline, 2002 ‹http://www.petitiononline.com/bates69/petition.html›.

40

THE CORPORATE TAKEOVER OF OUR MEDIA

In 1983, the first edition of Ben H. Bagdikian's *The Media Monopoly* raised alarms about the disturbing level of media consolidation. At the time, Bagdikian warned that "50 corporations dominated most of every mass medium."

20 years later, that number looks almost utopian in comparison to today's mere six: Time Warner, Disney, Bertelsmann, Fox, Viacom, and General Electric. Other lists make it nine by including Sony, Seagram, and AT&T, and there's some flux lately (most notably the disturbing rise of Clear Channel Communications). Whatever the list, these are the few major players influencing people's minds. And this only tells half the story: as Bagdikian points out, "The power and influence of the dominant companies are understated by counting them as 'six.' They are intertwined: they own stock in each other, they cooperate in joint media ventures, and among themselves they divide profits from some of the most widely viewed programs on television, cable and movies."

To be fair to Bush, this disturbing trend did not start with him. From 1983 to 1992, the number of media giants dropped from 50 to 14, and it continued to fall under Clinton. It may be amusing to some to hear leaders of the Democratic Party now decrying media concentration after cheering it on for so long. Indeed, much of the explosion in consolidation happened after the 1996 Telecommunications Act was easily passed by both houses of Congress and signed by Billy Boy with overwhelming bipartisan support. At the time, most controversy surrounding the legislation involved the Communications Decency Act, a doggie bone thrown (and since tossed out by courts) for religious conservatives to "protect children" from sexual material on the Internet. It turned out to be a red herring: the Telecommunications Act itself was fundamentally unsound, radically changing Federal law to allow even more control of public airwaves by even fewer hands. This was done, ironically, at a time when a new medium such as the Internet could have conceivably caused the reverse. (William Kennard, Clinton's Federal Communications Commission Chairman, now sits on the board of the Carlyle Group thanks to his work.)

But while the Democratic Party is guilty of predictable political hypocrisy, the Bush Team's crime is willingly pushing for a destructive agenda in the face of increasing public opposition. On June 2, 2003, the FCC (under Michael Powell, Colin's corporate bootlicking son) approved proposed changes to telecommunications regulations by a 3–2 vote, split on a straight party line. Under the new rules, among other changes, networks may own TV stations that reach 45% of the national audience, up from 35%, and a company may now own both a newspaper and a radio station in the same area. Powell smugly dismissed criticism of the proposal as stuck in a "bygone black-and-white era." Meanwhile, dissenting Commissioner Michael Copps warned of a "dark cloud now looming over the future of American media." His dim view was backed by hundreds of thousands of emails and letters from Americans concerned about the changes. Currently, the decision faces a stiff challenge in both courts and (surprisingly) in Congress, where even many Republican stalwarts, including the NRA, are disturbed by the proposals.

A cynic would suggest that the Democratic Party is only in opposition to corporate media consolidation now that the damage is hitting its members personally. FOX News is a prime example: the pseudo-news operation is a right-wing cheerleader, with hacks such as Levittown square Bill O'Reilly, transparent GOP mouthpiece Sean Hannity, and Shepard Smith (the Dan Quayle of news anchors) rarely concealing their support for the Bush agenda. Besides its ownership by Rupert Murdoch, FOX News is run by Roger Ailes, a longtime Republican supporter from the Nixon years. (Curiously, Murdoch's recent buyout of DirecTV for $6.6 billion was aided by the nullification of a previous deal by Echostar nixed by the FCC, a move that suggests political back-scratching.) Then there is the rise of Clear Channel Communications, the radio behemoth with over 1,200 stations in the U.S. (The maximum allowed was 40 before the 1996 telecom "deregulation.") Clear Channel was a major player in the Dixie Chick-bashing, blacklisting

their music from stations for Natalie Maines' solitary denounce-
ment of Bush during a European concert. It's a disturbing development that a single company could control public airwaves to
such a degree and silence someone for her politics—making it
even more suspicious is that Clear Channel is run by Chairman
Lowry Mays and Vice Chairman Tom Hicks, both of whom have
been close business associates of Dubya. (In fact, Hicks is the
man who bought the Texas Rangers from a consortium Shrub was
part of, making Georgie-boy a multimillionaire.) Clear Channel
also staged "patriotic rallies" across the country that were thinly-
veiled promotions of the Iraq war.

(All of this increasingly exposes the lie by right-wing mouthpieces who whine of a "liberal" bias in the media. As Al Franken
put it, "Asking if there is liberal or conservative bias in the media
is like asking if al Qaeda uses too much oil in the hummus. There
is a bias in the right-wing media. The right-wing media is FOX,
Washington Times, Ann Coulter, *Wall Street Journal* ed page and
talk radio. They will lie and cheat in talk radio . . . There is no
equivalency.")

Cynical politics aside, at least Democrat leaders have finally
awakened to the consequences of the policies they've resound-
ingly supported. Bush, Powell, and their allies appear ready to
retire any concept of public interest in fairly distributing airwaves,
and Bush has threatened to veto any law that reverses the FCC
decision. The bottom line: had any 2004 Democratic presidential
candidate made the FCC appointment, the new rules would not
be in place.

Sources:

Ahrens, Frank. "Unlikely Alliances Forged in Fight Over Media Rules." *The Washington Post*, 20 May 2003: E01

Alterman, Eric. *What Liberal Media? The Truth about Bias and the News*. New York: Basic Books, 2003.

Atrios. "Radio Ga Ga." *Take Back the Media*, 20 March 2003
‹http://www.takebackthemedia.com/radiogaga.html›.

Bagdikian, Ben H. *The Media Monopoly*. Boston: Beacon Press, 2000.

"The Bush-Carlyle Group Archive." *BuzzFlash*, 2002 ‹http://www.buzzflash.com/per-spectives/2002/Bush-Carlyle.html›.

"Corporate Ownership." Fairness & Accuracy in Reporting, 2003
‹http://www.fair.org/media-woes/corporate.html›.

Davidson, Paul. "Court Delays FCC Media Ownership Rules." *USA Today*, 3 September 2003 ‹http://www.usatoday.com/money/media/2003-09-16-senate-overturns_x.htm›.

Davidson, Paul. "Senate Votes No on New Media Rules." *USA Today*, 16 September 2003 ‹http://www.usatoday.com/money/media/2003-09-16-senate-overturns_x.htm›.

"FCC Clears Way for Media Monopolies." AFL-CIO, 2 June 2003 ‹http://www.aflcio.org/issuespolitics/ns06022003a.cfm›.

Franken, Al. *Lies and the Lying Liars Who Tell Them: A Fair and Balanced Look at the Right*. New York: E P Dutton, 2003.

McCullagh, Declan. "FCC Eases Rules on Media Ownership." CNET News.com, 2 June 2003 ‹http://news.com.com/2100-1028-1012027.html›.

Miller, Mark Crispin. "What's Wrong with This Picture?" *The Nation*, 20 December 2001 ‹http://www.thenation.com/doc.mhtml?i=20020107&s=miller›.

Nebel, Robert J. "Q&A: Al Franken." *AlterNet*, 2 September 2003 ‹http://www.alternet.org/story.html?StoryID=16696›.

Smith, Sam. "Slanted Stats." TomPaine.com, 9 January 2003 ‹http://www.tompaine.com/feature2.cfm/ID/7049›.

Solomon, Norman. "Break up Microsoft? . . . Then How about the Media 'Big Six'?" Fairness & Accuracy in Reporting, 27 April 2000 ‹http://www.fair.org/media-beat/000427.html›.

41

→ **HIS DADDY**

True, a man should not be held accountable for the sins of the father. However, sometimes the shrub doesn't stray far from the bush.

In the case of little Georgie, the legacy of his father seems like an inordinately important factor in the judgment of the younger. After all, Shrub's success could only have grown in the rich dirt of his inheritance. He makes Dan Quayle look like a self-made man. Would anyone take such a lightweight as Dubya even remotely seriously as a political figure (much less as a presidential candidate) if he had a different last name?

That said, what actually is the legacy of George Herbert Walker Bush? A pretty sordid one. Jonathan Vankin, in his journalistic volume on modern conspiracy theory history (*Conspiracies, Cover-Ups and Crimes*), devotes an entire chapter to Poppy Bush, who is linked to nearly every diabolical plot since the end of World War II. Indeed, GHW Bush was one of those rare figures who could unite the left and right fringe culture in a nonstop loathe-a-thon.

Biggie George was tapped for big things early on, when he (like his father Prescott, a well-connected fellow in his own right, and like his son) was selected in his senior year at Yale as a member of Skull and Bones, the powerful insider training ground posing as frat. After moving to Texas and working for Dresser Industries, he co-founded Zapata Petroleum in 1953, soon becoming CEO of Zapata Off-Shore. According to Colonel Fletcher Prouty, the man who secured for the Bay of Pigs (Code Name: Zapata) two naval ships, the boats were named "Barbara" and "Houston" for the CIA operation—the names of HW's wife and the city he lived in. This leads to the obvious question of whether Bush was involved with the CIA and the Bay of Pigs at the time. Of course, per policy, both GHW and the CIA deny this, but in 1988, an FBI memo signed by J. Edgar Hoover came to light revealing that on November 23, 1963 (one day after the JFK assassination) a "George

Bush of the CIA" was briefed "regarding the reaction of anti-Castro Cuban exiles to the assassination of President Kennedy." Among JFK assassination buffs, the most popular theories link the CIA, Texas oilmen, and pissed-off Cubans in a plot to kill the president, all of which intersects perfectly in the personage of Poppy Bush.

After serving four years in the House of Representatives (opposing the 1964 Civil Rights Act and strongly supporting the Vietnam War his son evaded), he lost in a second failed run for the Senate to Lloyd Bentsen. He was then appointed by Nixon as U.N. Ambassador (a bugaboo of the John Bircher set), and then, significantly, Republican National Committee Chairman throughout the Watergate scandal. The Watergate burglary, curiously, was done by a team of CIA operatives and anti-Castro Cubans, and Nixon was heard on his tapes worrying that the scandal could expose "the whole Bay of Pigs thing"—which White House aide H.R. Haldeman believed was code for the JFK assassination.

After Nixon resigned (at Bush's urging), he became the Envoy to Communist China, once again endearing him to the John Birchers. In 1976, he was appointed head of the CIA, at a time of congressional revelations of Agency-sanctioned assassinations, political coups, and creepy drug-induced mind-control operations. In his only officially acknowledged time of employment by the Agency, the senior Bush, thanks to his affable personality, was able to ease the intelligence agency out of the political jam with smiles and stonewalling.

During the Carter years, Bush was a Board Director of the pharmaceutical giant Eli Lilly. The Quayle family had a controlling interest in the pill titan, which perhaps explains Bush's appointment of the man almost as dumb as his son to a position one heartbeat away from leadership of the free world.

In 1980, Poppy was selected by Ronald Reagan to be his running mate, although Ronnie distrusted him, believing him to be an Ivy League wimp. (Score one for the Gipper.) Their victory over Jimmy Carter was suspected to have been ensured by "the October Surprise," a secret deal between representatives of the Reagan camp and members of the Khomeini government to shut off negotiations to free 52 U.S. hostages in Iran until after the election. Though the October Surprise theory has been mocked in the mainstream press, in 1995 journalist Robert Parry uncovered formerly classified Russian documents that backed up the claims and gave strong evidence that Bush himself was directly involved in the treasonous deal.

On March 30, 1981, George H.W. Bush almost achieved a feat his son would later succeed at: becoming president of the United States without winning an election. Ronald Reagan was shot by John Hinkley, Jr. and nearly died. The father of the assassin was a Texas oilman and close personal friend of George H.W. Bush. The same day Reagan was shot, Neil Bush had a dinner date with the would-be-assassin's brother, although it was cancelled when it was deemed inappropriate (much like being a bin Laden family business partner after 9/11).

Though Reagan survived, he never fully recovered, and remained a smiling figurehead of the push for the class-warfare-based Reaganomics. Meanwhile, Bush became a major player in White House-led covert operations. Chief among these, of course, was Iran-Contra, a plot that involved arming the Iranian government and the Nicaraguan Contra terrorists and sucking in a lot of cocaine profits. Despite his lame insistence that he was "out of the loop," all evidence and common sense suggest otherwise.

Despite the Wimp Factor, Bush managed to defeat a tank-driving Michael Dukakis (aided by the notorious Willie Horton ads and his "read my lips" pledge of no new taxes) in the 1988 election to become the United States' 41st President. Although he promised a "kinder, gentler nation," he quickly moved the already insane and failed "War on Drugs" into overdrive, attacking civil liberties and property rights in the process.

This didn't stop him from continuing to do business with Panama's Manuel Noriega. Stansfield Turner, who would replace Bush as CIA head in 1977, declared: "We all know that Bush met with Noriega, even though he was there only 11 months. And I will affirm that Bush had him on the payroll." Though Turner claims to have stopped sending checks to Noriega, after Reagan defeated Carter, Bush personally "met with Noriega and put him back on the payroll" of the CIA. The dealings between Bush, the CIA, and Noriega eventually turned sour, however, as Manuel's narco-baron made him a political liability. During the first Bush I years, Noriega was forcefully removed in a brutal attack on a sovereign nation with no sanction or support from the international community. In disregard for the Panamanian people, little money was put into the country to rebuild what the U.S. destroyed, and the hand-picked replacements for Noriega were as dirty with drug dollars as the pineapple-faced strongman.

Still, Bush later became incredibly popular at the height of the Gulf War, which followed an invasion of Kuwait okayed by April Glaspie, U.S. Ambassador to Iraq. When asked about Hussein's desire to invade Kuwait, Glaspie declared, "We have no opinion on your Arab-Arab conflicts, such as your dispute with Kuwait. Secretary Baker has directed me to emphasize the instruction first given to Iraq in the 1960s, that the Kuwait issue is not associated with America." At the peak of his popularity, Bush would creepily allude to the formation of a "New World Order," a phrase commonly invoked by would-be Illuminati throughout history.

Unfortunately for George, like his son, his immense popularity was brief, as a failing economy, weighted by an immense business scandal (the S&L meltdown) and a ballooning debt, undermined it. His only plan to deal with the gloomy economy? Tax breaks for the rich. American voters rightfully dumped him, thus giving hope that history can repeat.

Still, give Poppy Bush some credit. After all, in his book *A World Transformed*, he explained why he didn't "finish off Saddam" in 1991:

> Trying to eliminate Saddam, extending the ground war into an occupation of Iraq, would have violated our guideline about not changing objectives in midstream, engaging in "mission creep," and would have incurred incalculable human and political costs. Apprehending him was probably impossible. We had been unable to find Noriega in Panama, which we knew intimately. We would have been forced to occupy Baghdad and, in effect, rule Iraq. The coalition would instantly have collapsed, the Arabs deserting it in anger and other allies pulling out as well. Under the circumstances, there was no viable "exit strategy" we could see, violating another of our principles. Furthermore, we had been self-consciously trying to set a pattern for handling aggression in the post-Cold War world. Going in and occupying Iraq, thus unilaterally exceeding the United Nations' mandate, would have destroyed the precedent of international response to aggression that we hoped to establish. Had we gone the invasion route, the United States could conceivably still be an occupying power in a bitterly hostile land. It would have been a dramatically different—and perhaps barren—outcome.

Too bad *A World Transformed* wasn't a coloring book. Maybe then his son would've bothered to read his warning.

Sources:

Bainerman, Joel. *Crimes of a President*. New York: Shapolsky Publishers, 1992.

Bush, George, and Scowcroft, Brent. *A World Transformed*. New York: Alfred A. Knopf, 1998.

"George Herbert Walker Bush." *Encyclopedia Americana*, 2000 <http://gi.grolier.com/presidents/ea/bios/41pbush.html>.

Herer, Jack. *The Emperor Wears No Clothes*. Van Nuys, CA: AH HA Publishing, 2000.

Keith, Jim. *Secret and Suppressed: Banned Ideas and Hidden History*. Feral House, 1993.

"Looking Behind the Bushes." *Progressive Review*, 2000 <http://prorev.com/bush.htm>.

Moench, Doug. *The Big Book of Conspiracies*. New York: Paradox Press, 1995.

Parry, Robert. *Trick or Treason: The October Surprise Mystery*. New York: Sheridan Square Press, 1993.

Parry, Robert. *The October Surprise X-Files*. Arlington, VA: The Media Consortium, 1996.

Prouty, Fletcher. *JFK*. New York: Birch Lane Press, 1992.

Sutton, Anthony C. *America's Secret Establishment: An Introduction to the Order of Skull and Bones*. Waterville, OR: TrineDay, 2002.

Tarpley, Webster G., and Chaitkin, Anton. *George Bush: The Unauthorized Biography*. Washington, D.C.: Executive Intelligence Review, 1991.

Vankin, Jonathan. *Conspiracies, Cover-Ups and Crimes*. Lilburn, GA: Illuminet Press, 1996.

Vankin, Jonathan, and Whalen, John. *The Seventy Greatest Conspiracies of All Time: History's Biggest Mysteries, Coverups, and Cabals*. New York: Citadel Trade, 1998.

42

→ HIS GRANDDADDY:
HITLER'S AMERICAN BANKER

With GHW as his pappy and Neil as his brother, it would take a lot for Shrub to have a more loathsome relative. Still, there is a pretty good argument for his grandpa Prescott being the most despicable of all.

By most news accounts, Prescott Bush was a respected member of the American establishment. The truth in this statement is an indictment of the entire political elite in both the rise of Nazi Germany and the cover-up of U.S. business complicity afterwards.

In October 1942 (ten months after the U.S. entered WWII), the U.S. government seized all 4,000 shares of stock for the Union Banking Corporation. According to U.S. authorities, the set of shares was "held for the benefit of . . . members of the Thyssen family, [and] is property of nationals . . . of a designated enemy country . . ."

The "designated enemy country" referred to here is Hitler's Germany. Indeed, three directors of the UBC were Nazi officers Prescott Bush and three of his business associates owned the rest of the stock. UBC was a front organization for Fritz Thyssen, the German industrialist and primary financier for the Nazi movement. The UBC was formed in 1924 by W.A. Harriman & Co. to funnel capital into Germany during the 1920s–1930s. U.S. investigators stated that "the Union Banking Corporation has since its inception handled funds chiefly supplied to it through the Dutch bank by the Thyssen interests for American investment." In no small way, then, did UBC help finance the rise of the Third Reich.

The President and CEO of W.A. Harriman was George Herbert Walker, Prescott Bush's father-in-law and the namesake of both Poppy Bush and Shrub. The controlling co-owners of the corporation were W. Averell Harriman (hence the company's name) and his brother E. Roland, who went by the nickname "Bunny." Bunny and Prescott were both class of 1917 members of the Yale Skull and Bones. Prescott got on board in 1926 as VP of Harriman, which would later merge with the Brown Brothers investment house to become Brown Brothers Harriman.

Some writers have pooh-poohed the connections between Prescott Bush and the Nazis, pointing out that, of the 4,000 shares of UBC, only one was owned by Prescott. While that is true, it is only half of the story. First, besides his solitary share, Prescott was a UBC board director. Second, and perhaps more important, 3,991 shares were owned by Bunny Harriman, whose personal investments were managed by Prescott. As Bunny's investment manager, then, Bush controlled 99.8% of UBC stock. Besides all this, in October and November 1942, three other Nazi front organizations that the Bush-Harriman team ran were seized under the Trading with the Enemy Act.

Rather than confront these disturbing facts, many mainstream apologists have chosen to attack the messenger instead. The attacks have been aided by the fact that much of the exposure of Bush family ties to the Nazis has come from an unauthorized biography of George Bush senior written by Webster G. Tarpley and Anton Chaitkin and published by the Lyndon LaRouche organization. Still, whatever the merits of the LaRouche organization (a curious mixture of left- and right-wing fringe thought, laced with homophobia and anti-drug mania), the book itself relies on solid and sourced research.

To be fair, Brown Brothers Harriman was hardly alone in aligning with Nazi Germany. Among others, Standard Oil, GM, and Ford had close ties to Germany during Hitler's rise and reign. This hardly excuses the Harriman banking firm for its misdeeds. Nor can its business ties to the Nazis be excused as apolitical business transactions; indeed, considering the popularity of racist eugenics philosophies among Prescott and his crowd, as well as their opposition to Marxism, the work done for the rise of the Nazi cause could be called not so much a marriage of convenience as a merging of private and philosophical concerns.

In 1952, Prescott Bush was elected Senator in Connecticut, where he served until 1963. His ties to Nazi Germany were never raised as a campaign issue.

Sources:

Adams, Cecil. "Was President Bush's Great-grandfather a Nazi?" *The Straight Dope*, 14 February 2003 ‹http://www.straightdope.com/columns/030214.html›.

Ash, Marc. "Standing on the Dead." *Truthout*, 22 January 2003
‹http://www.truthout.org/docs_02/012303A.ma.dead.htm›.

Buchanan, John. "Bush-Nazi Link Confirmed." *The New Hampshire Gazette*, 10 October
2003 ‹http://www.nhgazette.com/cgi-bin/NHGstore.cgi?user_action=detail&catalogno=NN_
Bush_Nazi%20Link›.

Higham, Charles. *Trading With The Enemy*. New York: Delacorte Press, 1983.

Loftus, John, and Aarons, Mark. *The Secret War Against the Jews*. New York: St.
Martin's Press, 1994.

Salant, Jonathon D. "Bush Ancestor's Bank Seized by Gov't." *Truthout*, 17 October
2003 ‹http://www.truthout.org/docs_03/101903l.shtml›.

Sutton, Anthony C. *America's Secret Establishment: An Introduction to the Order of
Skull and Bones*. Waterville, OR: TrineDay, 2002.

Tarpley, Webster G. and Chaitkin, Anton. *George Bush: The Unauthorized Biography*.
Washington, D.C.: Executive Intelligence Review, 1991.

Rogers, Toby. "Heir to the Holocaust." John Loftus, 2003
‹http://www.john-loftus.com/Thyssen.asp›.

43

➡ TOTAL INFORMATION AWARENESS

One of the favorites of old-time conspiracy theories (along with ones about the JFK assassination and Roswell) has been that of a coming New World Order. The vision combines the worst of *1984* with creepy occultism, picturing a police state run by an omnipotent secretive cabal. At their worst, NWO plots are ludicrous fictions only a crackpot could take seriously.

That is, until now. In 2002, DARPA (Defense Advanced Research Projects Agency) released on its website information about a secretive project known as "Total Information Awareness" (TIA). TIA is a $200-million-per-year project described by its head as a way to "break down the stovepipes" between commercial and government databases, combing and combining records of citizens' credit card purchases, travel itineraries, telephone calls, email, medical histories, and finances. The logo for TIA (which appeared on, but was then removed from, the agency's website) depicts a globe with a pyramid behind it, topped with the Eye of Horus, shining a ray of light over the entire globe. At the bottom is the Latin slogan "Scientia Est Potentia" ("Knowledge Is Power").

It would've been easy to dismiss TIA as an Internet prank. Indeed, had it been exposed on any other website, it would've been dismissed as a paranoid delusion. But this was DARPA's own website promoting the Orwellian wet dream.

Even worse, the head of the sinister project was John Poindexter, the former National Security Advisor under Ronald Reagan who was convicted of five felony counts of lying to Congress during the Iran-Contra affair. ("Tia" is Spanish for aunt, inspiring Jeff Elkins of LewRockwell.com to refer to him as "The Man from Auntie.") While he was on the Reagan team, the National Security Council came up with the modest proposal known as REX-84, a nifty plan of the patriot Ollie North for using a state of national emergency to lock up political dissidents (up to 400,000) in concentration camps.

(Curiously, Poindexter, like North, was spared jail time by an appellate court's overturning of his convictions, with a ruling that he was indicted with the help of Iran-Contra testimony he gave under immunity. The soft-on-crime liberal judges who made that ruling included David Sentelle, who had been an aide to the ultra-right-wing former North Carolina Senator Jesse Helms, and Laurence Silberman, a right-wing Reagan appointee. These men later appointed the conflict-of-interest-plagued Ken Starr as an "independent" prosecutor of Bill Clinton. Silberman would later order Secret Service agents to testify in the Starr investigation, a violation of all historical precedents involving a group whose job is to protect the president, not spy on him during blowjobs.)

The good news: a backlash did develop against TIA. Matt Smith of the *SF Weekly* posted private information on Poindexter (who lives with his wife, Linda, at 10 Barrington Fare, in Rockville, Maryland) that he had gathered to point out the sinister side of government collecting information on individuals. Further, many conservatives spoke out vehemently against the program (including members of the Cato Institute and the free market advocates at LewRockwell.com). TIA was shut down, and DARPA removed the information from the website. However, as George Paine of warblogging.com put it, "Government efforts towards total information awareness are not over—only Total Information Awareness is over."

TIA did not develop out of thin air; it aims at a goal of surveillance dear to the Bush Team. With impressive intellectual agility, they argue for less privacy for the average American and ever more executive secrecy for themselves.

Sources:

Elkins, Jeff. "The Man From Auntie." LewRockwell.com, 19 November 2002 ‹http://www.lewrockwell.com/elkins/elkins72.html›.

Healy, Gene. "Beware of Total Information Awareness." The Cato Institute, 20 January 2003 ‹http://www.cato.org/dailys/01-20-03.html›.

Kick, Russ. "Information Awareness Office Website Deletes Its Logo." *The Memory Hole*, 18 Dec 2002 ‹http://www.thememoryhole.org/policestate/iao-logo.htm›.

Paine, George. "Total Information Awareness: Dead." Warblogging.com, 26 September 2003 ‹http://www.warblogging.com/archives/000738.php›.

Reynolds, Diana. "The Rise of the National Security State: FEMA and the NSC." *The Public Eye*, 1997 ‹http://www.publiceye.org/liberty/fema/Fema_1.htm›.

Smith, Matt. "Calling All Yahoos." *SF Weekly*, 27 November 2002 ‹http://sfweekly.com/issues/2002-11-27/smith.html/1/index.html›.

→ BET ON TERRORISM
FOR FUN AND PROFIT!

Granted, Total Information Awareness would be hard project to out-creep. Still, another proposed DARPA plan comes close enough to deserve honorable mention.

In July 2003, the Pentagon revealed another brilliant idea from the geniuses at DARPA, this time an online futures-trading market in which anonymous speculators could bet on forecasting terrorist attacks, assassinations, coups, and other political calamities. The DOD rationalized, "Research indicates that markets are extremely efficient, effective, and timely aggregators of dispersed and even hidden information. Futures markets have proven themselves to be good at predicting such things as elections results; they are often better than expert opinions."

Others weren't so thrilled. Senator Byron L. Dorgan of North Dakota asked, "Can you imagine if another country set up a betting parlor so that people could go in—and is sponsored by the government itself—people could go in and bet on the assassination of an American political figure?" Further, the morbid aspect of profit from tragedy disturbed many observers. As the Pentagon's own website boasted, "Involvement in this group prediction process should prove engaging and may prove profitable." Even worse, it seemed likely that terrorists themselves could participate in the scheme, because the traders' identities would be unknown. (Apparently, the Bush Team is more concerned with what the average American rents from Blockbuster than what wealthy insiders know about potential terrorist activity.) In conclusion, a letter by Dorgan and Senator Ron Wyden of Oregon stated, "The American people want the federal government to use its resources enhancing our security, not gambling on it."

In face of the swift and widespread criticism, Paul Wolfowitz would soon announce that the project would be terminated. As

Wolfowitz would explain with understatement, "It sounds like maybe they got too imaginative in this area."

The head of the program, incidentally, was John Poindexter again. After leading the two greatest flubs in DARPA's history in less than a year, Poindexter resigned from his post at the Pentagon, to which he had been appointed by George W. Bush.

Sources:

Courson, Paul, and Turnham, Steve. "Amid Furor, Pentagon Kills Terrorism Futures Market." CNN, 30 July 2003 ‹http://www.cnn.com/2003/ALLPOLITICS/07/29/terror.market›.

Hulse, Carl. "Pentagon Prepares a Futures Market on Terror Attacks." *The New York Times*, 28 July 2003 ‹http://www.nytimes.com/2003/07/29/politics/29TERR.html?ex=1069477200&en= 8388030111243007&ei=5070›.

Lindorff, David. "Poindexter the Terror Bookie." *CounterPunch*, 30 July 2003 ‹http://www.counterpunch.org/lindorff07302003.html›.

Phillips, Peter, & Project Censored. *Censored 2003*. New York: Seven Stories Press, 2002.

"Poindexter to Resign in Wake of Terror Market Flap." *USA Today*, 1 August 2003 ‹http://www.usatoday.com/news/washington/2003-07-31-poindexter_x.htm›.

"Policy Analysis Market—PAM." *Cryptome*, 30 July 2003 ‹http://cryptome.org/pam/pam-site.htm›.

45

➤ DUBYA'S USA: INTERNATIONAL PARIAH

If the bounce that Bush received after 9/11 improved his prospects in the U.S., internationally it was an astounding boon. Before September 11, U.S. relations with the world were certainly worsening. Mainly because of Shrub's Kyoto Protocol pullout and push for a renewed Star Wars program, the U.S. was kicked off the U.N. Human Rights Commission (of which it had been a founding member since 1946) and the International Narcotics Control Board in May 2001. This was an international message that Dubya's contemptuous style of foreign relations was not well received.

All this changed immediately after 9/11. The worldwide sympathy for the U.S. was unprecedented, and perhaps best exemplified by the *Le Monde* front-page headline on September 12, "We Are All Americans."

Osama's atrocities had given the U.S. an international blank check of goodwill, redeemable even in France. Bush and company wasted it on the equivalent of a coked and boozy gambling weekend in Vegas. And the American public didn't even get any free shrimp cocktails.

In the rush to bomb Iraq, an inept attempt was made to sell the world on the invasion. (Inept, but not half-assed: besides immense bribes and bullying to get nations on the U.N. Security Council to approve, a dirty-tricks campaign was uncovered by the *UK Observer*, which detailed plans by the NSA to bug the homes and offices of U.N. delegates.) When the modest Iraq proposal fell apart, unable either to get the minimum number of votes needed or to talk France or Russia out of their proposed vetoes, Shrub petulantly declared that he didn't need the U.N.'s approval in the first place, and the quiche-eating French became the scapegoats for the U.S. diplomatic failure.

Faced with a deepening quagmire in Iraq, Bush spoke before the U.N. on September 23, 2003, trying to sound defiant when he should have been pleading for help. In essence, the U.S. proposal was for other nations to supply troops and money for the Iraq war they had opposed and warned the U.S. not to launch, in exchange for nothing. After all, Dubya still wanted to control the entire occupation, including (most importantly) the giant contracts to be doled out afterward. The rest of the world said "no."

All of this makes one almost feel sorry for Colin Powell, the solitary figure in the Bush Team to show anything resembling decency since their illegal occupation of D.C. Powell, a top-notch diplomat, has continuously seen his skills wasted and his efforts undermined by the arrogance of his associates. Snide comments (such as Donald Rumsfeld referring to France and Germany as "Old Europe") have pointlessly alienated even previously avowed allies of the U.S.

Indeed, to even call the blunders in foreign policy a diplomatic failure would degrade the term "diplomatic." Nothing in the Bush Team's contemptuousness toward world statesmen and indifference to world opinion amounts to diplomacy.

Now, the chickens are coming home to roost. An expensive campaign wages on in Iraq. Peace in the Middle East seems an ever more distant dream, with little hope of the Arab world trusting the U.S. to be an honest broker. There seems little hope for improvement in the U.S.'s world standing until the little boy posing as Emperor is replaced.

Sources:

Bright, Martin, Vulliamy, Ed, and Beaumont, Peter. "Revealed: U.S. Dirty Tricks to Win Vote on Iraq War." *The Observer*, 2 March 2003
‹http://observer.guardian.co.uk/iraq/story/0,12239,905936,00.html›.

Colombani, Jean-Marie. "We Are All Americans." *World Press Review*, November 2001
‹http://www.worldpress.org/1101we_are_all_americans.htm›.

Conason, Joe. "Bush League." *Salon*, 8 May 2001
‹http://dir.salon.com/news/col/cona/2001/05/08/commission/index.html›.

Hohenadel, Kristin. "Formez Vos Bataillons!" *Salon*, 28 September 2001
‹http://dir.salon.com/people/feature/2001/09/28/france/index.html›.

Kaplan, Fred. "Bush to World: Drop Dead!" *Slate*, 23 September 2003
‹http://slate.msn.com/id/2088799›.

"Rumsfeld: France, Germany Are 'Problems' in Iraqi Conflict." CNN, 23 January 2003
‹http://www.cnn.com/2003/WORLD/meast/01/22/sprj.irq.wrap›.

Shalom, Stephen R. "Iraq War Quiz." *Truthout*, 1 April 2003
‹http://www.truthout.org/docs_03/040103H.shtml›.

Tran, Mark. "Finding a Way to Rebuke the U.S." *The Guardian Unlimited*, 4 May 2001
‹http://www.guardian.co.uk/bush/story/0,7369,485946,00.html›.

46

➤ NORTH KOREA

Israelis and their Middle East neighbors have been killing each other since the Jewish homeland was founded. India and Pakistan's feud isn't new, either. Behind the smiles at even the stillest of peacetimes, Europe, Russia, and China have waged a covert war with the U.S. over the control of world resources. And while the failed coup of Venezuela by a not-so-secretly U.S.-backed junta was embarrassing, it is not the worst example of American interference in Latin American politics. To cite any of these as examples of Shrub's policy failures would be unfair. With North Korea, however, the Bush Team has made grave diplomatic errors that invite disaster on a world-historical scale.

It didn't have to happen this way. That North Korean leader Kim Jong Il is a brutal dictator of dubious sanity, few would dispute. What is in dispute is how to deal with a North Korean state under his reign. That's what diplomacy is about: working for the best state of affairs available given the political constraints of the situation and personalities of those empowered to negotiate and decide.

One man who seemed to understand this was South Korean President Kim Dae Jung, whose efforts in dealing with his neighbor earned him a Nobel Peace Prize in October 2000. His goal of an eventual reunification of the Koreas seemed ambitious but not unattainable at the end of the Clinton years: North Korea, desperate for economic growth, could have been absorbed in a bloodless revolution much like the fall of the Soviet Union. Aiding this goal was the Clinton administration, which struck a smart deal to supply heavy fuel shipments and two light-water reactors to North Korea for ending its nuclear program. Far cheaper than a Korean crisis, the Clinton plan provided relief for an impoverished society in exchange for better international security.

All this began to change on March 7, 2001, when Bush, during a meeting with Jung, alleged that North Korea wasn't keeping to its agreement. "We look forward to at some point in the future having a dialogue with the North Koreans but . . . any negotiation would require complete verification. Part of the problem in dealing with North Korea is there's not very much transparency. We're not certain as to whether or not they're keeping all terms of all agreements." Dubya was unable to cite any grounds for suspicion, but the shift had started.

Hostility between the U.S. and North Korea increased that month, when North Korea accused the U.S. of fabricating missile threats from their nation to promote the Star Wars defense program. The North Korean state-run media declared, "If they continue to provoke military confrontation with North Korea—following this path to war—we will have no option but to respond with firm resolve." Much of this was cheap talk from a thuggish dictatorship trying to prove it wouldn't be pushed around. Behind the bluster, however, was a legitimate beef: the Bush Team appeared (in a suspicious precursor to the Iraqi WMD hysteria) to be pushing unsubstantiated claims of North Korean duplicity to boost a defense contractors' boondoggle. North Korea, along with Iraq, was cited as the "rogue nation" against which a missile shield was needed. Thus, the Star Wars plan could rightfully be viewed as a security threat by the North Korean state.

In June 2001, the other shoe dropped. North Korea threatened to restart missile tests if the Bush administration continued its hard-line policies. After completing its policy review, the Bush Team agreed to talk with North Korea, but with the condition that any new agreement must include reduction of North Korea's conventional forces. The following month, the State Department reported that North Korea had conducted tests of a long-range missile.

Shrub and his gang cited this as proof that the North Koreans couldn't be trusted and that Slick Willie had erred in negotiating with the communist regime. In truth, North Korea's actions are predictable results of dealing with a regime trying to undo the bargains made by its predecessor. Indeed, much of the North Korean crisis is the result of an attempt by the Bushistas to deny Clinton credit for his push for peace in the Koreas.

But a stronger motivation than hatred of Bill seems to be the Bush Team's hard-on for Star Wars. In essence, Dubya and his colleagues appeared to be promoting strife in the Koreas to justify the weapon system. Later, bewilderingly, Bush officials told the *New*

York Times that they wouldn't oppose China if it resumed nuclear tests, or—more disturbingly—increased from 20 the number of nuclear weapons capable of hitting the U.S. As one senior official put it, "Why panic? They are modernizing anyway."

On January 29, 2002, Dubya delivered his infamous "axis of evil" speech, citing North Korea, Iran, and Iraq as the greatest threats to world peace. The North Korean media called the speech "little short of declaring war." Reaction was swift: in summer 2002, the CIA concluded that North Korea was secretly pursuing a uranium enrichment program. In October, North Korea admitted to the program but refused to stop it. The next month, the U.S., Japan, and South Korea cut off the fuel shipments. In February 2003, North Korea restarted its nuclear program. Soon after, it tested two short-range missiles, intercepted and harassed a U.S. spy plane, and pulled out of the talks that started at the end of the Korean War. In two years, Bush and his pals had turned a promising détente into a potential nightmare.

How is it all going to end? Well, nuclear weapons are nothing to sneeze at, especially in the hands of a poor and desperate regime with little to lose. Even without nukes, confronting the immense North Korean Army would make Operation Iraqi Freedom look like patty-cake, even disregarding the likelihood that Russia or China would enter any Korean conflict. Of course, there's always a possibility of reconciliation, but with Shrub's track record in Korea, there's little reason to expect one while he remains in the White House.

Sources:

"Bush Talks Tough on North Korea." CNN, 7 March 2001 ‹http://www.cnn.com/2001/WORLD/asiapcf/03/07/korea.usa.meeting›.

Feffer, John and Lee, Karin. "Bush Policies Could Set Back Relations with North Korea." The Progressive Media Project, 29 March 2001 ‹http://www.progressive.org/pmpfm2901.html›.

"Kim's Nuclear Gamble." *Frontline* ‹http://www.pbs.org/wgbh/pages/frontline/shows/kim›.

"N Korea Threatens U.S., Japan Over Missile Shield." CNN, 28 March 2001 ‹http://www.cnn.com/2001/WORLD/asiapcf/east/03/28/nkorea.japan.U.S.›.

Palais, James B. "George W.'s Wrong-headed Approach to Korea." History News Network, 7 February 2003 ‹http://hnn.U.S./articles/1235.html›.

Rothschild, Matthew. "Bush's Nuclear Footsie with China." *The Progressive*, 6 September 2001 ‹http://www.progressive.org/webex/wx090601.html›.

Tapper, Jake. "Did Bush Bungle Relations with North Korea?" *Salon*, 15 March 2001 ‹http://dir.salon.com/politics/feature/2001/03/15/north_korea/index.html?pn=1›.

47

CUTTING THE FORESTS TO SAVE THEM

The Bush Gang loves Orwellian anti-logic. Perhaps the best example of their fuzzy thinking is Bush's ridiculously named "Healthy Forests" initiative.

The "Healthy Forests" plan would allow loggers back on to ten million acres of woods that have been off-limits for three decades. Both the National Environmental Policy Act and the National Forest Management Act would be sawed for the plan. More than 2.5 million acres of federal forests would be logged over a decade, and logging projects affecting less than a thousand acres would no longer need environmental studies.

Shrub claims, unconvincingly, that the initiative aims to protect fire-prone forests. Senator Joe Lieberman of Connecticut sneered that it "should be called the No Tree Left Behind plan."

Bill Meadows of the Wilderness Society warned, "This is part of Bush's irresponsible anti-environmental agenda. The truth is that waiving environmental laws will not protect homes and lives from wildfire." He added, "Wilderness and roadless areas are too valuable to be handed over to the logging industry in the name of 'fuel reduction.'"

Despite widespread opposition from environmental groups, the plan has a good chance of becoming law. It was aided in the summer of 2003 by vast wildfires. In August 2003, Shrub toured an Arizona wildfire site, claiming that his plan would save homes and lives. Never mind that this would hardly solve the problem. As noted by Jeffrey St. Clair in *Counterpunch*, "The last thing a burned over forest needs is an assault by chainsaws, logging roads and skid trails, to haul out the only living trees in a scorched landscape. The evidence has been in for decades. Proof can be found at Mt. St. Helens and Yellowstone Park: unlogged burned forests recover quickly, feeding off the nutrients left behind by dead trees and shrubs. On the other hand, logged over burned forests rarely recover, but persist as biological deserts, prone to mudslides, difficult to revegetate and abandoned by salmon and deep forest birds, such as the spotted owl, goshawk and marbled murrelet." But such logic competes feebly with the emotional punch of seeing Bush at a burned-out site, feigning concern for victims and promoting his absurd solution.

This isn't the first time that Dubya has cynically exploited disaster for political gain.

Sources:

"Bush Unveils 'Healthy Forests' Plan." CNN, 22 August 2002 ‹http://www.cnn.com/2002/ALLPOLITICS/08/22/bush.timber/index.html›.

"Joe Lieberman: On Wilderness Protection." The League of Conservation Voters ‹http://www.lcv.org/Campaigns/Campaigns.cfm?ID=1696&c=4›.

Johnson, Eric. "Bush's War against Nature." *AlterNet*, 18 April 2003 ‹http://www.alternet.org/story.html?StoryID=15672›.

Lindlaw, Scott. "At Wildfire Site, Bush Calls for Thinning." *The Mercury News*, 11 August 2003 ‹http://www.bayarea.com/mld/mercurynews/news/6505885.htm›.

St. Clair, Jeffrey. "Chainsaw George." *CounterPunch*, 24 August 2002 ‹http://www.counterpunch.org/stclair0824.html›.

48

→ HE'S A RECOVERING ALCOHOLIC, DRUNK DRIVER & COKEHEAD

Leader of the Free World is a high-pressure job. It could make mincemeat out of most, and the demands sometime lead to destructive pathological behaviors, such as getting blowjobs from chubby interns. No wonder Poppy Bush kept looking at his watch during his debate with Bill Clinton in 1992: he knew he wasn't up to snuff, and could barely wait to hightail out of there.

Granted, Shrub has been a major slacker during his years of squatting on Pennsylvania Avenue, so he, like Ronald Reagan, may evade the stress fairly well by flying on auto-pilot. But then again. . .

That Georgie was an alcoholic is undisputed. He himself owns up to everything but the label, claiming that he couldn't remember a day he didn't have a drink during one period. As *Newsweek* put it, Bush "went to Yale but seems to have majored in drinking at the Deke House." For over 20 years of his life he drank heavily.

On at least one occasion, Dubya's drunkenness turned potentially deadly. On September 4, 1976, state troopers in Kennebunkport, Maine saw his car swerve onto the shoulder of the road. He was pulled over and failed an alcohol test. Shrub pleaded guilty, was fined, and had his license suspended. He didn't own up to his drunk-driving conviction until a Maine television station uncovered it. While admitting to the crime, he alluded to the timing of the revelation (just days before the 2000 election) and whined that it was part of some liberal conspiracy against him. The station that uncovered the story was a FOX News affiliate, casting doubt on this theory.

There may have been other drunk-driving escapades in Texas. When he became governor, a new driver's license with a new ID number was issued him, an action that destroyed the records of his previous license. What offenses may have besmirched those records is anyone's guess, but a safe bet would be at least one DUI. Bush would only need two DUIs to match the total of his 2000 VP pick Dick Cheney. (These guys know how to party.)

Driving drunk is only part of his pathological past: three independent sources confirmed to author J.H. Hatfield that Shrub was arrested in 1972 for possession of cocaine. He avoided jail or formal charges through a community service program, working for troubled inner city youths in Houston. A judge friendly to the Bush family expunged the record as a favor. (According to Bill Minutaglio's *First Son*, the community service deal was arranged by his daddy as well.) The coke rap would certainly explain his sudden desire to do charity work, which he had never done before and has not done since.

Alas, the cocaine charges were never investigated further, in part because of the fishy history of Hatfield, the man who uncovered them. Hatfield was once convicted of attempted murder for hiring a hit-man to kill a former boss. Like Bush, Hatfield lied and covered up his shady past. When this was revealed, St. Martin's Press, the original publisher of *Fortunate Son*, recalled the biography and burned all the printed copies. Soft Skull Press later published the book, but the damage had been done, to the story (which has yet to be debunked) and to Hatfield (who died in 2001 of a drug overdose suicide after his life went into a tailspin following the book-burning). For the record, Bush will only insist that he hasn't taken any illegal drugs since 1974, while he leads an extremely harsh anti-drug campaign that imprisons youth less well-connected than he was.

Dubya claims that he gave up drinking after his 40th birthday. While that may be true, it would be evidence of unusual self-discipline, something that Bush hasn't shown otherwise. But whether or not Bush really quit cold turkey, as the saying goes, once an alcoholic, always an alcoholic. A malady known as Dry Drunk Syndrome is often manifested by persons who formerly abused alcohol, a predictable pattern of compensation for the loss of getting blitzed as an outlet. Among the traits of a dry drunk: exaggerated self-importance and pomposity, grandiose behavior, a rigid, judgmental outlook, impatience, childish and irresponsible behavior, illogical rationalization, projection, and overreaction. In Bush's case, the diagnosis is clear.

Sources:

"A Bush Family Book Burning." *The Consortium*, 17 November 1999 <http://www.consortiumnews.com/1999/111799a.html>.

Crowly, Candy. "Bush Acknowledges 1976 DUI Charge." CNN, 2 November 2000 <http://www.cnn.com/2000/ALLPOLITICS/stories/11/02/bush.dui>.

"George Bush's Arrest Record." *The Smoking Gun*, 3 November 2000 <http://www.thesmokinggun.com/archive/bushdui1.html>.

"Bush Jr.'s Skeleton Closet." *Skeleton Closet* <http://www.realchange.org/bushjr.htm>.

Hamod, Sam, and Cassel, Elaine. "G.W. Bush: Drunk on Power." *CounterPunch*, 9 May 2003 <http://www.counterpunch.org/hamod05092003.html>.

Hatfield, J.H. *Fortunate Son: George W. Bush and the Making of an American President.* Brooklyn: Soft Skull Press, 2001.

Kranish, Michael. "Bush Denies Allegation of '72 Drug Arrest in Book. *The Boston Globe*, 20 October 1999: A1).

Minutaglio, Bill. *First Son: George W. Bush and the Bush Family Dynasty.* New York: Crown, 1999.

Thomas, Evan. "The Sons Also Rise." *Newsweek*, 16 November 1998: 44–48.

Van Wormer, Katherine. "Addiction, Brain Damage and the President." *CounterPunch*, 11 October 2002 <http://www.counterpunch.org/wormer1011.html>.

49

HE'S PRO-LIFE:
WHEN THE BABY ISN'T HIS

Few topics divide the American public as abortion does. While the public is now leaning strongly in favor of women's right to abort, emotional and sometimes violent disagreement continues. Getting the American public to agree on anything about abortion is difficult. One thing, however, would elicit unanimity from people of all stripes: the corruptness of a politician who vocally opposes abortions but secretly arranges one. Depending on your view of abortion, such a hypocrite would be either an enemy of basic individual liberties or a murderer of babies.

On October 20, 2000, *Hustler* publisher Larry Flynt declared on CNN's *Crossfire* that the anti-abortion Dubya had knocked up a girlfriend in the early '70s and then arranged for her to get an abortion in a Houston hospital. This all took place before *Roe v. Wade* made abortion legal. Flynt claims to have four affidavits from girlfriends of the woman, and claims to know the name of the doctor who performed the procedure. The only thing holding Flynt back from disclosing these names, he insists, is that the patient herself is unwilling to go forward.

CNN, apparently concerned over the reliability of the claim, took the transcript of the charge and the video of the program off its website within 48 hours of the broadcast.

Is there any truth to Flynt's assertion? By Shrub insiders' own accounts, he has a checkered history. When Bush hired a private dick to investigate his past for dirt (apparently to anticipate anything the Democrats could dig up on him), he wasn't too happy with the outcome, though the details have remained under wraps. (One Bush confidant did insist, superfluously, that the PI found "no handcuffs or dwarf orgies.")

Although the mainstream media dropped the story like a hot potato, Jackson Thoreau (author of the book, *We Will Not Get Over It*) dug in. He apparently came away with information that

Bush impregnated four women other than his wife and arranged abortions for all. One was sent out of the U.S. to get it done, and another was under the age of 18.

Thoreau's claims of multiple abortions aside, Larry Flynt has a good track record of backing up his sensationalistic claims. And the picture he paints is believable in light of other better documented tales of Bush: a smirking boy who thinks he is above the very laws he pushes upon and preaches to others. After all, Bush claims to be "pro-life" and supports a "Human Life Amendment" to the Constitution to rescind the freedoms created by *Roe v. Wade*. He also signed 18 anti-abortion laws as Texas governor, appointed anti-choice judges to U.S. courts, and claims that his favorite Supreme Court judges are Antonin Scalia and Clarence Thomas, who, besides helping rig his election, strongly oppose abortion rights. Such political positions and personal practices are entirely out of whack, unless we assume that Bush's political stance is a cynical lie to cater to the religious fundamentalist right. But then, what does he care? Wealthy and connected men like himself can always arrange an abortion, no matter what the law is.

Sources:

"Bush Jr.'s Skeleton Closet." *Skeleton Closet* <http://www.realchange.org/bushjr.htm>.

"Desperate Measures: George W. Bush & Abortion." *Bartcop* <http://www.bartcop.com/bushabortion.htm>.

Elliot, Jeff. "The Unexamined Man." *Albion Monitor*, 8 November 2000 <http://www.monitor.net/monitor/0011a/election2000.html>.

Thoreau, Jackson. "Bush Hypocritically Pushes Anti-Abortion Agenda." *Democracy Means You*, 1 August 2003 <http://www.democracymeansyou.com/columns/thoreau/8-1-03-abortion.htm>.

"Was George W. Bush 'Involved' in an Illegal Abortion??" Democrats.com <http://democrats.com/display.cfm?id=159>.

50

→ KARL ROVE

Last but not least comes the only man arguably owed as much for Shrub's ludicrous but dangerous political career as his daddy, Karl Rove, the man best described as "Bush's Brain." (Somebody has to fill that void.)

While Bush likes to feign being a "shoot-from-the-hip" kind of guy, this is disproved by former insiders' accounts. For example, John Dilulio, a former Bush advisor and director of the Office of Faith Based and Community Initiatives, told *Esquire*: "There is no precedent in any modern White House for what is going on in this one: a complete lack of a policy apparatus. What you've got is everything—and I mean everything—being run by the political arm."

Dilulio describes Rove and his minions as the "Mayberry Machiavellis," unscrupulous architects of simplistic policies. Politics in the Bush White House is a game of cynical reductionism and demagoguery.

Part of the game is hardball, an area of expertise of Karl Rove. The crude smearing of John McCain during the 2000 GOP primaries was his project. And whether or not Rove leaked to the press that Joseph Wilson's wife was a CIA agent, he did call other journalists afterwards to declare her "fair game." Of course, Rove may have become (like Bush) power-drunk from his success. His gloating smile from the pages of *Esquire* and *Time* seems to exceed even Shrub's in smugness. Unfortunately for him, he may have taken his scheming too far: besides his involvement in Leakgate, Rove's plotting appears to be all over the backfired "Mission Accomplished" stunt by Top Gun Bush.

The last test for Rove's shameless ploys before the 2004 election will come in September 2004, during the GOP convention. The convention will take place in New York City, later than usual. The September 2 date for the last day of the convention comes strategically near the third anniversary of 9/11. With the powerful memories of the day still in people's minds, Bush will be there wearing that shit-eating smirk as the Republicans lay claim to God and country. That's not the only thing they'll be claiming: New York Governor George Pataki has arranged for the laying of the cornerstone of reconstruction at ground zero to occur during the GOP Convention. In the *New York Times*, Rove could barely conceal his glee at the plan, which he described as a "checkmate result."

In *New York Magazine*, Michael Tomasky wrote, with rightful outrage, "you might think that someone in the media would step in and say, just for the record, and just in case they are considering it, what everyone who gave the matter two seconds' thought was thinking—namely, what an unimaginably offensive idea this is. Picture it. During the most political event American politics has to offer, a quadrennial nominating convention, the assembled honchos trudge down to ground zero and perform their ceremony. . . An event like this would make every person who died on the site a martyr—to a reelection campaign. If that's not politicizing 9/11, there is no such thing."

Of course, it has become clear that Bush, Rove, and the rest of the gang of White House thieves are not above such things. The only question left is how the American public will respond.

Sources:

Allen, Mike. "Ex-Official Blasts White House." *The Washington Post*, 2 December 2002: A07.

Clines, Francis X. "Karl Rove's Campaign Strategy: It's the Terror, Stupid." *Common Dreams*, 10 May 2003 ‹http://www.commondreams.org/views03/0510-03.htm›.

Dubose, Lou, Reid, Jan, and Cannon, Carl M. *Boy Genius: Karl Rove, the Brains behind the Remarkable Political Triumph of George W. Bush*. New York: PublicAffairs, 2003.

Meyerson, Harold. "The Cult of Karl." *The American Prospect*, 30 December 2002 ‹http://www.prospect.org/print/V13/23/meyerson-h.html›.

Moore, James, and Slater, Wayne. *Bush's Brain: How Karl Rove Made George W. Bush Presidential*. Hoboken, NJ: John Wiley & Sons, Inc., 2003.

Suskind, Ron. "Why Are These Men Laughing?" RonSuskind.com, January 2003 ‹http://www.ronsuskind.com/writing/esquire/esq_rove_0103.html›.

Tapper, Jake. "The Brains Behind Bush." *Salon*, 21 January 2003 ‹http://www.salon.com/books/feature/2003/01/21/rove›.

Tomasky, Michael. "Anything Goes." *New York Magazine*, 14 July 2003 ‹http://www.newyorkmetro.com/nymetro/news/politics/columns/citypolitic/n_8937/›.

→ AFTERWORD

This book had a December 2003 deadline and was limited to 50 reasons to make timely publication possible. A couple of developments since the list was completed are worth commenting on.

First, as the mainstream media repeatedly intoned, "We Got Him!" Saddam Hussein, of course, has a history of loathsome behavior and will not be missed by the Iraqi people. But his capture doesn't make things any safer for the American people, as is proven by elevated terror alert levels before Christmas in 2003. The flag-waving after the Saddam capture made good theater, a distraction from the deaths of hundreds of American soldiers and the waste of billions of dollars on a mission falsely sold to the American people as part of the war against terror.

The second important development is the supposedly booming economy, which grew by 8.2% during the third quarter. Astute observers rightfully shrug and ask: "So what?" 8.2% growth doesn't seem impressive (or sustainable) following record federal budget deficits and rates of job losses unseen since the Great Depression. Which leads to a pressing question about the "recovery": where are the jobs? Even Bush's greatest supporters concede that job growth over 2004 will be by fewer than 200,000 per month—less than the average gain in employment under Bill Clinton over his entire eight years, and not enough to bring job growth to a surplus during Bush's illegitimate regime.

The capture of Saddam and the hollow economic boom are emblematic of Bush's presidency, the stuff of sound bites without substance. In the end, the best symbol of Bush's performance in office may be the inedible, tarted-up fowl he posed with when he visited troops in Iraq on Thanksgiving. Having squandered billions of dollars on tax cuts for the rich and thousands of lives on fraudulent wars, he smilingly offered the camera a bogus turkey. Come November 2004, Americans had better say "no thanks."

—Robert Sterling

WOMEN AND CHILDREN FIRST

→ **LYDIA LUNCH**

Women and children first
Women and children first
Women and children are
The first casualties of War

And the War is never over. . . the War is never ending
The War is just an orgy of blood and guts
Masterminded by testosterone fueled dirty old men
Who in order to pump up that last fading trickle
Of their waning sexuality
Get off on raping the entire fucking planet

War is just menstrual envy. . .
If men bleed every month as much as I do
Please. . . just grant me five minutes alone in the White House. . .
Maybe they wouldn't have such incredible blood lust

Did you ever notice that when you turn on the TV
To get your daily update from the "Cradle of Civilization"
That they never show the women and children
They never show the women and children
Starving to death living on dry grass and sand
Widows and orphans marching to the Border. . . any Border

Did you ever notice that a woman
Has never started a World War
Is that because we're still so busy playing the victim
Or expending so much energy on NOT BECOMING ONE
Waging our own preposterous Battle of the Sexes
That we just don't have the energy to go out
AND BLOW UP THE KILLING FIELDS

Did you ever notice that a woman
Has never STOPPED A WORLD WAR EITHER
Is that because
WE STILL DON'T HAVE ENOUGH AMMUNITION, LADIES?
Maybe we needed to go into Afghanistan and Iraq
AND ARM THE FUCKING WOMEN. . .
Gun drops alongside the rice and Pop Tarts

Hundreds of thousands of young virile men
Their fists raised in the air waving Uzis
Dressed in the spitting image of their Gods
The Gods of War
Simulcast by satellite on the Nightly News
To fear and fawn over

HOLY WAR! HOLY WAR!
BULL FUCKING SHIT!
EVERY WAR IS A HOLY WAR
EVERY WAR IS ABOUT ONE OF THREE THINGS. . .
GOD, LAND, OIL

I think it's time we got rid of God
It's time we got rid of God

GOD GAVE US WAR, THE GODS OF WAR
AND MAN PLAYING GOD WILL DO WHAT GOD HAS DONE
DESTROY, MUTILATE, TERRORIZE, PENALIZE AND PUNISH
THE EARTH

Maybe if we outlawed God
Maybe if we got back to the Goddess
You know what the Goddess said?
You know what Durga said?

DURGA SAID CUT OFF YOUR OWN FUCKING HEAD
DURGA SAID CUT OFF YOUR OWN FUCKING HEAD

You wanna go on a Suicide Mission
THEN BUY A ONE WAY TICKET FOR ONE PERSON
Leave the women out of it

Leave the children out of it
Leave the innocent male civilians out of it

If Bush wanted to "take out" Saddam. . .
Why didn't they just stage a Celebrity Death Match
Mano à Mano. . . one on one. . . Man to Man
Hand to hand combat. . .
Don King could have promoted it. . .
Televised it on Pay Per View at 30 bucks a pop
And wiped out the National Debt in no time
Then Junior would have finally gotten the ass kicking
He should have been given after his third DUI. . .

They call themselves Freedom Fighters
We call ourselves Freedom Fighters
Oh yeah. . . Freedom and Liberty for all
The Good Fight. . . Might Makes Right
Good Cop versus "Evil Doers"
You want Evil?
You want Evil?
Then look no further than
1600 Pennsylvania Avenue
HOW THE HELL DID THEY MISS THAT TARGET ANYWAY???

America is the ULTIMATE Terrorist
We've killed more than eight million civilians
Since World War Two
We're the Bullies of the Planet
Sticking our nose in everybody else's business
BUT ONLY WHEN THERE'S SOMETHING TO GAIN
Which is why we let Milosevic get away with it for so long
Killing tens of thousands of his own People
NO CASH COW HERE
They haven't figured out a way
To turn corpses into fuel yet
But when they do. . . Watch out. . .
The Killing has only just begun.

We pride ourselves on Force Feeding
The rest of the World

The Hypocrisy of Democracy. . .
Preaching Human Rights
While 33 million people in the United States live in abject poverty
32 percent of the U.S. Population
Live hand to mouth, month to month
While working 40 hours a week for six bucks an hour. . .

There are 600,000 people left homeless every night
and that's just a head count of the lucky ones
being warehoused in shelters
200,000 of them in Texas alone
Why do you think Bush left the state. . .
40% of men made homeless have served in the armed forces
risk your life to serve this country
and you just might score a warm bed and a bologna sandwich
down at the Salvation Army

Yeah Freedom and Liberty. . .
If you can afford it
But NOT for the over TWO MILLION PEOPLE
INCARCERATED IN THE UNITED STATES RIGHT NOW

YEAH! WE'RE NUMBER ONE!
NUMBER ONE!
MORE PRISONERS THAN RUSSIA OR CHINA
Most of them on petty Drug Charges

They must assume we're all on drugs!
And so stoned that we'll turn a blind eye
To the fact that the "presidential election" was a hoax
And now we're all forced to suffer the Sins of the Father
The Sins of the Father . . . that Fucker
Who used the CIA to seduce, arm and train Terrorists
Like Noriega, Saddam Hussein, Idi Amin and Bin Laden
Sucking up to them as long as they did our dirty work
Turning the Poppy Fields into the Killing Fields

And Bush. . . being Bush. . .
Was stupid enough to give the Taliban
243 million dollars in 2001

Like paying off the drug pusher
EVER GOT RID OF THE DRUG PROBLEM
EVER ENDED THE DRUG WAR. . .

And what the fuck does that mean?
The Drug War???
Another farce played out behind our backs
Meant to steal a little bit more of our Freedom and Liberty
Shit. . . the billions wasted every year on the "DRUG WAR"
Could ensure that we were all higher than Kingdom Come
Just like W's drunken daughter and junkie niece
Who got ten days added on to her sentence for
Sneaking Crack Cocaine into her Country Club Rehab Center. . .
If she would have been the Average African-American
man, woman or child. . . would have gotten ten years
in State Prison. . . ten fucking days!

You'd think that having an alcoholic, ex-coke freaking father like
Georgie Boy, he'd be a little more lenient. . .
But Ole "W" Daddy Warbucks is not satisfied just punishing
His own sons by locking millions of them up
In their room in the Big House. . .
Three Strikes You're OUT!
Life Without Parole!
A California Initiative!
But his megalomaniacal Father Complex ensures
That he sees fit to torture the sons and daughters
Of families from Cuba to Kuwait
Since the sons of terrorists MUST be terrorists too
And at least there he lives up to his own perverted theory
Because THE GUILTY ARE ALWAYS SUSPICIOUS

The REAL TERRORISTS are the COPS amongst us. . .
The FBI, CIA, SCOTLAND YARD, THE DEA, ATF, WTO
Who are waging REAL WARS EVERY DAY
Against our Freedoms, our Liberties and our Privacy.
Mail is being X-Rayed. . . phones are tapped
The Internet is not secure. . .
There's surveillance cameras in every school, supermarket
Liquor store, bodega, burger joint, bank and coming soon

To every street corner and dash board near you
I don't know about you. . . but they got my date of birth,
Expected date of death, passport #, social security # and
Bank accounts all hooked up to a Central Database. . .

There's Spy Cameras in Outer Space

They've got my DNA on file thanks to my dentist
My medical records are in review thanks to the extortionists
In the American Medical Association who won't drop
Their exorbitant fees in order to assure affordable health care
Because in AMERICON
LIFE IS CHEAP. . . DEATH IS FREE. . .
But if you get sick because the food is genetically modified,
The meat isn't inspected, the air is polluted
The water is contaminated, the chemtrails are proliferating
Cancer is a curse on all of us and the Doctors are crooks. . .
DON'T SAY I DIDN'T WARN YOU

A billion dollars a month to keep 9000 troops in Afghanistan
Rebuilding the infrastructure that we destroyed
While in the Good Ole USA . . . unemployment soars,
Community Health Clinics close, schools collapse,
Welfare is abolished, the minimum wage stagnates
Fear and Panic Run Rampant
The real issues are avoided
AND I'M LOSING MY FUCKING MIND, MAN

Which cannot even configure how many trillions of tax dollars
Are going to be wasted painting the desert red with the blood of
Innocent men, women and children
Because our recently "elected" FASCIST DICTATOR
FEELS THE NEED TO SETTLE A BEEF HIS DADDY DIDN'T
By sending 250,000 troops on a WILD GOOSE CHASE
To Catch a Fox that never sleeps in the same bed twice
AND WE STILL HAVEN'T FOUND BIN LADEN. . .
We were REAL SMART about "SMOKING HIM OUT"

Shit. . . . we can't even find the Vice President!
And never a more appropriate moniker. . .

For that oil grubbing, money laundering invisible racketeer
Whose probably so embarrassed by the Bush Baby's flagrant idiocy
that he's all but disappeared, holed up inside
His manmade underground bunker
Shuffling stocks, buying and trading bonds
And stockpiling so much loot
That he'll be able to buy himself another planet
Once they succeed in blowing this one up. . .
Hell. . . we got 22,369 NUCLEAR WARHEADS in this country alone.

Why should we be worried about North Korea
With their three or four measly bombs???

Yeah yeah yeah. . . little girl BIG MOUTH
AND NOT ENOUGH NUKES OF MY OWN
To make enough noise to rattle
The Deaf Dumb and Blind in D.C.
WHO WON'T EVEN ACKNOWLEDGE THAT WE HAVE ALIENATED
THE ENTIRE REST OF THE WORLD. . .
NO ONE WANTS "IN" ON THE WAR WHORE'S "EVIL" ORGY
THIS PREPOSTEROUS IMPERIALIST BLOOD FOR OIL CHARADE THAT
WILL ASSURE THAT THE TEXAS FUEL BARONS MAKE OUT LIKE
THE BANDITS THEY ARE, AS WE'RE STUCK AT THE EXXON
STATION HOLDING GAS PUMPS IN OUR FISTS LIKE BIG LIMP
DICKS THAT WE PAY OUT THE ASS TO GET PERPETUALLY
FUCKED BY

And PLEASE don't accuse me of being paranoid!
I've been predicting this bullshit for the past two decades
And all my worst premonitions have come true
Like a No-Wave Nostradamus. . .
AND I DON'T HATE MEN
I'm just sick of being gang-raped by the patriarchy
A HOODLUM ELITE
Of greedy, money grubbing, power hungry fuckwads
That never gave a shit about you in the first place
Who LIED, CHEATED AND BULLIED THEIR WAY INTO POSITIONS OF
POWER
BACKSLAPPING THEIR BUTT-BUDDIES ON THE WAY UP TO THE TOP
OF THE CORPORATE LADDER. . .

And the REAL "Evil-Doers" are the Corporations who
Puppeteer the Politicians who are Bankrupting
The entire Planet: Enron, Exxon, Shell, DuPont, Dow Chemical,
General Electric, Boeing, Lockheed, Hughes Martin. . .
Who get off on dangling the endless carrot of Western Corruption
In the face of those who
Don't want it
Won't buy it
Can't afford it
Can see right through it
AND HAVE EVERY RIGHT TO BE PISSED OFF ENOUGH
TO GIVE IT AS GOOD AS THEY GET IT

You Reap what you fucking Sow. . .

And in the end. . . it's only We The People who are getting screwed
The innocent will always suffer
The guilty will always be set free
Ignorance is Bliss
War is Peace
AND PEACE IS NOT PROFITABLE

Through music, books, spoken word performances, film, video, photogra-
phy, poetry and a multitude of creative endeavors, Lydia Lunch has been
one of the most daring artists of the current era. She is the co-editor (with
Adam Parfrey) of the coming *Sin-A-Rama: Sleaze Sex Paperbacks of the
'60s* (Feral House).

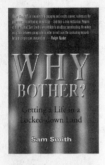

E STOLE THE 2000 ELECTION ★ WHERE'S OSAMA?

11: HE KNEW ★ THE CORPORATE TAKEOVER OF OUR MEDIA

HE IRAQI QUAGMIRE ★ "VICTORY" IN IRAQ

OHN ASHCROFT IS WATCHING ★ ENRONGATE

E'S A PATHOLOGICAL LIAR ★ HE'S BANKRUPTING THE USA

CREWING OUR TROOPS ★ "BRING 'EM ON!"

HE BUSH FAMILY BUSINESS PARTNERS—THE BIN LADENS

ALLIBURTONGATE ★ THE HOMELESS CRISIS ★ LIARGATE

SAMAGATE ★ WHERE ARE THE TALIBAN?

'S STILL THE ECONOMY, STUPID ★ FUZZY MATH & TAX CUT VOODOO

NRON & THE CALIFORNIA ENERGY SWINDLE

HE NORAD STAND-DOWN ★ "ANOTHER PEARL HARBOR"

ET ON TERRORISM FOR FUN AND PROFIT!

EOCONS GONE WILD! ★ CHICKEN-HAWKS ON PARADE

OTAL INFORMATION AWARENESS

E'S A PSYCHOPATHIC KILLER ★ HE'S AN ENEMY OF THE PLANET

IS GRANDDADDY—HITLER'S AMERICAN BANKER

EAKGATE ★ SHRUBONOMICS ★ KARL ROVE

UBYA'S USA—INTERNATIONAL PARIAH ★ NORTH KOREA

HE CORPORATE CROOKS ★ HARKENGATE

E'S A COWARD ★ HE'S A WIMP ★ HE'S A DUMBASS

UTTING THE FORESTS TO SAVE THEM

E'LL DESTROY OUR COURTS ★ JEB, KAT, & THE SUPREMES

E'S A RECOVERING ALCOHOLIC, DRUNK DRIVER & COKEHEAD

A CARPET OF GOLD OR A CARPET OF BOMBS"

HE SUPREME COURT ★ ELECTRONIC VOTING ELECTION THEFT

E'S PRO-LIFE—WHEN THE BABY ISN'T HIS

HE CHENEY ENERGY PROGRAM ★ HIS DADDY